William Mackergo Taylor

The Boy Jesus

And other sermons

William Mackergo Taylor

The Boy Jesus
And other sermons

ISBN/EAN: 9783337114480

Printed in Europe, USA, Canada, Australia, Japan

Cover: Foto ©Lupo / pixelio.de

More available books at **www.hansebooks.com**

THE BOY JESUS

AND OTHER SERMONS

BY

WILLIAM M. TAYLOR, D.D., LL.D.

PASTOR EMERITUS OF THE BROADWAY TABERNACLE, NEW YORK CITY

New York
A. C. ARMSTRONG AND SON
51 East 10th Street, near Broadway
1893

University Press:
John Wilson and Son, Cambridge, U.S.A.

PREFACE.

In the Providence of God I have been laid aside from the ministry of the pulpit, but there is still left to me that of the press ; and in my months of silence I have had great comfort under my affliction in the selection and preparation for publication of the discourses which form this volume.

I hope also in this way to prolong my usefulness as a preacher of that gospel to the furtherance of which I gave my life at first, and would give it again, only with more intensity than ever, if I had the opportunity.

Praying that, as in the preaching of them originally, so now in the printing of them, these sermons may, in the hands of God's Holy Spirit, be the means of blessing to many souls, I lay them upon his altar, as a thank-offering for countless mercies.

New York, October, 1893.

CONTENTS.

		PAGE
I.	THE BOY JESUS	1
II.	THE GOSPEL ACCORDING TO JOHN THE BAPTIST	17
III.	RISEN WITH CHRIST	29
IV.	EARLY PIETY	41
V.	SEEKING GREAT THINGS	57
VI.	HIM WITH WHOM WE HAVE TO DO	74
VII.	"I KNOW WHERE THOU DWELLEST"	90
VIII.	THE SILENCE OF JESUS	105
IX.	THERE CAME OUT THIS CALF	119
X.	THE RESIDUE	129
XI.	THREE ESTIMATES OF ONE CHARACTER	140
XII.	SATAN'S ESTIMATE OF HUMAN NATURE	153
XIII.	THE WAY AND THE LEADING	167
XIV.	THE HOLY SPIRIT AS A FACTOR IN OUR PRAYERS	182
XV.	VISIONS	194
XVI.	THE PROVINCE OF FEELING IN RELIGIOUS EXPERIENCE	206
XVII.	THE PLACE AND POWER OF INDIVIDUALITY IN CHRISTIAN LIFE AND WORK	218
XVIII.	THE READINESS OF THE GOSPEL OF PEACE	231
XIX.	THE INTERPRETING INFLUENCE OF TIME	242
XX.	PRAISE	255
XXI.	THE IRREPRESSIBLE IN CHRISTIAN TESTIMONY	263
XXII.	CHARACTERISTICS AND TRIALS OF REVIVAL	277
XXIII.	THE PLAGUE OF THE HEART	290

SERMONS.

I.

THE BOY JESUS.

A CHRISTMAS SERMON.

The boy Jesus. — LUKE ii. 43 (Revised Version).

I PREFER the reading of the Revisers, because it marks the difference between the original word, which in the common version is rendered "child" in the fortieth verse, and that which is translated by the same English term in the text. In the Greek, the former is ($παιδίον$) the diminutive form of the latter ($παῖς$). The former denotes a little child, and is especially appropriate to one in the years of early infancy; the latter signifies a young person, and is used of one at any age from infancy up to manhood. Besides, having regard to the statement of the forty-second verse, that he was now "twelve years old," nothing could be happier or more idiomatic than the rendering given by the Revisers, "The boy Jesus."

Our subject, then, this morning is the boyhood of him whose coming into the world is uppermost to-day in all our thoughts. Now, when we turn to the Gospel narratives, with the view of learning what they contain in reference to this portion of the life of Christ, we are at once impressed by two things, — first, the marvellous silence which the Evangelists have maintained concerning the years between his infancy and manhood; and second, the still more marvellous character of the records which they have preserved belonging to that interval.

We notice, first, a marvellous reticence. We have full particulars regarding his birth, and the wonders which were attendant thereon. Luke tells us of the annunciation made by the angel to the Virgin; of the appearance of the angel to the shepherds, and of the song of the heavenly host. And Matthew gives us an account of the coming of the wise men to Bethlehem under the guidance of the star; of the flight of the Holy Family into Egypt, and of their return to Palestine, where they took up their abode in Nazareth. But from that point on, till his baptism at the Jordan, we have only one incident of his life recorded. That, as we shall see before we close, was remarkable enough; it is even more so than the silence of the authors of the Gospels concerning everything else. Now, when we remember how, in regard to others whose lives have been afterward noteworthy, whether as warriors or teachers, the tendency of all biographers has been to gather up every trifling detail which might help to show that the boy was "father to the man," and magnify it into importance; above all, when we know what manner of things have been told in the Apocryphal Gospels in regard to the doings of Jesus himself during his boyhood, — it is impossible to believe that this silence of the Evangelists is altogether accidental. They had ample opportunities, either by application to Mary herself, or by referring to the brothers of Jesus, who were brought up beside him, and who at a later date became his disciples, of acquainting themselves with the real facts; they were themselves men of like passions with others, and if left to themselves they would have been just as likely to insert these in their memorabilia as ordinary biographers are to dwell upon the child-life of their heroes. Whence, then, this reticence? The only satisfactory answer, as it seems to me, which can be given to that question is that they were under supernatural guidance; and few stronger confirmations of the inspiration of the Evangelists are to be found than that which one receives from the contrast between the Apocryphal Gospels and the narratives of Matthew and Luke in this regard. As one has said of these spurious productions, "They are particularly full of the sayings and doings of the childhood of Jesus. But they only show how unequal the human imagination was to such a theme, and bring out by the contrast of glitter and caricature the solidity and truthfulness of the Scripture narrative. They make him a worker of frivolous and useless marvels, who moulded birds of clay and made them fly, changed his playmates into kids, and so forth. In short, they are compilations of worthless and often blasphemous fables."[1] This wonderful silence of the Evangelists, therefore, tantalizing as we may sometimes feel it to be, becomes, when rightly regarded, a valuable and striking proof of their divine inspiration.

But still the question presses for an answer in another shape, "Why were they guided by the Inspiring Spirit to preserve this reticence?" and to that, perhaps, no complete answer can be given. But one has been offered, and may be mentioned here, as suggesting a profitable train of thought. As I have already incidentally hinted, there were other children besides Jesus in the house of Joseph. They are called in the narrative "the brothers of the Lord;" and there has been much

[1] Stalker's Life of Jesus Christ, p. 18.

controversy as to who they were, — whether the children of Joseph by a former marriage, or the first cousins of the Lord on his mother's side, or the children of Joseph and Mary born subsequently to the birth of Jesus; but it would not be profitable to enter here upon the merits of that discussion. Suffice it to say, that with Neander, Farrar, and not a few others, I have been led to adopt the view that these brothers were the children of Joseph and Mary. They were, of course, younger than Jesus, but they shared the Nazarene home with him for many years; and it is noteworthy that both Mark and John agree in the statement that they remained unbelievers in his claims to the Messiahship until after his resurrection. Now, this fact may help to explain the silence of the Evangelists concerning the boyhood of the Lord. As Neander says: "It is not to be wondered at that the prophet was without honor among those who dwelt under the same roof, and saw him grow up under the same laws of ordinary human nature with themselves. True, this daily contact afforded them many opportunities of beholding the divinity that streamed through the veil of his flesh; yet it required a spiritual mind and a lively faith to recognize the revealed Son of God in the lowly garb of humanity. The impression of humanity made upon their *senses* day after day, and thus grown into a habit, could not be made to yield to the divine manifestations, unless in longer time than was required for others; but when it *did* yield, and after such long-continued opposition they acknowledged their brother to be the Son of God and the Messiah, they only became thereby the more trustworthy witnesses."[1] But if the record of such a life as that which they thus daily observed had been given by the

---

[1] Neander's Life of Christ, p. 33.

Evangelists, then it might have done for others what the observance of that life did for them; and so it might have kept its readers from fully realizing the deity of the Son of Man. As Ellicott has observed: "The material and familiar was a hindrance to their recognition of the spiritual, — a hindrance, be it not forgotten, which in their case (that is, the case of the brothers of the Lord) was removed, but a hindrance in the case of those who could not have their advantages, which might never have been removed; an obstacle to a true acknowledgment of their Lord's divinity, against which faith might not have been able to prevail."[1] If that view of the matter be correct, then it is easy for us to see that in this particular portion of the sacred history, "the prerogative of solemn reserve," which Scripture has assumed to itself, is for us a matter of thankfulness rather than of regret.

But now, in the second place, we find that such records as are given of the Saviour's boyhood are even more marvellous than is the general silence to which we have referred. Exclusive of the account of the visit to the Temple when he was twelve years old, these records are entirely comprised in the following statements: "And the child grew, and waxed strong, filled with wisdom; and the grace of God was upon him." "And he went down with them, and came to Nazareth; and he was subject unto them." "And Jesus advanced in wisdom and stature, and in favour with God and men." Now, I have said that these utterances are more marvellous than the silence. Ordinary writers of such a history, standing merely on the human side, would have given us records of wonders that revealed his deity, and would have been most concerned to estab-

[1] Historical Lectures on the Life of the Lord Jesus, p. 101.

lish the reality of that; but these statements are all concerned with his humanity, and go to prove the genuineness of that. The Apocryphal Gospels invent miracles rather than have none at all; but the inspired Evangelists dwell on the reality of the boyhood, and on the evidence thereby furnished of his true humanity. Does not that suggest that the Gospels were written under the guidance of the Holy Spirit, and from the divine standpoint? From that standpoint it was the humanity that was the miracle. Of that, therefore, chief mention is made. To us the mystery of the incarnation is that deity should tabernacle in humanity; but to the celestial ones the mystery of it is that humanity should be the tabernacle of deity. Merely uninspired writers, therefore, might be expected to put forward the marvels that indicate to men the presence of deity, while those inspired by the Spirit of God speak, as we see here, of the proofs of the fact that it was a true humanity in which deity did dwell. And, in all soberness, the words of Luke, in the verses which I have quoted, take us into the very heart of the mystery of the incarnation. We do not marvel to read that "the grace of God was upon him." But when we remember that we are reading of him who was the Word, who as the Word was God, and who became flesh, and then pause over the phrases, Jesus "advanced in wisdom and stature and in favour with God and men," we are enveloped in mystery. We do not, it is true, as a general rule, feel so much difficulty over the assertion that he increased in stature, as we do over the saying that he increased in wisdom; and yet it was just as natural that he should do the one as the other, and there is really as much of mystery in the one as in the other. What the Evangelist means to tell us is that Jesus was a real boy, and that his human growth and development were subject to the ordinary laws of child and boy life. From his birth, indeed, deity tabernacled within him; but, however great the mystery, that did not interfere with his progressive human life. It conditioned it, indeed, so that it was entirely sinless, — a perfect life; yet, thus far, only the perfect life of a boy; and as a boy he had no advantage over other boys, save in the moral safeguards which were furnished by the residence of deity within him. When he came to earth, as Paul tells us, "he emptied himself," — that is, as I understand the words, he laid aside, not his deity, but all the accessory advantages which belong to him in right of his deity, or what the same apostle calls the "form of God;" and he took upon him "the form," with all its limitations and conditions, first of a little child, then of a boy, then of a man. He had to learn to speak like other children. He had to learn to think like other children. He had to learn to read like other children. None of these things came to him by virtue of his divine omniscience. He had to acquire them all just like other children. That belonged to the limitation which his incarnation imposed on him. Indeed, it was involved in his incarnation. He grew in knowledge just as he grew in physical stature.

Now, with these things in our minds, let us go down with him to Nazareth. He was "brought up" in the household of Joseph, who is described as a "just" or "righteous" man, and must, therefore, have been a pious Jew; while all that we know of Mary — the most exalted among women — proves her to have been a woman of genuine piety, of great strength of mind, and of far more than average intelligence. Their home was that of working people, — simple, unpretending, pious. And as Lois and Eunice instructed Timothy out of the

Scriptures, so, we may well believe, would Mary and Joseph talk to Jesus of the wonderful things in their national history. They told him, doubtless, the stories of Abraham and Isaac, of Jacob and Joseph, of Moses and Samuel; and perhaps in the home, certainly in the synagogue, — when he was old enough to understand the readers there, — he would become acquainted with the Psalms of David, and the ritual and history of his people.

Then, after the custom of the Jews at that time, when he was six years old he would be sent to school. For by an accomplished writer we are told that "eighty years before Christ, schools flourished throughout the length and breadth of the land. These schools were free, and were for all alike. Education was taken up as a national work, and laws were passed fixing the location and the form of school buildings, the number of children to one teacher, the age of pupils, and the duty of parents in preparing their children for school, and in watching over their studies. By much effort a law was passed making education compulsory; but at first that law did not apply to Galilee, yet Galilee had its village schools which were open to all. We know that Jesus could read and write; and we may well suppose that at the usual age he was sent to school with the other children of the village. This school at Nazareth was not like the high schools in our great cities, or the academies of our large towns and villages, where children are taught a little of almost everything; but it was a sort of parish school, kept by an officer of the synagogue, and the children were taught to read, to write, and to cipher, and were made to learn by heart the Bible history and the Psalms that were used in public worship. Besides this, they had lessons in the meaning of the sacred law, and in the moral duties of life. . . The teacher wore a turban, and a long robe or gown, fastened with a girdle, around his waist. He sat upon a cushion, with his legs crossed under him, . . . and the children sat cross-legged in a circle upon cushions on the floor. They had no desks, but held their books or scrolls in their hands; and whatever the teacher told them they would repeat together after him at the top of their voices. One can see just such schools now in Egypt and Syria."[1]

This account may help us, without doing any violence to probability, to realize the school-life of "the boy Jesus;" and I am particular to bring it out to-day, for two reasons: first, because it may tend to reconcile the boys and girls among us to what they sometimes think is the drudgery of school-life, to remember that "the boy Jesus" went to school just as they are doing now. He did not shrink from all that was required of him there, in order that he might fit himself for the work which he was afterward to accomplish; and if he who came to be our Saviour did all that for our sakes, it is only showing gratitude to him when we seek to make the best of ourselves through education for his sake. What a school-boy he must have been! Such school-boys try you to be; and when you come to hard places in your lessons, or to difficulties in your intercourse with school-fellows or teachers, then lift your hearts in prayer to him who was once at school himself. You will be sure of his sympathy, and you will not be left without his assistance.

But I have dwelt thus on the school-life of "the boy Jesus" for a second reason; namely, that I might show you how impossible it is to account for the intellectual greatness of Christ by the environment in which

[1] Jesus of Nazareth, a Book for Young People, by Joseph P. Thompson, D.D., LL.D., pp. 76, 77.

we find him. Think of the carpenter's home and the village school of Nazareth; then read the Sermon on the Mount, and the discourses reported in John's Gospel, and say if it be possible to believe that a young man of thirty, who was no more than a mere man, and who had only these advantages, could have been their author. Surely, the question of the Jews themselves is in order here, "How knoweth this man letters, having never learned?"—that is, having never been at any such recognized seminary as those of Hillel and Gamaliel. There is no doubt that Jesus, being a young man, did make these discourses, which by common consent have been regarded as the greatest utterances formulated in human speech; there is just as little doubt that he had in his boyhood no greater advantages than we have described, and so, not to speak at all of his moral perfection, his intellectual pre-eminence becomes an enigma for which nothing short of miracle can account.

But in speaking of what we may call the education of "the boy Jesus," we must not forget the locality of Nazareth. The place itself, indeed, had no enviable notoriety in the land, and there was ground enough for the question of Nathanael, "Can there any good thing come out of Nazareth?" but its situation was one both of beauty and of interest. The valley to which it gives its name is hidden among the hills that bound the northern edge of the plain of Esdraelon, and forms a pretty basin about a mile long by a quarter of a mile broad. To the northwest is a hill much higher than the others, the side of which is marked by little ridges, and along these the houses stand in rows, as one has said, "like a handful of pearls in a basin of emerald." Down among some olive-trees in the valley is a spring, now called the Fountain of the Virgin, to which, perhaps, Jesus may have accompanied his mother when she went to draw water; and when he was old enough, he must have gone often to the top of the hill behind the town,— from which at a later date his townsmen were for casting him down,— and there feasted his eyes on the magnificent panorama that opened before him. It was not only a goodly prospect in itself, but it was covered with the most spirit-stirring historical associations. On that great plain before him many decisive battles had been fought. Far away yonder was Carmel, where Elijah confronted the prophets of Baal, and Elisha had his quiet retreat. Within sight, also, were Gilboa, on which Saul fell before the Philistines; and Tabor, where Deborah rallied the armies of Israel against Sisera. Yonder, again, was Jezreel, where the Tishbite bearded Ahab in the vineyard which he had made his own by murder. Wherever he looked he was confronted by some historical association, and so such a prospect was to the Jewish boy much what the view from the battlements of Stirling Castle is to the young Scotchman with the halo of piety added to that of patriotism; and even to look intelligently upon it, would be itself an education. It was thus a fitting locality for the training of him who came to set up the kingdom of God on the earth, and to reclaim the allegiance of the nations to their God.

These, then, were "the schools and schoolmasters" of "the boy Jesus,"— Joseph, his mother Mary, the school, the synagogue, the locality; and under the combined influence of them all he grew until he was twelve years old, when the one recorded incident of his boyhood occurred, and to that I must now very briefly direct your attention. Though his mother taught him much, there is no evidence to show that she said anything to him about the circumstances of his birth, or the mission on which, according to the saying of the angel, he was sent. The probability rather is that she kept all these things in her heart, and waited with patience for the manifestation of anything in himself which might give token of the fulfilment of her anticipations. The truth in all likelihood was that as he grew in intelligence, so he grew into the knowledge and recognition of the deity which from the first dwelt within him. There were probably landing-places in the stairway up which he ascended to the full recognition of his own divine Sonship and Messianic dignity; but he went up that stairway gradually, and perhaps the attainment of the first of these landing-places by him was connected with the visit to Jerusalem which now he made. At least, it was during that visit that he made the first recorded utterance which indicated that already he felt within him and recognized the stirrings of that divine indwelling with which from the first he had been endowed.

The occasion is familiar to you all. When among the Jews a boy had reached the age of twelve, he became what was called "a son of the law," and was expected to conform to all the requirements of the Mosaic ritual. Hence it was usual for him to be taken then for the first time to the Temple of Jerusalem, to the greatest of the three annual feasts. Such an occasion was always an epoch in the history of a youth, for the scenes which passed before his eyes, both on the way to Jerusalem and in the Holy City itself, were well calculated to awaken his mind to earnest thoughtfulness. It was in fact the mental birth-time of many. The songs which the pilgrims chanted on their journey; the beauty of the country through which they passed; the magnificence of the city to which they went; above all, the grandeur of the temple, with its imposing worship, — all combined to make this first visit memorable to a boy, and gave to his after life a new significance. It stimulated curiosity, it evoked power, it turned the mind into the direction of holy things; and as Jesus was a real boy, we have every reason to believe that this going up to Jerusalem for the first time would be quickening to him in the highest degree. We do not wonder, therefore, that most of all in the metropolis he was attracted to the schools of the Doctors, and that with the eagerness natural to his age he took advantage of the opportunity to ask such questions as he had been pondering in his heart. Nay, so absorbed did he become in this employment — as interesting and suggestive to the teachers, we may believe, as it was instructive to himself — that when it was time to take their departure Joseph and his mother could not find him. At first they supposed that he was with some companions in the caravan, and they went a day's journey on their homeward way; but when after search that evening he was not found in the company, they returned to the city, where, on the following day, after a long search, they discovered him, much to their surprise, among the students. "Son," said his mother, "why hast thou thus dealt with us? Behold, thy father and I have sought thee sorrowing." And he replied, "How is it that ye sought me? Wist ye not that I must be about my Father's business?" "My father," as if he had said, "did not require to seek me. He knew — what it is strange you did not know — that I must be about his work." Thus he indicates his realization of his divine Sonship, and makes plain that he has come to the perception of his true life-work. The words must have gone to Mary's heart as with an electric thrill, reviving in her the memories of the Annunciation and of Bethlehem; so she said nothing in reply, but laid the saying away among those which she had so often pondered, and all of which were yet to be so completely fulfilled. But now he returns with her to Nazareth,—recognizing *that* as an essential part of his Father's business,—and patiently, through eighteen years, he wrought at the carpenter's bench, waiting the time for his fuller manifestation, when to this earliest word of Messianic consciousness he should add these others, "My meat is to do the will of him that sent me, and to finish his work." "I must work the work of him that sent me while it is day; the night cometh when no man can work;" and not to cease until he could say, "I have glorified thee on the earth; I have finished the work which thou gavest me to do." "It is finished."

I have left myself no time to draw any lessons from this review of the Saviour's boyhood. I name only three inferences from this first recorded saying of the Lord:

It is a great thing to find out that God is my father. This never can be true of any one of us in precisely the same sense as it was true here of "the boy Jesus;" but in a very real sense we must live beneath the level of our true selves until we discover that we are the children of God. We are all familiar with the story which tells how a poor dissipated man was roused to reflection and reformation by overhearing a little boy protesting against the cruelty which some children were inflicting on a kitten, in these words: "You must not hurt it, for it's God's creature." But a deeper and more powerful influence comes into the heart with the assurance that we are God's sons; and to have that assurance we must be "born again." The new birth is the doorway into the new relationship, and "to as many as receive him, to them does Christ give power [or the right] to become the sons of God, even to them that believe on his name, which are born not of blood, nor of the will of the flesh, nor of the will of man, but of God." This is fundamental. If we have not begun here we have not begun at all. We must be born again, and that birthday is the grandest anniversary to us of all the year.

But further, here be it observed that this consciousness of God's fatherhood involves in it the obligation to be about God's business. Duty springs out of relationship, and so the son must render filial service to his father. I am aware, indeed, that some would render this memorable sentence thus: " Wist ye not that I must be in my Father's house?" But our preference here is very decidedly for that translation to which we have been so long accustomed, and so taken it furnishes a suggestive example for us. The Heavenly Father must have our highest love, and our most devoted service. When Joseph Neesima was meditating his flight from Japan, in order to get the education for which he longed, he was held back for a great while by that regard and reverence for his earthly parents which Buddhism had instilled into him. After a time, however, he found some Christian primers from which he learned that he had a Father in heaven; and believing that when He called His authority was supreme, the way was opened up for his setting out on that perilous but most interesting enterprise, which finally took him back as a Christian teacher to his native land. Now, similar it is with every man who comes to the discovery for himself of the great fact that through the new birth he has become a son of God. Every other relationship becomes henceforth subordinated to that. The Father's business is now the supreme end of life, and anything he does is done by him as a department of that. Here is a test that will infallibly reveal to us whether or not we are the children of God. Let us apply it honestly, and see truly whose we are. Is God's business our constant care; or do we make it merely an appendix to that which we regard as our true life-work?

Finally, true earnestness comes when we can say, "We *must* be about our Father's business." That is not the "must" of external constraint or compulsion, but the outburst from within of that which has become irrepressible. It is like the "cannot but" of the Apostles, and it is the germ of all that came after in this perfect life. Let us not be content with anything short of it in ourselves; and if you desire to know how to attain to it, Paul will instruct you in these words: "The love of Christ constraineth us . . . to live to him who died for us and rose again." The effect of our believing perception of Christ's love to us in his death will be to concentrate us on this as the one business of our lives. To such faith, and such concentration, I call you now; and in the measure in which you obey, there will be new happiness in your hearts and new earnestness in your lives.

II.

THE GOSPEL ACCORDING TO JOHN THE BAPTIST.

Behold the Lamb of God which taketh away the sin of the world. — JOHN i. 29.

EVERYTHING which the Evangelists tell us concerning John the Baptist is unique. The asceticism of his life in the desert; the startling message with which he broke the silence maintained by the spirit of prophecy for four hundred years; the incorruptible sincerity of his humility, out of which no allurement could bribe him; the fearless honesty of his words; and the tragic horror of his death, — all combine to give him a peculiar and distinctive place on the page of Scripture. But these things were, after all, only the indications and accompaniments of the singularity of his official position; for, indeed, he stands alone among the servants of God. He came, no doubt, in the spirit and power of Elijah, and his dress was not the only thing about him that reminds us of the prophet of Gilead; but yet, take him for all in all, there is no one to whom he can be properly compared. He stood between the Jewish and the Christian dispensations, having much that connected him with both, and yet belonging exclusively to neither. He had more knowledge of the nature of the person and work of the Messiah than any of his predecessors among the prophets, and yet "he that is least in the kingdom of heaven is greater than he." Thus he is the connecting link between the two economies, and his messages ally him to them both.

This is very apparent in those two utterances of his which mark the flood-tide of his prophetic inspiration; for when he said of his greater successor, "He shall baptize you with the Holy Ghost and with fire," the very term "baptize" connects his thought with "the divers washings" under the old dispensation, while the words, "with the Holy Ghost and with fire," forcherald that ministration of the spirit which was ushered in on the day of Pentecost. So, again, when he exclaimed, "Behold the Lamb of God which taketh away the sin of the world!" the phraseology in which he describes the great propitiation of Christ is seen at once to be derived from the typical sacrifices with which as the son of a priest he was perfectly familiar; while the mention of "the world" gives a wider range to the efficacy of the Atonement than the common Jew would have assigned to it, and is the prelude of the great commission, "Go ye into all the world and preach the gospel to every creature." In the former instance it would almost seem that he had received a vision of the upper room at the moment when, to the disciples assembled in it, there appeared "cloven tongues like as of fire, which sat upon each of them." In the latter he appears to have had a revelation of the uplifted Christ on Calvary drawing all men unto him.

Thus we have, even from the forerunner of the Lord, a clear proclamation of the two great things which he was coming to bring,—namely, a sacrifice for human guilt, and a cleansing from human pollution; and it is interesting to mark with what equal distinctness these stand out in the brief records of the Baptist's ministry.

Spiritual regeneration and power given to man by him who won them for man through the offering of himself a victim for the world's sin; the baptism of the Holy Ghost dispensed by the pierced hands of him who went from the cross of Calvary to the throne of heaven,— these were the things which John saw in his moments of loftiest inspiration; and in making announcement of them he rose above all the prophets who preceded him, albeit he did not attain to the elevation of the Apostles by whom he was succeeded.

But now, leaving the singular character and position of him whose message these words were, let me fix your attention a little more particularly on the words themselves. Do they really mean all that I have indicated; or, in so explaining them, have I been guilty of putting into them a significance which is not legitimately there? The question is important by reason of its bearing on the great doctrine of the Atonement, and we must endeavor to answer it fairly and honestly. On the one hand, some have alleged that the lamb is here used by the Baptist simply as an emblem of those personal qualities of meekness, patience, and gentleness for which Jesus was pre-eminent; and on the other, it has been maintained that the allusion of John is to that servant of Jehovah of whom Isaiah has spoken in the fifty-third chapter of his prophecies, as bearing "the sins of many," and whom he has described as "brought as a lamb to the slaughter." Others still have contended that the expression in my text, without intimating that Jesus is the antitype of any particular lamb,— whether that of the Passover or of the trespass offering,— does yet describe him as the substance of which all the Mosaic victims, each from its own particular angle, were but shadows, and so represents him as God's Lamb, "appointed and consecrated for the highest work of sacrificial suffering and death." Now, to me it does not seem difficult to decide between these views. If the words had been simply, "Behold the Lamb of God," and if there had been no Old Testament at all, then we might have been contented to accept them as a figurative indication of the peaceful meekness of the Lord Jesus; but when he is styled "the Lamb of God which taketh away the sin of the world," the case is entirely altered. For then we come upon phraseology which, in the Old Testament, is connected exclusively with sacrifice; and it is impossible, having a due regard to that fact, to reach any other conclusion than that Jesus stands in reality to human sin in the same relation as the lamb of sacrifice stood to the iniquities of the congregation of Israel. Nor, in adopting that view, is it necessary to maintain that John had not in his mind the wonderful prediction of Isaiah, to which we have alluded. On the contrary, it is, to me, highly probable that he was at the moment thinking of that very oracle. We know that he was familiar with other utterances of the Evangelical prophet; for when he was required by the Jews to define his own position, he did so by quoting from him the words, "The voice of one crying in the wilderness, 'Prepare ye the way of the Lord.'" It is, therefore, every way likely that when he sought to describe the Messiah, he would draw from the same source. But the fact, if it be a fact, that he drew immediately from Isaiah does not imply that there was in his words no reference to the sacrificial system of Moses. For behind the predictions of the prophet are the book of Leviticus and the history of the Jewish nation; and his language receives all its meaning from these sacrificial and historical associations.

They suggested to him the material out of which, under the guiding Spirit of God, he wrought his description of the priestly work of the Messiah; and so John, in appropriating his words, refers, through him, to that without which his prediction would have been unintelligible, and thus, as one has said, he "condenses the whole sacrificial system into one burning word based upon Isaiah's oracle touching the suffering servant of Jehovah."

Thus far all is plain. Jesus Christ is the antitype of Old-Testament sacrifice, because "he taketh away sin." But what precisely do these words mean? In the margin of the ordinary version we read, "beareth away" the sin of the world; and in that of the revised version it is given simply, "beareth the sin." But perhaps the full significance of the word is to be had alone by the union of both the textual and marginal renderings, for the term in the original is the equivalent of a Hebrew word, which sometimes denotes the bearing of the punishment of sin, and sometimes the making of expiation for sin; and so, as Alford well remarks, "it will in our verse bear either of these meanings, or both conjoined, for if the Lamb is to suffer the burden of the sins of the world, and is to take away sin and its guilt by expiation, this result must be accomplished by the offering of himself." Thus the doctrine which we distil from the Baptist's words is that Jesus Christ, by his sacrificial death, makes expiation for the world's sin; and so the forerunner of the Lord is in perfect accord with the Apostle who said, "Ye were not redeemed with such corruptible things as silver and gold, but with the precious blood of Christ, as of a lamb, without blemish and without spot;" and with the Apocalyptic elder who described the white-robed company before the throne as having "washed their robes, and made them white in the blood of the Lamb." Jesus Christ, the holy Lamb of God, took on him the load of our sins, and suffered even unto death, as if he had been guilty, that we might be forgiven; thus he beareth, and by bearing taketh away, the sin of the world.

Now, if this exposition be correct, we begin to see what must be meant by the phrase, "The Lamb of God." For an ordinary victim could make no such expiation as that which we have just described. In vain here is the blood of bulls and of goats; for the only efficacy *that* ever had was due to its relation to the blood of Christ, and in itself, considered apart from that, it is worthless. In vain, too, is the offering up of a fellow-man, even if he were voluntarily to give himself up to death for us; for his life is already forfeited by his own sin, and therefore his death can have in it no vicarious merit. Besides, it is against God that we have sinned, and only a victim satisfactory to him will meet the case. The lamb to be offered must be the Lamb of God, — that is, the lamb of his appointment and approval. The nations of the earth, like the young Isaac, found no answer to the question, "Where is the lamb for a burnt offering?" But the believing Abrahams rested in the assurance that God would provide himself a Lamb; and when the fulness of the time had come, lo! there he is, — having the dignity of deity united to the perfection of humanity, — a victim of infinite excellency whose offering is "the propitiation for the sins of the whole world."

But how was John the Baptist so sure that Jesus of Nazareth was this Lamb of God? Let him answer for himself in these words, which are in the immediate neighborhood of my text: "I knew him not, but he that sent me to baptize with water, the same said unto me, upon whom thou shalt see the Spirit descending and remaining on him, the same is he which baptizeth with the Holy Ghost." Thus by the hovering dove-like descent of the Holy Spirit upon him Jesus was designated to John as the Lamb of God; and on the day of his baptism he was, as it were, adorned with the garland which marked him for the altar.

Still further, if this be a true description of the meaning of the phrase, "the Lamb of God," we have no difficulty in comprehending how it is "the sin of the world" that he beareth and taketh away. For the dignity and worth of the victim give unlimited sufficiency to his atonement, and its efficacy is not confined within the boundaries of locality or race, but any man believing in him may be saved through him. No sin could be taken away except through such a sacrifice; but no greater sacrifice is needed for the taking away of any sin. The blessed Redeemer has removed all obstacles from the salvation of any man, so far as these lay with the violated law of God; and now all that the sinner has to do is to "behold" him with that eye of faith which looks with expectant appropriation to him.

Thus expounded, these words of the Baptist are a strong assertion of the doctrine that the Lord Jesus Christ offered himself as a true and proper sacrifice for the sins of the world. It does not seem to me possible, on any fair and rational principle of interpretation, to bring anything else out of his language. To say, as some have done, that his expression is a mere metaphor, drawn from the ritual system of the Jews, is to reverse the true state of the case; for that system was itself the metaphor, and the whole drift and purpose of the Epistle to the Hebrews is to show that the sacrifices under the law were types, figures, or, if you will, metaphors, of the great reality in the sacrifice of Christ. To affirm, therefore, that Christ's death was only figuratively a sacrifice, is to reverse the relation subsisting between the two; to put the metaphor in the place of the reality, and the reality in the place of the metaphor, and so to make them both alike shadowy and unsubstantial. Nothing can be more apparent, even to the superficial reader of the Old Testament, than that the doctrine of sacrifice pervades the Mosaic system. Now, as an eminent expositor has said: "If there is nothing of this in the New Testament; if this is Jewish only, and not Christian as well; if Christ, for instance, is only the Lamb of God because of his innocence and purity, and not because of his sacrificial death; if he takes away the sin of the world only in the way of summoning and enabling men to leave off their sins," (then) "all bonds between the New Testament and, at least, the Levitical sacrifices of the Old are broken. These last point to nothing. They are a huge husk without a kernel; types without their antitype; shadows, but not the shadows of the true; and thus with no substance following, a promise without a performance, an elaborate and enormous machinery for the effecting of nothing."[1] Thus there is no getting rid of this doctrine without setting ourselves above the Scriptures, and repudiating or explaining away their statements.

But some one objects that the statements referred to seem to run counter to the plainest principles of morality. "Can it be just," he asks, "to compel the innocent to suffer for the guilty?" But such a way of putting the case, first mis-states it, and then founds a criticism on the mis-statement; for there was no compulsion. The Lord Jesus Christ was not dragged unwillingly to

[1] Trench.

the Cross. He was a voluntary victim. He laid down his life of himself. The necessity that there should be an atonement in order to the forgiveness of sin is one thing; the compelling of a particular person to make that atonement is quite another. But in the minds of most objectors to the doctrine of Scripture on the subject, these two things are often confounded. We admit the necessity, but we deny the compulsion. A thing may be necessary in an emergency; and though you cannot justly compel any man to do it, yet if one should volunteer to do it, and successfully carry it through, he thereby takes his place among the worthies of the land. Now, there is no talk of injustice in such a case; and why should there be any such criticism in the matter of the atonement of Christ? Here was the emergency. Man could be redeemed only by the death of a victim of a certain character, and the Lord Jesus Christ eagerly came forward and offered himself as that victim; but if you praise the hero who sacrificed his own life at the helm of the burning ship in order that he might save those of the passengers and crew, how can you stand chaffering about injustice at the foot of the Cross, or refuse to recognize the death of Jesus thereon as the noblest heroism the universe has ever seen? Either blame them both or praise them both; but if you blame them both, then the instinct of humanity is against you, and every man would cry out against your utter selfishness. Thus that which you could not righteously compel another to bear, may be so taken by another upon himself, and so borne by him as to prove at once his courage and his love; and every such instance may help to illustrate, on a lower level, the sacrifice of Christ; so that we come back with deeper emphasis than ever to the assertion of the old truth, that "in him we have redemption, through his blood, even the forgiveness of sins."

So much, then, for the teaching of the text. Let us now, in conclusion, use it briefly for three practical purposes:

It may serve, in the first place, to direct the sinner to the source of salvation. If there be one here this evening burdened with a sense of guilt, then I give him the direction of the Baptist, "Behold the Lamb of God that taketh away the sin of the world." Mark, the *sin*. That is the very thing that is troubling you. Other things do not so much distress you; but the thought that you have disobeyed or dishonored God overwhelms you. That is the sharpest sting wherewith your conscience pierces you, and your most earnest anxiety is to have that removed. Here, then, is one who taketh just that away. Look unto him, and he will save you.

Mark, again, "the sin of *the world;*" not merely that of the Jew, or that of the generation which was alive when he was crucified, or that of any small section of humanity, but that of the world. So you may be sure that yours is included. No matter, therefore, who you are, or whence you have come, or what you have done, there is here salvation for you if you will accept it.

Mark, again, "he *taketh* away the sin of the world." It is a present thing. He was bearing sin in sacrifice even as John spoke the words; and he is bearing it now in intercession before the mercy seat on high. We have not to do, therefore, with one who lived and died eighteen hundred years ago, and then ceased to have any connection with us. We have to do with a living Redeemer, of whom it is said that "he is able to save unto the uttermost all that come unto God by him, seeing he ever liveth to make intercession for them." We cannot "behold" him with the bodily eye, just as Andrew and John saw him when he was pointed out to them by the Baptist: but we can recognize the Lamb of God in him precisely as they did, and we can make spiritual application to him for salvation; and if we do we shall not make it in vain.

But this text may serve, in the second place, to stimulate the Christian to earnest gratitude. How much do we owe our divine Redeemer? He has taken away our sin. He has given us peace with God, and imparted to us peace of conscience and joy in the Holy Ghost. And he has done all at the sacrifice of himself. Surely, then, it becomes each of us to ask, "What shall I render unto the Lord for all his benefits?" The Apocalyptic seer tells us that he heard multitudinous voices singing, "Worthy is the Lamb that was slain to receive power and riches and wisdom and strength and honour and glory and blessing." We hope to join at length in that glad acclaim; but why should we wait until we are in heaven before we begin? Nay, if we do not begin here, it is certain that we shall not join in it there. But what is it to join in it here? Is it merely to employ the words? Nay, verily. It is to have our lives set to the key of its celestial music, and thus harmonized into a song of which these words are the verbal interpretation, "Worthy is the Lamb that was slain to receive power."—that is, to have absolute dominion over *my* heart and life; "and riches," that is, to have the sovereign disposal of *my* possessions and belongings; "and wisdom," that is, to have all the wisdom that he has given *me* employed in his service; "and strength," that is, to have *my* strength of body and mind consecrated to him and used for him; "and honor," that is, to have the supreme place in *my* regard, and to be made the depositary of all the honors I may receive on earth: "and glory," that is, to receive all the credit for what *I* have and am and have done; "and blessing," that is, to be the theme of all *my* praise, and the object of all *my* gratitude. This is what such a song means now and here for you and me. Oh, let us not make it a mere mockery, but stirred again by the contemplation of the sacrifice of Christ, let us dedicate ourselves anew to his service, and keep ourselves wholly for his glory.

Finally, this text may serve as a pattern to the preacher of the Gospel. Indeed, the whole ministry of the Baptist is full of richest suggestiveness in this regard. He never put himself first. Always he pointed away from himself to the Christ. He sought not to make adherents to himself, but his peculiar joy was to introduce those who thronged around him to his Lord, the personal Messiah, the sacrifice for human sin, and the Dispenser of the great baptism of the Holy Spirit.

If he preached repentance, it was because Christ was at hand. If he urged baptism, it was but as a symbol of that divine ordinance which only Christ could administer. If he besought men to flee from the wrath to come, it was because that wrath was the wrath of the Lamb, and as such all the more terrible. Thus Christ was the background of all his utterances, and his great ambition was to make ready a people prepared for the Lord. Now, in all this he was an ensample to every preacher of the Gospel whose aim ought ever to be to proclaim faithfully and earnestly the truth as it is in Jesus. Not to seek a new Gospel, but to stand continually at the foot of the cross in the spirit of him who sang, —

> "Happy if with my latest breath
> I may but gasp his name,
> Preach him to all, and cry in death,
> Behold, behold the Lamb!"

III.

RISEN WITH CHRIST.

AN EASTER SERMON.

If ye then be risen with Christ, seek those things which are above, where Christ sitteth on the right hand of God. — COLOSSIANS iii. 1.

THIS exhortation is based on a fact and a principle. The fact is, that Jesus Christ has risen from the dead, and is now at the right hand of God ; the principle is, that faith in that fact ought to affect the estimate which we form of the relative value of things on earth and things in heaven. I do not intend, this morning, to enter upon the proof of the fact, inasmuch as on former occasions of this sort I have gone fully into the consideration of the evidence by which it is established. But what about the principle which the Apostle has here connected with the fact? Probably there is no one here to-day who thinks either of doubting or denying that Jesus actually did rise from the dead ; but how many, if I should not rather say how few, of us have gone on a step farther and asked if it be true that Jesus rose again, what then ? Can I continue to live as if no such event had occurred ? Has no light been shed by it on my duty and my destiny ? Or does it not rather open up to me new views, supply me with new motives, and give me new inspiration, so that the moment I grasp it, I begin to live for other objects than those which formerly engrossed my whole attention? It is one thing to have a doctrine, or a fact, as an article in our creed, and another to have it as a power in our lives; and so to-day, when the Resurrection of Christ is uppermost in all our minds, we may profitably occupy ourselves with the consideration of the question, how our belief in that great unique fact in the history of our race ought to affect our characters and lives upon the earth. Accepting it as a fact that Jesus Christ died and rose again from the dead, what ought to be the practical outcome of our belief in it on our present earthly life?

Now, in answer to this inquiry I remark that an intelligent belief in the Resurrection of Christ ought to give us a new ambition in life. Many would decry ambition as if it were in itself and always an evil thing. But it is a natural principle in the human soul, and becomes evil only when it is directed to an improper object. The ivy will climb upwards, if only it can but lay hold on some tall object to which it may adhere; but if no such support presents itself, it will creep ignominiously along the ground. Like it, ambition will mount heavenward, if it be fixed upon some heavenly thing; but left to itself, it will trail along the earth. But because it may degenerate into one of the worst of things, we must not forget that rightly directed it may become one of the best. Take ambition out of the heart and you paralyze the life; for then there will be no plan or purpose, no concentration of energy, no subordination of means to ends, no ardor, and no enthusiasm in the soul of the man. Bad, therefore, as ambition is in some men, they would I verily believe be worse if they had none. For the evil is not in the existence but rather in

III.

RISEN WITH CHRIST.

An Easter Sermon.

If ye then be risen with Christ, seek those things which are above, where Christ sitteth on the right hand of God. — Colossians iii. 1.

This exhortation is based on a fact and a principle. The fact is, that Jesus Christ has risen from the dead, and is now at the right hand of God; the principle is, that faith in that fact ought to affect the estimate which we form of the relative value of things on earth and things in heaven. I do not intend, this morning, to enter upon the proof of the fact, inasmuch as on former occasions of this sort I have gone fully into the consideration of the evidence by which it is established. But what about the principle which the Apostle has here connected with the fact? Probably there is no one here to-day who thinks either of doubting or denying that Jesus actually did rise from the dead; but how many, if I should not rather say how few, of us have gone on a step farther and asked if it be true that Jesus rose again, what then? Can I continue to live as if no such event had occurred? Has no light been shed by it on my duty and my destiny? Or does it not rather open up to me new views, supply me with new motives, and give me new inspiration, so that the moment I grasp it, I begin to live for other objects than those which formerly engrossed my whole attention? It is one thing to have a doctrine, or a fact, as an article in our creed, and another to have it as a power in our lives; and so to-day, when the Resurrection of Christ is uppermost in all our minds, we may profitably occupy ourselves with the consideration of the question, how our belief in that great unique fact in the history of our race ought to affect our characters and lives upon the earth. Accepting it as a fact that Jesus Christ died and rose again from the dead, what ought to be the practical outcome of our belief in it on our present earthly life?

Now, in answer to this inquiry I remark that an intelligent belief in the Resurrection of Christ ought to give us a new ambition in life. Many would decry ambition as if it were in itself and always an evil thing. But it is a natural principle in the human soul, and becomes evil only when it is directed to an improper object. The ivy will climb upwards, if only it can but lay hold on some tall object to which it may adhere; but if no such support presents itself, it will creep ignominiously along the ground. Like it, ambition will mount heavenward, if it be fixed upon some heavenly thing; but left to itself, it will trail along the earth. But because it may degenerate into one of the worst of things, we must not forget that rightly directed it may become one of the best. Take ambition out of the heart and you paralyze the life; for then there will be no plan or purpose, no concentration of energy, no subordination of means to ends, no ardor, and no enthusiasm in the soul of the man. Bad, therefore, as ambition is in some men, they would I verily believe be worse if they had none. For the evil is not in the existence but rather in the misdirection of ambition. Its range is most frequently bounded by the horizon of time and sense. Its object is too generally some earthly thing, such as riches, honor, pleasure, fame, power, and the like. Now that would be rational enough, if there were no revelation of a future life, or if the present state were proved to have no sort of connection with that which is to come. There is no resisting Paul's logic when he says, as an inference from these premises, "Let us eat and drink, for to-morrow we die." But the Resurrection of Christ and his ascension into glory have so far lifted for us the veil that conceals the future as to let us see the certainty of the life to come, and the intimate relation which exists between our character here and our destiny hereafter. Thereby, therefore, they have opened up a new field for our ambition and stirred us up to lay hold on eternal life. That empty grave has demonstrated that death is not non-existence. Usually we look only on one side of death, and so we are tempted to think of it as a cessation of life; but here we are permitted to catch some glimpses of the other side, and we learn that in the case of the Christian it is only the passing from one form of life into a higher. When the chrysalis has become the butterfly, if we were to look only at the caterpillar carcass which it has left behind, we might imagine that the insect had simply ceased to be; when the bird has burst the shell, if we were to regard only the fragments of its former abode, we might be apt to think that the egg and its inmate had been destroyed together; but in both cases what has occurred has been that one form of life has been exchanged for another which yet is only an outgrowth and development of the former. There has been a death in the putting off of an old body, and a birth in the taking on of a new and higher kind of life. Now, it is similar with man: when you look at a dead body you are apt to say that all is over; but when you take in the full significance of the Resurrection of Christ, as not the coming of the Lord back to the life of earth but his going forward to a new and more glorious form of life adapted to the heavenly state, you discover that what on the earthly side is a death, is on the other side of it a birth into a higher form of human existence.

But this is not all. If the Resurrection revealed only the fact of future existence, without showing us that there is any intimate relation between the life that now is and that which is to come, it is conceivable that a belief in it might not operate much in changing or moulding our present character. But when we view it in connection with the ascension of Christ into heaven and with the statements which he and his Apostles have made upon the subject, we become convinced that the position which we are to occupy hereafter will be fixed, not in any arbitrary and capricious manner, but by the character which we have formed and the work which we have done here. In the Resurrection body of the Lord, there were the marks of his sacrificial death, and the height of his exaltation now is proportioned to the depth of his voluntary humiliation when he was on earth. The cross was the precursor of the crown; and just in so far as we approach to the likeness of our Lord Jesus here, we shall attain to the measure of his glory hereafter. The present is the embryo of the future; and what I attain to on earth is the germ of that which I shall be in the world beyond. Now if these things be so, what an influence they ought to have on our ambition? Here is the field of eternity opened up before us, and as the brightest glory there, the throne of Christ is unveiled to our enraptured gaze. We are assured also that on that throne we may have a seat, and that in the royalty of the king to whom of right it belongs we may have a share, if only through faith in him we employ the present life in acquiring and maintaining a character like his.

Now, in the light of considerations like these, do not merely earthly objects fall into a secondary and subordinate position? No longer do they appear to be ends which we may seek for themselves alone; but they become valuable to us only as means in the right and Christian use of which we may attain to the higher end of conformity to the image of Christ. Riches must be left behind us when we leave the body; earthly honor is for this life alone; pleasure is but as " the lightning, which doth cease to be ere one can say, It lightens;" but character remains, and only that character which is Christ-like on earth shall have Christ's honor on high. Salvation is not mere deliverance from punishment, — it is the attainment and development of holiness; and earthly things are valuable only in so far as they can be made to minister to that, because the measure of our attainment here will be the measure of our glory hereafter.

Here, then, is an ambition worthy of immortal beings. Let me fire you with it now. By the empty sepulchre of the Lord, all other questions merge into these vital inquiries, What am I? What sort of a resurrection am I preparing for myself? For I am living, I must die, and I, yes, I am to rise again with my eternal state rooted in and growing out of my present character. Thus even as a lens concentrates the rays of the sun into one burning spot, so by faith in the Redeemer's Resurrection the whole infinitude of eternity is focussed for each believer on the narrow and intense point of the present life, and he feels himself constrained to live not unto himself, but unto Him who died for him and rose again; not for things on the earth, but for those things that are above; not for things that are material, but for those that are spiritual and divine.

I remark, in the second place, that an intelligent belief in the fact that Christ has risen from the dead ought to give us a new support through life. Writing to the Corinthians, Paul uses these words regarding the resurrection of Christians as made sure by that of Christ: "If the dead rise not at all, why stand we in jeopardy every hour?" And again he asks: "If after the manner of men I have fought with beasts at Ephesus, what advantageth it me if the dead rise not?" So, also, at the conclusion of his great argument, and as the practical inference from the whole chapter, he says: "Therefore, my beloved brethren, be ye steadfast, immovable, always abounding in the work of the Lord, forasmuch as ye know that your labour is not in vain in the Lord." In the same strain he says elsewhere: "Knowing that he which raised up the Lord Jesus shall raise up us also by Jesus, and shall present us with you, for which cause we faint not." Once more he declares that "If we suffer with Christ, we shall also reign with him;" and the words, "Remember that Jesus Christ, of the seed of David, was raised from the dead," which occur in the immediate context, show that when he spoke of reigning with Christ, he was thinking of that as one result of his Resurrection.

But we are not left merely to argue that this practical influence is a direct result of Christ's Resurrection; we see it actually producing this effect in the case of the Apostles. The most casual reader of the Gospels and the Acts of the Apostles cannot but remark that there is a wonderful difference between the dispositions and actions of the same Apostles before and after the Resurrection of their Lord. Prior to that event they were timid, halting, irresolute, clinging to the hope of earthly glory, and seeking worldly security. After it they were brave, determined, spiritual, heroic. Peter no more seeks self-preservation in denying his Master; but before rulers and councillors, and at the risk of imprisonment and death, he proclaims the truth to all. And as it was with him, so it was with the others.

Now, how shall we account for that? By the descent of the Holy Spirit, you reply. And you answer correctly; but then the Holy Spirit works by means, and the means through which, in this case, he accomplished this wondrous transformation was their belief in and realization of the fact that Jesus had risen from the dead. He was a living person; he was not now to them as one dead. They had seen him; they knew that they should see him again, and should be received by him at last as the result of their steadfastness. So they faced every danger at his bidding. Now, if we have anything like an intelligent realization of the great fact which this day commemorates, the same effect should be produced on us; yet I fear that it is just here that most of us egregiously fail. Our faith takes up this marvellous event simply as one that occurred eighteen hundred years ago. We look on it as something far away from us; and we do not see its connection with ourselves here and now, because we forget that he who then rose from the dead still lives and reigns as Lord. When we think of Jesus now, are we conscious of making any difference in our minds between his present mode of existence and relation to us, and those of our fellow-men who have gone into the world unseen; or is it not rather the case with many of us that our idea regarding him is very much like that which we have of some departed relative of our own? I press these questions, for they touch the very quick of the subject here, and may reveal to us the secret of much of our spiritual weakness. One writes of those "dead but sceptred sov'rans whose spirits rule us from their urns;" and it is to be feared that multitudes place Jesus simply at the head of these. But to think of him thus is not to believe in and realize his Resurrection. He does not rule us from an *urn*. He rules us from a *throne*, whereon he sits endowed with "the power of an endless life." "Being raised from the dead he dieth no more; death hath no more dominion over him." So he lives still, the same as he was during those forty days between his Resurrection and ascension; not like the departed dead, who live as spirits disembodied, but as he who alone could say, "I am he that liveth, and was dead, and behold I am alive for evermore." He lives as near us as he was when he appeared to Mary, to Thomas, to the disciples on the shore of the Galilean lake, and to Paul on the way to Damascus. Ah! if we but dwelt on this aspect of the matter, what a power would come from the risen Lord to vitalize and ennoble all our conduct, and to sustain us under all difficulty and trial! We cannot long continue to live contrary to the world's maxims and fashions if we are not upheld by a strength that is not of the earth. We must have meat to eat of which the world knows not. We must be able in time of conflict and weariness to fall back upon some source of support which is higher than the world can furnish; and that is opened up to us by the Resurrection of our

Lord, for that tells us that he who conquered death lives yet as our friend, and can and will help us in every time of need. I have read of a tree in a Scottish valley which was planted by the side of a little brook, where there was no kindly soil in which it could spread its roots, and by which it could be nourished. For a long time it looked stunted and unhealthy; but at length, by what the writer who describes it calls "a wonderful vegetable instinct," it sent out a shoot along a narrow bridge which had been rudely made for the sheep, and this, rooting itself in the rich loam which it found in the opposite bank, enabled it to draw sap therefrom, so that it speedily became strong and vigorous. Now, what that tiny bridge was to the tree, that in the higher realm of spiritual life the Resurrection of Christ is to the believer. The Christian's life on earth is rooted in unkindly soil, and if it can find no better nutriment than that can furnish, it must droop and wither; but taught by the Holy Spirit it sends, through faith in the Resurrection of Christ, a rootlet across the river into the better land, whence it draws all it needs to keep it fresh and fruitful.

But I remark, in the third place, that an intelligent belief in the fact of the Resurrection of Christ ought to give us comfort when we are bereaved of Christian friends, and to give us calmness in the contemplation of our own departure from the world. How unutterably dark must have been the desolation of the mourner's heart before life and immortality had been brought to light by the Gospel! The classical scholar finds few passages in ancient literature so full of sadness as those in which Cicero laments the death of Tullia, his daughter. But now, though the Christian parent who is in circumstances similar to his, sorrows, yet he sorrows "in hope;" and his hope is that he shall see his loved one again, and their hearts shall rejoice. "Now is Christ risen from the dead, and become the first fruits of them that slept." "Them that sleep in Jesus will God bring with him." Sore is the heart-wrench as the beloved object is torn from our embrace; keen is the pang of separation. But the angel of the Resurrection forbids us to linger in the place of sepulture, or to "seek the living among the dead." He tells us that our loved ones are not there. He points upward, and affirms that they are spiritually with the risen Lord. He points forward, and assures us that they shall rise again; and so even as the weeping Mary thrilled with glad emotion at the sound of the well-remembered voice, the believing mourner is sustained and soothed as he sings, in words familiar to every Scottish boy, —

> "The saints of God, from death set free,
> With joy shall mount on high;
> The heavenly hosts, with praises loud,
> Shall meet them in the sky.
>
> "Together to their Father's house
> With joyful hearts they go,
> And dwell forever with the Lord
> Beyond the reach of woe.
>
> "A few short years of evil passed,
> We reach the happy shore,
> Where death-divided friends at last
> Shall meet to part no more."

Then, again, why should we fear death for ourselves, since Christ has risen? That victory over death achieved by Christ has changed the relation of death to all Christ's people. He is no longer what he was, even to the saints before the advent. Some of them, indeed, reached a lofty mountain-top of faith, from which they saw a glimpse of the truth; but the many were still in darkness. But Christ's Resurrection brought us light. For his people's sake, Christ, when he died, went into the domain of the King of Terrors, where he grappled with and overcame the grim monarch; and whence the conqueror brought him as a captive slave, to be employed as the porter in his palace in opening the door for his friends into the chamber of his presence. The King of Terrors is now the servant of Christ; and so he may well be said to be "abolished" for those who belong to Christ's household. The grave thus illumined becomes but the robing-room for heaven, where we put off the garment of corruption and put on our incorruptible attire. Between the two, indeed, the putting off of the one and the putting on of the other, there may be a long interval; but it will not seem long, because throughout it the spirit of the believer shall be "at home with the Lord." So, if we but receive and rest on Christ and live for him, we need not fear to die, for now since Christ has risen, —

"Death seemeth but a covered way,
  Which opens into light;
Wherein no blinded child can stray
  Beyond the Father's sight."

Many other points about the Resurrection might be specified and illustrated; but of design, to-day, I have waived all consideration of them, that I might set the more distinctly before you its practical bearing on present character and life. It is in vain that we seek to keep a Lord's Day in every week, if on all the other days the Resurrection of Christ has no influence on our conduct

It is to no purpose that we keep an Easter Day in every year, if at all other times we forget that Christ is risen, and live as if his body were still in Joseph's tomb; and my discourse at this time will not be altogether unblessed if it only rouse you to reflect on the effect which your faith in the fact that Jesus Christ rose again from the dead should have on your daily lives. Go, then, from this house, to-day, not to levity and frivolity, not to exchange complimentary commonplaces with each other, or to indulge in aimless day-dreaming by yourselves, but to ponder these questions: If it be true that Christ has risen from the dead, am I what I ought to be; or am I living as I ought to live? Have I risen with Christ, and am I seeking, as the result of that, to walk in newness of life?

IV.

EARLY PIETY.

And Eli perceived that the Lord had called the child.
1 SAMUEL iii. 8.

MANY things in the early history of Samuel combine to give it that wonderful charm by which it fascinates every reader. At the very opening of the book our sympathy is at once enlisted on the side of Hannah by the rehearsal of the indignities to which she was subjected; and when at length the prayer which she offered with tears at the gate of the tabernacle is answered, and she takes the little one whom she had received from God, and gives him back to God for his service in His house, and leaves him there, we join most heartily with her in that grateful song which formed the ground-work of the Virgin's Magnificat over the birth of the Messiah, and which has given expression to the gladness of motherhood in every after day.

Then in spite of the one dark shadow resting on his character, because of his over-indulgence of his sons, we have a very tender interest in the venerable Eli, and can well understand why he took so kindly to the prattling boy at his feet, and allowed him in his tiny ephod to be to him a kind of acolyte as he "ministered before the Lord." The disappointment which he had experienced in his own sons sought to solace itself in the childish attentions and simple piety of his little companion, and so he lavished on him the love of his heart, and we love him for loving Samuel.

And who can help being attracted by the boy himself? He makes no fuss over being left by his mother away from home in Shiloh, for she had trained him to look upon that as the special honor as well as the peculiar service of his life; and he went forward to it with a real joy, which held him up through his daily duties. Then on those annual red-letter days so long anticipated before they came and so fondly looked back upon after they had gone, when his mother came and clothed him with the new coat, into every stitch of which she had sewed her love, and left him again with wistful affection but with no regrets, we feel for her a new admiration and have in him a deeper interest, which increases as we watch him tripping day by day at Eli's feet and ministering before him unto the Lord.

But the first section of the story has its climax in the incident from the account of which my text is taken. It was night in the tabernacle. The little boy had been long asleep; the aged priest himself had been for hours in bed; and the sacred light in the holy place was burning low, betokening that the morning was not far away. It was in fact in Nature — as it was just then also in the history of Israel — the darkest hour before the dawning of a new day, when, startled by the hearing of his name, the little Samuel, with an alacrity that shows how ready he always was to answer Eli's call, rose from his couch and went to the bedside of the aged priest, and said, "Here am I." But the venerable man had not spoken, and bade him lie down again. A second time he went with the same impression, and received the same reply. But when he went a third time, it flashed into the mind of Eli that God had called the child; and he enjoined him if the voice should come again to make this reverent reply, " Speak, Lord, for thy servant heareth." Following that injunction, the boy Samuel received his first direct and special communication from Jehovah, and entered there and then into " the goodly fellowship of the prophets." The message with which he was intrusted must have wrung his heart with sadness, for it told of the extinction of the family of his venerable instructor; but it had to be delivered, and when it began to be fulfilled, " all Israel knew that Samuel was established to be a prophet of the Lord."

Now, of course this was a special call to a special office, and we cannot reason from it in every particular to our common and ordinary experience. Nevertheless, there is enough of similarity between what is here recorded and the procedure of God in the calling of his people generally to himself, to warrant us from this text to speak of the piety of children, and the proper treatment of it by the grown-up people under whose care they are.

With that object in view, then, let me remark, in the first place, that God frequently calls his people in their childhood. We have such cases in the Holy Scriptures, as those of Daniel, Jeremiah, Timothy, and others, who were, as the sacred writer phrases it, "sanctified to the Lord from their birth;" and the annals of Christian biography are rich in the records of many who so grew up in the knowledge and love of the Saviour that neither they themselves nor those around them could tell when they entered upon the path of life. Their piety seemed to be almost coeval with their birth. It grew with their growth, and strengthened with their strength, so that it could be said of them as it is here of Samuel, that "they grew on and were in favour both with the Lord and also with men." Indeed, as I read the Sacred Scriptures, and ponder over the fact that throughout their pages the promise is to believers and their children, I reach the conviction that the ideal of home-training which they set before us is that we should seek by prayer and patience and precept and godly example so to bring up our children that the progress of piety in them shall be like the dawning of the morning or the opening of the petals of a flower to the sunshine,—a thing so gradual in its on-coming that we can hardly tell when it begins or what its stages are, but can only say it is there. I do not deny the necessity of the new birth, for the law is universal, "Except a man be born again he cannot see the kingdom of God." But I speak now of the manifestation of the new life. Only grant me that the new birth may be away back in the earliest years, and then the development of the new life will be largely a matter of unconsciousness to the child, and will not be marked by anything like crisis.

Now, that, as it seems to me, is the ideal, after the attainment of which in the case of all the members of their families Christians are to pray and labor. I do not mean to assert that godly parents are invariably blessed with godly children; for the case of Eli here is an evidence to the contrary. But that case was largely the result of Eli's own faultiness; and though we must admit the existence of many other instances, we must still affirm that, as a general rule, Christian parents are warranted to expect that *if they use the appointed means* their children will so grow up within the kingdom of Christ that it shall be true of them that they never remember the time when they did not seek to serve the Lord.

The well-known treatise by Dr. Bushnell on Christian Nurture may have pushed this principle in certain directions a little too far; but there is no doubt in my mind of the soundness of the principle itself, and the excess into which here and there he ran with it, may be accounted for by the fact that, as advocated by him, it was a reaction from the opinion largely prevalent in New England in his earlier days, which seemed to cast suspicion on all piety that did not begin in the shock of a violent crisis, and go through all the distinct and well-defined stages of awakening, contrition, and conversion. The doctrine of depravity was held in such a way as to imply that even the children of Christian households must grow up in sin, and that they could not become the called of God, except through a spiritual upheaval as real if not perhaps as great as that which marked the conversion of Paul.

With such a state of things around him Bushnell may be excused for the lengths to which he carried the principle which he enunciated; but although his advocacy of it brought it very prominently before the minds of the Christians of his day, it was not in itself a new principle. It was as old as the epistles of Paul and the teachings of our Lord himself, and it has found a place in the confessions of many of the churches. We need, of course, to state it guardedly and with caution. On the one hand, we must admit that grace does not run in the blood. Piety is not a mere matter of heredity, and we have no right to anticipate that simply because we are believers in Jesus our children will grow up into that faith without any effort of our own. But on the other hand, we must distinctly recognize that there is such a thing as piety in childhood, and parents are encouraged to hope for its appearance in their offspring, provided they will use the means which God has authorized and appointed for its development. The church is to increase by the nurture of the children who are born within it, as well as by the conversion of those grown up persons who have been all along outside of its pale; and the true ideal of a Christian household is when all the children in it grow up into the love and service of Christ as naturally as they do into the likings and dislikings of their parents in other and less important respects.

Do not say that such a thing is impossible, for many of God's most eminent saints have had just such an early history; and every pastor can speak of cases, the genuineness of which has been attested by life-long devotion to Christ, and which were precisely of the same sort. "How long have you felt as you now describe?" said a minister to a boy of fourteen who was seeking admission into the church. "*All my life*," was the prompt and open-hearted answer. "And when did you begin to have these experiences?" said the same pastor to another member of the same household at a separate interview. "I never *began* to have them," was the naïve reply, "I have had them always;" and the thrill which vibrated in that minister's heart as he heard the words was all the more ecstatic because the children were his own.

Do not say either that all piety must be discredited which cannot tell the day of conversion; for if you do, you will invalidate the genuineness of the Christianity of many who have adorned the doctrine of God their Saviour by most consistent lives, and are to-day in places of honor and usefulness in the church. Nor let yourselves be tempted to object that such childish piety must needs be short-lived, for Christ always keeps a firm hold of his own; and after forty years' experience in the pastorate I deliberately affirm that the stability of those who enter the ranks of church membership in early days is, to say the very least, equal to that of those who make their confession in maturer years. I know that there comes a time to every soul when the traditional faith of childhood has to be exchanged for the personal conviction of manhood; and that in days of unsettlement like those in which we live, that time is likely to prove one of great anxiety. But still the experience of the effects of their childhood's faith is not a tradition. That is a part of their own personal history, and with that it is easier for them to keep hold of the faith than it would be without it. There may be some, I believe that there are some, who lose their faith in spite of their early experience. But they do so with regret, like that of him who wrote, —

"It was a childish ignorance,
But now 't is little joy
To know I 'm farther off from heaven
Than when I was a boy."

And to counterbalance these there are many more, who, after being tossed to and fro upon the sea of doubt, come back at length to their old anchorage in the faith of their childhood. Therefore, let there be no ungenerous suspicions of the genuineness of the piety of children, and no dark forebodings of its lack of permanence. God has often moved upon the hearts of little ones, and we should labor and pray that the young people of our homes and of our churches may grow up from their earliest years in the love and service of the Lord Jesus.

But now let us pass on to consider, in the second place, what those marks are by which we may perceive that God has called a child. And here we must begin negatively that we may come at length to a more definite, positive conclusion. Let it be remembered, therefore, that I am speaking of the piety of *children*, and that we must not expect to find in that qualities which belong to maturer life. For example, we should not look in a child for such a sense of guilt as we find in those who, after years spent in sin, have been brought to a knowledge of their danger, and have fled for refuge to lay hold of the hope set before them in the Gospel. When I go over to the Cremorne Mission, or go down to the Discharged Convicts' Home, or go up to the Christian Home for Intemperate Men, and listen to the testimonies which are given there, I hear from the inmates of these institutions a great deal of confession of sin. I hear much too of former helplessness, and I am profoundly stirred by the song which celebrates the praise of Christ for the great deliverance which he has wrought out both for them and in them. But all those things would be unnatural in a child who has known nothing save the sheltering protection and holy influences of a Christian household. You would call the testimony of such an one fictitious if he began to speak of sin, as, for example, Augustine speaks of it in his Confessions. For a similar reason you would not credit the rehearsal by such a child of anything like such a conversion as that of Charles Finney, or that of Adoniram Judson. A child is a child, and his piety will show itself in a way natural to himself, even as he has his own childish fashion of manifesting his love and reverence for his parents. His heart will be attracted by Jesus before it will be repelled by sin, and his horror of sin will be the result of his love of the Lord rather than the impelling motive that determines him to make application unto Christ.

Then again, we need not expect in a child a well-formulated system of Christian doctrine. That may come in later life, or it may not. Opinions differ as to whether it is desirable at any age, though for my own part I have no hesitation in saying that I regard it as highly desirable, especially in days like these; but still it is not to be looked for in a child. His piety is of the heart rather than of the head, and it may be recognized by the presence of these three things: first, a tender love for the Saviour, which is founded on the simple story of his love to men, and which delights to dwell on his winning words and kindly deeds and sacrificial death; second, a sensitiveness of conscience, which shrinks from doing anything that Christ would disapprove, and is eager to do always those things that please him. Of this conscientiousness the spring is not fear, but love; not the terror of punishment, but the desire to give delight to Christ. And third, a keen relish for the Gospel narratives, together with a simple trust in prayer. When your child speaks to you again and again with delight of Jesus and his love, or in simple and direct language, which has in it the ring of truth, tells you that this or that course of conduct has been taken by him because Jesus would rather have it so; or is seen by you to carry troublous things to Jesus in prayer, — then I think you may conclude that God has called him, and may see the beginning of the answer to your prayers regarding him. You do not ask that the earliest letter which your boy writes to you should be as beautiful in penmanship, as correct in spelling, as elegant in style, as full of thought as those which you are receiving from correspondents who have had a collegiate education and a large experience. It is enough that it is legible and true and genuine. You do not want in it the presentation of sentiments which a master has dictated, or the utterance of things which he thinks may evoke your approbation, though at the moment he feels nothing of them all; but you are content, yea delighted, with it simply because it is *his own*, and all so like himself. So piety must always have the stamp of individuality, and a child's piety cannot but be childlike. It would not be real if it were anything else. But it is piety none the less, and it reveals its presence by the steadiness of its love and obedience of Christ.

What then? The question now becomes, and this is the third head of my discourse, how we are to treat those children whom we thus recognize that God has called. Now here the first thing to be said is that we must be on our guard against causing them to stumble by our own inconsistency. Example is more powerful than precept. Little eyes are very sharp, and see a great deal more than they often get credit for. They are particularly quick in marking everything that is out of keeping with the professed principles of the man; and if our children once get the idea that in our inmost hearts we have no regard for that which by our words we recommend to them, they will very soon cease to be moved by our exhortations. If the injunctions point in one direction, and the life goes in another, they will ultimately follow the life, however much for a time they may have been moved by the appeals. The sight of any of those marks of childish piety, therefore, should make those round about the little one more than usually careful in their conduct and conversation, lest they should come within the sweep of the Master's words: "Whoso shall cause one of these little ones to stumble, it were better for him that a millstone were hanged about his neck, and that he were drowned in the depths of the sea."

Again we must beware of doing or saying anything that would make light of their experience. We must not bid them "Go lie down again." We must not say to them that they are as yet too young to think or speak of such sacred things, and that they had better take no more heed to them until they are older. Above all, we must not ridicule their sentiments, or laugh at their modes of expressing themselves. We must not hold them back in any of these ways from the Saviour, but rather gladly suffer them to go unto him, that they may learn of him. Nor is this mere negative treatment enough. We ought in every possible way to encourage them to open their hearts and minds to the teachings of the Lord Jesus in his Word. We should endeavor to bring them to say to him, "Speak, Lord, for thy servant heareth." For all this the responsibility primarily rests on the parents; and that they may rise to their obligations, they should seek to be much with their children, and to cultivate their confidence. It is sad to think that often the father and mother are those who know least about their own children, and the reason of that is because they are very seldom with them. They see little or nothing of them. They rarely speak to them except in the most casual way about anything, much less about Christ and his salvation, and they excuse themselves by pleading the claims of business and the demands of society. But what is a parent's business if not to look after the training of his children; and what society ought to be preferred by a parent to that of his own children? Many years ago I read a sermon by the late Dr. Raleigh of London from the text in Job, "When my children were about me," and I have never forgotten the force with which he illustrated the first head of his discourse, which he thus announced: "*When our children are children they should be about us.*" Oh! if Christian parents would only realize that more, they would be more frequently gladdened by the sight of the piety of their children. But either they keep themselves so engaged that they see nothing of their children, or they send the children away from home altogether; and so they become virtual strangers to each other, and drift away apart through life in opposite directions. If you wish God to call your children, you must get to know them yourselves; and when you see that he has called them, you ought to go with them into the closet, and say with them and for them, "Speak, Lord, for thy servants hear."

But the church also shares the responsibility in this matter with the parents. The pastor ought to make a point of knowing the children of his flock as far as may be, that they may come to him with all confidence, and may not be afraid to tell him all that is in their hearts. He must not neglect them in the public ministrations, but seek in all his discourses to speak in such a way as shall interest the youngest as much as the oldest of his hearers, and he will do that best by keeping as close as possible to the exposition and illustration of the historical portions of the word of God.

But the members of the church ought to realize that they also have a duty to perform in this regard. The children of the church ought to be under the watch and care of the church, and here is the *raison d'être* for the Church Sunday-school. In the outset of its history indeed, under Robert Raikes a hundred years ago, the Sunday-School was a purely missionary institution. It was designed for the instruction of the children of the careless and the godless. But as the years have rolled on, we have come to look on it as not merely missionary for the inbringing of those outside of the church, but also educational for the upbringing of those within the church. And I suppose that each of us is conscious in his own history of a change like that which has come over the church as a whole. At all events I remember that when first I became a Sabbath-school teacher, I said, with some enthusiasm, "Church members ought to teach their own children. I will have nothing to do with *them;* but I will go to the children of ' the ignorant and them that are out of the way,' and seek to instruct them." And I acted on that principle for years. But when I became a pastor, and was constantly receiving children in the name of Christ in baptism, I saw at once that the church, being a party to the administration of that ordinance, had a responsibility resting on her in regard to the children to whom it was administered, and ought to take some part in their religious training.

But the responsibility of the church as a whole is that of each of her members, and that being admitted, no better way of meeting it has been devised than that afforded by the Sunday-school. It does not take the place of the parents, or remove the work out of their hands; but it comes to their assistance, and rightly improved by them, it may be of immense advantage. For the lesson, especially now when it is uniform for all classes, may become the religious theme for the week in the home. The Sabbath will thus give the keynote to all the other days, and there need never be any hesitation about referring to that in the study of which all are alike engaged. Am I wrong, my brethren, in affirming that if all parents were to work thus along with the Sunday-school they would more frequently see in their children the evidence that God had called them? And when they saw that evidence, they would find in the Sunday teacher, next only to the pastor, their most effective and interested ally in securing the desired result.

But now I must leave these thoughts with you, and ask you to ponder them prayerfully, that you may see what God would have you individually do in this important matter. Let the pastor realize how much rests on him; let parents take to themselves the hints which have been furnished them; let the Sunday-school teachers note how honorable their position is in being intrusted by the church with the duty of instructing the children in her name; let church members generally observe that as the teachers are doing work as their representatives, they ought to be sustained by their prayers, encouraged by their gratitude, and furnished with the means of carrying on the work by their liberality; and let the dear children themselves give heed to the meaning of all this effort on our part to lead them to Jesus. By your parents, by your pastor, by your teacher, the Lord is calling you just as truly as he did Samuel here. What answer will you give him? Away back among the earliest memories of my childhood I see at this moment a beautiful picture in my mother's Bible. It was an engraving of Sir Joshua Reynolds's great painting representing little Samuel, in the undress of the night, kneeling on his bed, and with outstretched hands looking up to the glory-light, which shone through the darkness, while beneath were the words, "Speak, Lord, for thy servant heareth." Often as I sat by my mother's side in church I lifted her book, and as often as I did so, I was fascinated by that engraving. I was never weary of looking at it, and it may be that in some hidden way the words which it thus forced upon my attention have had deep influence on my life. Would that they might impress themselves deeply now upon your hearts, and help to mould your characters! And that they may do so, let me repeat to you some beautiful verses founded on this whole history, which has always been so great a favorite with the young.

"Hushed was the evening hymn,
 The Temple courts were dark,
The Lamp was burning dim
 Before the sacred ark,
When suddenly a voice divine
Rang through the silence of the shrine.

"The old man, meek and mild,
 The prince of Israel, slept;
His watch the Temple child,
 The little Levite, kept;
And what from Eli's sense was sealed,
The Lord to Hannah's son revealed.

"Oh, give me Samuel's ear, —
　The open ear, O Lord!
　Alive and quick to hear
　　Each whisper of thy word;
Like him to answer at thy call,
And to obey *thee* first of all.

"Oh, give me Samuel's heart, —
　A lowly heart that waits
When in thy house thou art,
　Or watches at thy gates
By day and night, — a heart that still
Moves at the breathing of thy will.

"Oh, give me Samuel's mind, —
　A sweet unmurmuring faith,
Obedient and resigned
　To thee in life and death;
That I may read, with child-like eyes,
Truths that are hidden from the wise."

V.

SEEKING GREAT THINGS.

[PREACHED TO THE GRADUATING CLASS OF THE UNIVERSITY
OF THE CITY OF NEW YORK, JUNE 10, 1888.]

Seekest thou great things for thyself? seek them not.
JEREMIAH xlv. 5.

THE careful reader of the book of Jeremiah soon discovers that its chapters do not always come in chronological order. It is very difficult, perhaps, indeed, it is now impossible, to find out what principles were followed in the arrangement of the materials of which it is composed; but the probability is that, as Jeremiah died in Egypt among those who were bitterly opposed to his instructions, his literary remains were hastily put together by some posthumous editor, possibly by the very Baruch to whom the text was addressed, who, in the circumstances, was more anxious for their simple preservation than for their exact sequence. In any case the fact is apparent that the prophecies do not come in the order in which they were given. Thus, to take one illustration: we have a message that belongs to the beginning of the reign of Jehoiakim followed by one dated in the reign of Zedekiah, and that again followed after an interval of some chapters by one which takes us back to the days of Jehoiakim. Now, the failure to perceive, and make the necessary allowance for that, has kept the merely cursory reader in many cases from getting the full force of the message which he has been perusing. In the chapter before us, for example, though the date and the occasion of its original utterance are clearly enough given in the first verse, yet unless we have fully in memory all the facts which are there alluded to, we may easily glance over the message which it contains without the perception of any pertinence in it to anything in particular. But when, marking that date, and taking thoroughly in that occasion, we lift this chapter as a whole, and put it where it belongs chronologically into the early part of the thirty-sixth chapter, we then obtain such an intensification of the lesson which it teaches as must indelibly imprint it on our hearts.

Let me endeavor to do this for you now. The date, you observe, is the fourth year of Jehoiakim, which was that of Nebuchadnezzar's first invasion of Palestine and conquest of Jerusalem. It had seen the triumph of Babylon over Egypt at Carchemish, and the consequent subjugation of Judah by Babylon; so that now, instead of being tributaries of Egypt, Jehoiakim and his subjects had become the vassals of Nebuchadnezzar. But this was not the worst that was to happen, for unless the people repented and returned to Jehovah, Jeremiah kept continually warning them that they would be carried away captive to Babylon. Hitherto these warnings had been disregarded, but the time was now favorable for their repetition. The people had just seen that in all his past protests against the policy which linked them to Egypt the prophet had spoken truly, and it was therefore possible that after such an experience they would be more willing to hear him. It was thus an important, even a critical time; so he determined to see whether his countrymen might not be induced to turn unto the Lord and live. And it was with that object in view that at the bidding of the Lord he prepared the book referred to in the first verse of our chapter.

Sending for Baruch, the grandson of that Maaseiah who had been governor of Jerusalem under Josiah, he secured his services as amanuensis, while he dictated to him all the oracles which he had publicly delivered. Then as he was himself in some way hindered from appearing before the people, Jeremiah told Baruch to take the roll in which he had inscribed the prophecies and read them in the audience of all who chose to hear. The day was a fast day, and Baruch took up his position in one of the chambers connected with the Temple, where he had a goodly congregation. Some of his hearers told something of what they had heard to the princes, who sent for Baruch and made him read the whole over again to them. They in their turn were so deeply moved by what they heard that they eagerly desired to bring it before the king; so they went and told him the substance of the oracles, having first taken the precaution of asking both Baruch and Jeremiah to hide themselves. When the king was informed about the roll, he sent his servant Jehudi to bring it; and sitting the while in his winter parlor with a fire burning in a brazier beside him, he listened to the reading of a few leaves. Then he rose and took the roll in his own hands, cut it into pieces with his knife, and cast them, against the entreaty of his best friends, into the fire. Nor was this all. He was so mad with rage, that he gave orders for the apprehension of both Baruch and Jeremiah, intending, doubtless, to put them to death; but the Lord had hidden them, and they could not be found.

After this Jeremiah, at the command of God and with the assistance of Baruch, prepared another roll containing all that had been in the former, with the addition of many similar communications, and he sent a terrible message to the king, which predicted the degrading manner of his death and burial, so that the monarch was utterly baffled in his attempt to silence the messenger of the King of kings.

Now it is somewhere in this history that we must insert the chapter from which my text is taken; and having regard to the date (for the public reading in the Temple, according to chap. xxxvi. 9, was in the fifth year of Jehoiakim) we are inclined to put this chapter into the thirty-sixth, at a point between the seventh and the eighth verses of that chapter. The commission to go into the midst of the Temple and read out of the roll filled Baruch's heart with dismay. He was afraid for his life, with good reason, too, as we have seen; and the coming of such harm upon him was regarded by him as an utter breaking up of the scheme of life which he had formed for himself. For he was naturally of an ambitious disposition, and being of noble birth, he appears to have looked forward to high honor and the possession of "great things." So when he was ordered to go on this dangerous service, he said, "Woe is me now! for the Lord hath added grief to my sorrow. I fainted in my sighing, and I find no rest." And it was to meet that state of mind that this message, which is not one of consolation more than of reproof, came unto him. It bids him give up all his great dreams of personal ambition, and tells him that if he means to serve God at all, especially in such times as those in which his lot was cast, when Jehovah was breaking down what He had built and plucking up what He had planted, he must lay his account with hardship and distress. As a great favor, indeed, his life would be preserved, and he might go and do his work in the Temple without any fear on that score; but he was not to look for luxury or affluence, or what the world calls "great things." His reward was to be in the blessedness of doing the work of God, and in the favor and friendship of God himself. "Seekest thou great things for thyself? Seek them not, for behold I will bring evil upon all flesh, saith the Lord; but thy life will I give thee for a prey in all places whither thou goest." In all this Jeremiah was only giving, by divine inspiration, a lesson to his amanuensis out of his own experience; and when long after, in Egypt, humbled by years and by the weight of public calamity, and deprived of the fellowship of his prophet master, Baruch added this chapter to the book of which it is probable that he was the editor, he would read it, as one has said, "with very different feelings than those which filled his mind, when in his youth its words came to him to rebuke his ambition and to frustrate his plans."[1]

You see, now, how much my text gains in intensity and significance, when we put the chapter in which it is found into its true chronological and historic setting. And in this, its original application, it is a solemn call on all who would serve the Lord, and especially on such as are ministers of the Gospel, to renounce all dreams of self-aggrandizement and self-glorification, and to seek only and always to do the Lord's work, be the consequences what they may. "Dismiss," it says to all such (and I beg all students of theology to heed the warning), "dismiss all personal ambitions from your minds. Seek not for a quiet home, a liter-

[1] Dean Payne Smith in "Expositor."

ary life, and an opportunity for professional study. Set not your heart upon a rich living, a wealthy congregation, a city charge; aim not after a professor's chair with all its dignity and influence. Be willing to go where God sends you, and to do what he requires of you, even if it should seem to involve nothing but conflict and distress. If you can speak a word for him in the midst of abounding indifference; if you can bear any testimony against the sins of your countrymen; if you can in any way lessen the griefs and lighten the labors of the noble Jeremiahs, who are bending under the weight of their responsibilities, do it with all your might, and take patiently and thankfully what comes. But seek nothing for yourselves; for 'he that loveth his life shall lose it, and he that loseth his life, for Christ's sake, shall keep it unto life eternal.'" The greatness is in the *man*, not in the *things* which he gathers round him; and the measure of the greatness in the man is that of his self-sacrifice in the service of his God, and of his generation by the will of God. And where among mere men shall we find a better example of this than in Jeremiah himself? His name is so associated with the book of Lamentations, indeed, that men usually call him "the weeping prophet." But in truth, not even Elijah in his dauntless defiance of Jezebel was more heroic than he. Standing almost alone, repeating Cassandra-like prophecies which no one would believe; giving advices which no one would accept; accused even of treachery to his nation in the crisis and climax of its agony; imprisoned by the king; maltreated by the princes; maligned by the prophets; misunderstood by the people as a whole, — he yet held on his way, preaching the preaching which God bade him. I regard him on the whole as one of the

SEEKING GREAT THINGS. 63

greatest men in Jewish history. His example is for
stimulus and encouragement to all those who find
themselves in hardship and isolation because of their
loyalty to God. And sooner or later, in some form or
other, every faithful minister, wherever his lot is cast,
at home or abroad, east or west, in the vast city temple
or in the small village church, will have experiences
through which he will enter into fellowship with Jeremiah. Well for him, then, if whatever be his secret misgivings on his knees and in his closet, he can maintain
as unflinching a front before his fellows as the prophet
did! We glorify Luther before the Diet, and I would
not in the least diminish his greatness, even if I could;
but many a country church has seen as great a triumph
over self, when the pastor, with no encouragement from
Elector This, or Duke That, or Landgrave Thus, has
under constraint of conscience uttered words which he
knew would cost him his pulpit or diminish his already
far too scanty income. And if Luther was a hero, shall
we deny the name to the obscure witness-bearer in our
own age and land? That was the heroism to which
Jeremiah here incited Baruch; and that is the spirit
in which the Christian ministry is to be entered upon
and prosecuted to-day.

But the lesson of my text which is thus peculiarly
appropriate to those who are called to convey God's
message to men is broad enough to include all of us,
whatever our special work on earth may be. As the
servants of Christ, we are not to seek great things for
ourselves. The terms of discipleship are these: "If
any man be willing to come after me, let him renounce
self." There is no following of Christ otherwise. The
crucifixion of self is the very touchstone of Christian-

ity. And by the crucifixion of self I mean not the giving up of individual luxuries or the submission of one's self to voluntary indignities, but the repudiation of self as the guide of our lives, the renunciation of self-seeking in any form as an object of ambition, and the enthronement of Christ in our hearts instead. We cannot be God's servants at all on any other terms than these.

But is it so great a hardship after all to give up seeking great things for ourselves? Consider how many seek them and never get them. We have numerous books written on great successes in life, and the minds of youthful enthusiasts are fired by reading how here one and there another obtained immense fortunes and died millionnaires. But what a book that would be that should treat of the untold multitudes who have toiled on through life and were to the end, in spite of their dreams, only hewers of wood and drawers of water? In the race of life they were jostled aside by some stronger runner, or thrown down and trampled upon by the crowd that pressed behind them, and they sank into unknown graves. We hear of the wealthy successes, but not often of the poor broken-hearted failure, unless perchance in his despair he has leaped into the river, and as men dragged out his lifeless corpse, they found upon his person something that indicated that he had grown sick of existence in the weary monotony of disappointed hope and baffled effort.

Consider again, that great things, even when men get them, cannot satisfy the soul. One must have something better than "things," however great, before he can be happy. The wealthy man must have something else and something better than his wealth, before he can enjoy that wealth itself. And there are many homes — no, I cannot call them homes; let me say

SEEKING GREAT THINGS. 65

houses — among us in which you may find the costliest furniture, the finest specimens of art, the greatest "things" which genius can produce or taste can select or money can purchase, but into which happiness never enters even as a guest for a brief sojourn. Only God can fill and satisfy the soul; and the godless house and the godless heart lacks the one grand essential to satisfaction and delight.

Consider again that even if great things could satisfy the soul, we cannot have them always. *They* are perishing, but the soul is immortal; and when they perish, or when the soul is separated from the body, its portion has forever disappeared. You remember that old story which the father of history tells of Crœsus. The conqueror Cyrus had taken him prisoner, and was leading him out to execution. On the way the victim kept continually calling upon Solon and praising the wisdom of the Greek law-giver; and Cyrus, curious to know what he meant, asked him for an explanation. "Long ago," was the answer, "when I was in my palace, Solon came to visit me, and after I had shown him all my wealth, I asked him if he did not regard me as the happiest of mortals. He replied, 'No.' Whereupon I begged him to tell me what was needed to complete my happiness. He answered, 'Permanence.' I made merry then over his conceit; but now, stripped of my territory, my royalty, my palace, and my wealth, and soon to be deprived of my life, I see how truly he did speak." Ay, great things have no permanence, and therefore it is madness to make them the objects of our ambition, as if our highest felicity depended upon them. Indeed, history is full of salutary warning here, and the sands of time are covered with the wrecks of those who in seeking "great things" for themselves have lost both the "great things" and themselves. Wrecks, yes, and these of no mean craft either. For among them I see that of Nebuchadnezzar, who ate grass among the beasts of the field; that of Alexander, who sank with an aching heart into a premature grave; that of Cæsar, who fell by the assassin's dagger at the base of Pompey's statue; that of Napoleon, the splendor of whose tomb beneath the gilded dome of the Invalides cannot hide the fact that at the last, like an eagle chained to a rock, he fretted his life away as a captive in that far-off Atlantic isle. And of them all we may exclaim, —

> "Ah, who would climb the solar height,
> To set in such a starless night?"

"What, then," says some one, "must we have no ambition at all? Is the very emotion wrong?" To which I answer that whether it is right or wrong depends entirely on the object on which it is set. If that be purely selfish, then the emotion is essentially selfish, and so sinful. But if it be an ambition to serve God, and to serve our generation by his will, then that is a noble aspiration, and is to be followed out no matter what the cost. But then that is self-sacrifice and not self-seeking, and is like the spirit which was manifested by him who said, "The Son of man came not to be ministered unto but to minister, and to give his life a ransom for many." The real truth here is that our care should not be for the "things" at all, but only for the service of God where he has put us; and we should not allow either the promise of great things to allure us away from that service, or the fear of great sufferings to keep us from entering upon it. Our supreme desire should be to do our best, with

God's help and for Christ's sake, and we should leave all else to him. Then at the end, when we have not been thinking of them, the great things — ay, the greatest of all things — will come, when he shall say, "Well done, good and faithful servant; thou hast been faithful over a few things, I will make thee ruler over many things; enter thou into the joy of thy Lord." Remember, then, the great care of the Christian man should be for the service which he renders to God, rather than for any personal object or ambitions.

But still another objects: "Am I never to think of getting on in the world at all ? Must I not try to better myself? Is it not better to be comfortable than to be struggling, to be a foreman than a workman, to be an employer than an employee, to be rich than to be poor ?" Now the answer to that question takes us to the very core of the Christian philosophy of life. You say, "Am I never to think of getting on in the world ?" and I answer, "Yes, you may, provided you remember that the important thing is, that *you* are to get on, and not simply your circumstances." As another has said: "The circumstances are precious because and in so far as they minister to true progress in you. Seekest thou great things for thyself, thyself remaining the same? Seek them not. For then, like rank manure to a sickly plant, they can only come as a bane. But seekest thou, through fulfilment of the duties and submission to the burdens of the present, to fit thyself for a greater future? Seek on, for that future will full surely come, and will enlarge and enrich thy life." By all means try to "better yourself," but then see that it is *yourself* you are bettering, and not your circumstances; and the only way to better yourself in that sense is to do, in the name of the Lord Jesus, the present duty which

God has given you, however lowly or dangerous or distressing it may be, with all your might. That will qualify you for the doing of something better; and when you are thus qualified, God will open the door to that better thing, and so, up and up you will go, not by your seeking of great things, but by great things seeking you. Then when you get them, you will hold them not for *yourself*, but for God. They will become a part of the estate which Jehovah has given you to manage for him, and you will seek, as "good stewards," so to manage it, that you may be found faithful at the last.

Thus we have got the harmonizing principle between the Christian graces of contentment and laudable ambition. The man is content until it is God's time for him to rise; nay, he realizes that God has put him where he is, and he does faithfully the duties of his sphere out of love to Christ, knowing at the same time that he is thereby fitting himself for something better, when God shall see it fitting to bestow that upon him. But his happiness is not in the better thing which he has not yet attained; it is in the glow of inner joy which he has in the work that he is doing as work for God. The emphasis of the text thus may be best put on the words "for thyself;" and so understood, it is the negative form of that affirmative precept which Christ enjoined when he said, "Seek first the kingdom of God and his righteousness, and all these things shall be added unto you." That will reconcile you to the absence of great things; and it will make great things safe for you, if they should come. Admirably has it been said in this connection, "The man who will get on according to the will of God leaves to the same will his promotion. Whom the Lord commendeth is commended; whom the Lord promoteth is promoted; whom the

Lord calls victor is crowned. Opportunity never yet failed, and under God's rule never can fail to wait on faculty. Fit yourself for great things, and the great things are then fitted for you. The Lord needs men to promote more than you need promotion. Get ready. He is waiting. Show yourself approved in the lower, and you will swiftly pass into the higher room. This is the true joy, the true glory, — to feel that the Lord has called you up, and that all good beings ratify and rejoice in it. There is a glow in such success, of which no triumphant knave ever even dreamed. Fear lest you should kill such joy by restless, selfish ambition. Fear lest you should imperil your decisive promotion by weakly snatching at the prize. Work, work, work, 'at the present service which your Lord assigns,' and then await the Master's summons, 'Friend, come up hither, thou hast won the crown.'"[1]

Here, as I have said, is the harmonizing principle between contentment and aspiration. Here, too, let me add, is the true and only solution of those questions which are pressing in these days for settlement, and of which socialism in its varied forms is the cheap and easy, and, alas! also alluring and deceitful answer to the superficial and selfish thinker. Let the principles which we have now announced be accepted, and the laborer will fit himself for something nobler by diligence and devotion where he is; while the capitalist will regard himself as the steward of God's manifold bounties, and become considerate of his men as men and not machines. But so long as self-seeking holds sway in both, there will be nothing but conflict; for selfishness on one side or the other or on both is at the bottom of every dispute, and under the iron rule of

[1] Baldwin Brown's Christian Policy of Life, pp. 159, 160.

the survival of the strongest, the weakest will go to the wall. On the other hand, let the law of love and self-sacrifice be accepted by all alike at the foot of the cross, and then the rivalry will be one of beneficence according to that priceless utterance of Christ: "He that will be greatest among you let him be your servant, even as the Son of man came not to be ministered unto but to minister, and to give his life a ransom for many." This is the loftiest Christianity and the deepest philosophy. Oh, that the men of our generation would hear and heed, would learn and practise its far-reaching principles! To seek great things in selfish ambition is to lose all the brightest things that life can give; to seek to serve God where we are, out of love to Christ, is, without making it an end in itself, to secure both the life that now is and that which is to come. "Seekest thou great things for thyself? seek them not;" but if when thou art quietly and diligently serving God where thou art, "great things" seek thee, accept them and use them not for thyself, but for him, in the service of thy generation by his will. And if no great things come, and thou art fain to be content with receiving thy life as a prey, then look for thy compensation in the present satisfaction of serving God, and in the future glory of being with God. Remember him who for the joy that was set before him, endured the cross, despising the shame, and is set down at the right hand of the throne of God.

GENTLEMEN OF THE GRADUATING CLASS:

I congratulate you on the position which now you occupy. Having finished your course of study at the University, the time has come when, with honor to yourselves and the indorsement of your teachers, you are to begin the active work of life. That which has been thus far the goal which you have been striving to reach becomes, now that you have reached it, the starting-point of another and more arduous race; and as to-night you think that you have not passed this way heretofore, you may be feeling a little anxious about that which is before you. I could have wished that your honored chancellor had been here himself to give you such words of cheer and counsel as he knows so well how to speak; but in his absence and as his substitute, permit me to commend to your earnest attention the thoughts which I have endeavored to set before you in this discourse. Remember, I beseech you, that your highest aim ought not to be to get "things," but to form and maintain a noble Christian character. What you are is infinitely more important than what you have; what you become in your own manhood is vastly more momentous than what you acquire of the world's good things. Character is the true success. But what is character? It is not genius; it is not intellectual ability; it is not reputation, — though that is oftentimes mistaken for it. It is an inward thing and not an outward; and when we come to analyze it we shall find that it consists in conscience enlightened by an intelligent acquaintance with the Word of God and obeyed with courage. Conscience gives us the distinction between right and wrong. Intelligence, enlightened by the Word and Spirit of God, enables us to see what things are right and what are wrong; and courage sets itself manfully to carry out these convictions in the face of every opposition. Conscience is thus the backbone of character; and therefore, as the secret of all real manhood, I would say to you, accustom yourselves to look at every question of conduct in the light of conscience. I know that it is the fashion in these days, in some quarters, to sneer at such advice, and to preach up the importance of getting position, property, wealth, and the like, no matter how; but I would not have you to belong to the molluscous class of moral invertebrates, who yield to every external pressure, and wriggle from side to side as interest or fashion may dictate. Take your stand on conscience, and let your conscience be rooted in the Word of God. Reverence such a conscience as your king, and let your deciding question in all moments of hesitation be not, Will it pay? or, Will it please? or, Will it bring me reputation? but, Is it right? Lord Jesus, "What wilt thou have me to do?" Look well to that, and let other "things" look after themselves; nay, rather believe that while you hold to that, God will look after all other things for you. Never forget the advice which Tennyson, after his manner, has packed into these lines: —

> " Self-reverence, self-knowledge, self-control, —
> These three alone lead life to sovereign power.
> Yet not for power, — power of herself
> Would come uncalled for; but to live by law,
> Acting the law we live by without fear,
> And because right is right to follow right,
> Were wisdom in the scorn of consequence."

And now, as I bid you heartily God-speed, the scene of the moment fades from my view, and I think of life as itself a series of training times, each graduating into something that must be higher or lower than itself, according as we have used or abused its opportunities. The school-boy graduates into the student, the student into the professional man or the merchant, the professional man or the merchant into the man of retirement, the man of retirement into — what? Life itself into — what? Gentlemen, when that last graduation-day arrives, may there be for you and me, in the Well Done of that great Examiner, a better diploma than that which this week you are to receive, and an abundant entrance into the everlasting Kingdom of our Lord and Saviour Jesus Christ. May God bless you. Amen.

VI.

HIM WITH WHOM WE HAVE TO DO.

Him with whom we have to do. — HEBREWS iv. 13.

THE phrase which I have taken as my text at this time has been explained in three ways. Literally rendered, it is "Him to whom is our word," the writer using the same term which he has employed in the clause "the word of God," in the beginning of the twelfth verse, and thus pointing an antithesis between God's word to us and our word to God. But it is hard to see in what precise sense "our word to God" is to be understood. Some, taking the term "word" to mean discourse, would paraphrase the expression thus, "concerning whom our discourse is," or "about whom we are now speaking;" but such an exposition is not only inconsistent with the common use of the Greek preposition which is here employed, but is also in itself so tame as to make the phrase an anti-climax, altogether out of harmony with the sublimity of the sentence of which it is the close.

Others, therefore, with a finer exegetical instinct, would take the term "word" here in the sense of "account," as indeed it is rendered in the seventeenth verse of the thirteenth chapter of this same epistle, "They watch for your souls as they that must give *account*," thus restricting the reference of the expression simply to our responsibility to God. This is every way better than the former, because it is in perfect harmony with the construction of the original, and entirely agrees with the scope of the passage; for the Apostle is speaking of judgment, and the mention of him with whom our reckoning must be made forms a most appropriate conclusion of his appeal. At the same time this explanation seems to me unduly to narrow that which in the phrase itself is expressed in the most general manner. That it includes accountability and the last judgment, is undeniable; but its sweep is vastly wider than that, taking in our entire relationship to God, of which responsibility is only one particular. Accordingly I am disposed to agree with Alford, when he says, "There could not be a happier rendering than this 'with whom we have to do' of the English version, expressing our whole concern and relation with God, one who is not to be trifled with, considering that his Word is so powerful and his eye so discerning." It is in this broad sense that I will take the passage now, while I proceed to illustrate its truth in the several departments of the divine administration.

First of all, then, I remark that we have to do with God in the operations of nature. It is true, indeed, that the advance of science has revealed order, regularity, and law in the physical universe; but that is only what we might have anticipated, if, as the Bible declares and we believe, the world was called into being at the first, and is still sustained by the power and wisdom of the Most High, for "God is not the author of confusion." We are not surprised, therefore, to find that he proceeds upon fixed principles; but we must beware of allowing that which we call a law to hide from us the ever active agency of him whose orderly method of operation that law is. We must bear in mind that "Nature is but the name of an effect whose cause is God," and in redeeming men from the superstition which saw a divine frown in every eclipse and a divine judgment in every hurricane, we must not rush into the opposite extreme of excluding the Creator from the Universe which he has made. For what are the laws of nature, as men call them, but just the observed modes in which the forces of nature work? The laws do not enforce themselves. They are only the methods in which the energies behind them put forth their might. And what are these energies? If you put the question to science, she has, as yet, no answer ready. But in the doctrine of the conservation of energy she tells us that the sum of the actual and potential energies in the universe is a constant and unalterable thing, unaffected by the mutual interaction of these forces themselves: and in the doctrine of the correlation of forces she informs us that one force may be transmuted into another; and so she prepares the way for the inference drawn by one of her own apostles, Mr. Alfred Wallace, to wit,— to the effect that all force is at last resolvable into will force, and that there is behind the operations of all secondary causes a guiding force in the will of the Supreme intelligence. And so at length, as the latest conclusion of one of her own disciples, science has reached the earliest postulate of revelation, and is acknowledging that the laws of nature are the common operations of divine power, depending entirely for their existence and continuance on the divine wisdom and will.

Now, if this view be correct, what men call gravitation is just the power of God putting itself forth in the regulation, according to certain fixed principles, of the relation of material bodies to each other; and what they call electricity is the power of God exerting itself on certain other conditions and in certain other circumstances. Some ten years ago, when the members of the Corean Embassy visited the Western Union Building, So Kiang Pom, the secretary of the legation, who was always very quiet and never lost an opportunity to make a few notes in a book which he carried for the purpose, put a poser to those who were explaining things to him, when, after having heard a great deal about the electrical system, he asked, with much simplicity, "What, then, is electricity?" They tried to tell him that nobody knew just exactly what it is, and the anxious inquirer put up his pencil and his book in disappointment. But man is always speechless, no matter how intelligent he may be, when he is brought face to face with God. And it would have been well if some one had boldly answered the heathen prince after this fashion: "Electricity in the last resort is the power of God put forth in a certain set of circumstances and in accordance with certain conditions, which, in the course of our investigation of his creation, we have discovered." The same is true concerning attraction and cohesion in chemistry; and, in a word, that which in physical things makes a cause a cause, the nexus which secures that what we call an effect shall result from that which we call its cause, is always and everywhere the power of God. Hence when we employ an agent in nature to produce a certain result, the power which we are utilizing is the power of God, and the highest of all is seen thus to be the servant of all. When in the workshop the artisan invokes the aid of steam, his moving of the handle which sets the engine in motion is, unconsciously it may be, yet really a calling for the help of God through that peculiar channel of his power; and when the merchant sends his message to the telegraph office, he is virtually, though perhaps unwittingly, beseeching God to use his power for the transmission of his dispatch. And so in all similar cases. Some men ridicule the very idea of prayer, and think it absurd that God should answer the appeals of his people; and yet in this way every day they live and every hour of every day they are really, albeit unconsciously, invoking his aid and receiving his assistance; for even in these departments of nature it is with God that they have to do.

What a new dignity is given by these considerations to that which men call nature! What a new interest to science! What a new importance to our common labor! How absurd, too, when we look at the matter in this light, are all the fears entertained by simple-minded believers regarding science, as if it could ever in the long run undermine revelation! The world and the Bible are works of the same author, and rightly interpreted can never be antagonistic. Science properly prosecuted will come at length to be the theology of nature, even as theology, correctly understood, is the science of Revelation; and though the interpreters of the two may occasionally fall out, we may rely upon it that they are themselves always in harmony. Let us not, therefore, be jealous of science; for in so far as it advances in its discoveries, it will only reveal to us more clearly how true it is that in nature it is God with whom we have to do.

But in the second place I remark, that we have to do with God in the overtures of the Gospel. I do not require here and now to enter into an elaborate proof of the fact that the Gospel is from God. That has been established over and over again, and needs not to be done anew. When an advocate is intrusted with a cause headed, "The people versus so and so," he does not feel himself under obligation to show that the government of the State is a rightful and legitimate "government of the people, for the people, and by the people." The conflict of a hundred years ago settled that, and he very naturally takes it for granted. In like manner, when the preacher speaks of the overtures of the Gospel as from God, he is not now to be stopped on the threshold of his case with the demand for proof of the divine origin of the Gospel; that has been settled by the conflicts of eighteen hundred years, and may now be warrantably enough assumed, especially when he is dealing with those whose very presence in his audience is a tacit admission of their assent to his statement. Therefore, without hesitation, I adopt Paul's language, and say that "the Gospel is the power of God unto salvation."

Now, going back on what we have already advanced about God's power in natural agents like water, steam, and electricity, we may find that some things about them throw considerable light upon the Gospel. Thus, if we want to avail ourselves of the force which God has put into and maintains in electricity, for example, we must comply with the conditions on which it is generated and becomes operative. The man of science does not presume to dictate to the agent with which he is dealing. He never says, "It ought to do thus and so, and because it does not, I will have nothing more to do with it." Rather he investigates by patient research the methods of its operation, and then sets himself in conformity with these to avail himself of its help. He seeks it in the way in which he has discovered that it is to be found, and he uses it according to its own laws. Now, in the same way, if the Gospel is God's power for a certain purpose, and we wish to take advantage of it for that purpose, we must comply with its conditions and laws. These are faith in Jesus Christ as the only Mediator, Redeemer, Sacrifice, and Lord, and repentance unto life. To say that they ought to have been different is just as unphilosophical on the part of the sinner as it would be on the part of the man of science to allege that electricity should have been generated in some other way than God has chosen for that purpose; and to know that they are as they are, ought to be enough to stir us up to compliance with them.

If you ask me why in order that the Gospel should be God's power unto salvation there should be needed, on the one hand, the incarnation of Deity in Christ, the death of Christ on the cross for human sin, the resurrection of Christ, the ascension of Christ, and the mission of the Holy Spirit, and on the other the sinner's faith and repentance,—then I will answer you when you can tell me why certain ingredients and not others are needed in the electric battery for the generation of that mystic power of which we have been speaking; why a wire is needed for its transmission, and why contact with a peculiar sort of substance is absolutely indispensable for its discharge. If again you affirm that it is unreasonable to ask you to take advantage of the Gospel for salvation unless I can unfold to you the *rationale* of all these things, and tell you precisely what the virtue is that comes from Christ for our salvation, then I will send you down to the

Western Union office with the question of the Corean ambassador, — "What, then, is electricity?" — and I will show you those men availing themselves all the while of an agent of which not even the wisest among them knows what it is, but only how it works. Oh, if you would only do with the Gospel as the power of God for your salvation what you are always doing with other powers of God for your service, you would immediately conform to its conditions and turn to Christ in faith and penitence! When you do thus comply with its conditions or laws, then you will be saved; for no power of God ever fails. That is why we speak here with such unqualified confidence. If the result depended on anything else or anything less than God's power, we should fear to exaggerate; but we are absolutely sure of that.

Then, finally, because it is God's power, it is not a thing to be trifled with. You know what happens when a man fools with electricity; let him violate any of its conditions, and he is instantly destroyed. And so if you refuse to avail yourselves of the Gospel's power of salvation according to its conditions, and approach it as an antagonist or a railer, the very fact that it is God's power will work to your perdition, and you will be struck down by the outflashing of "the wrath of the Lamb."

But the suggestiveness of this parallel between the power of God in nature and in grace has led me a little away from the precise point on which I wished, first of all, to insist; this, namely, that if you have to do with God in the overtures of the Gospel, then the hearing of its proclamations assumes a very serious character indeed. For in such a case you have to answer not the herald, but God. The minister is but a man: he may be also a very poorly furnished man, and if he were talking on other subjects, he might show himself much inferior to you in his acquirements and abilities; but if he is proclaiming the Gospel, — if, as tested by the statements of this Book, his representations are true, — then he has been the instrument of bringing before you the message of God to you, and from that point on you have to do not with him, but with God. The most he can say is what Gad said to David, — "Advise now and see what answer I shall return to him that sent me;" but the answer is made to God, not to him. Have you thought of that sufficiently, my hearers? It may be an easy thing to put me off. It would be no great matter to despise me. It might even be venial enough to amuse yourselves, if you chose, over my words and ways. That were little, if that were all. But in so far forth as I publish God's declaration that "he was in Christ reconciling the world unto himself, not imputing their trespasses unto them, for he hath made him to be sin for us who knew no sin, that we might be made the righteousness of God in him," then it is with God that you have to do, and not with me. That is the significance of this open Bible on this desk. That is what makes the enjoyment of gospel privileges so solemn. It is a great opportunity, but it is a great peril; an opportunity of salvation, but a peril of peculiarly aggravated perdition. I implore you to consider well all that these things imply, and to remember that you are dealing with God in the overtures of the Gospel.

But I remark in the third place that we have to do with God in the dispensations of Providence. By Providence I understand God's overruling care over all events in nature and all the actions and circumstances of men. Now in his Word it is clearly and repeatedly asserted that he has a purpose which he is evolving from age to age in the history of the human race as a whole, and of every individual in it. "There are many devices in a man's heart, nevertheless the counsel of the Lord, that shall stand." "The hearts of all men are in his hands, and he turneth them whithersoever he will." "A man's heart deviseth his way, but the Lord directeth his steps." "A sparrow shall not fall on the ground without your father." "The very hairs of your head are all numbered."

Such are a few of the expressions used in the Sacred Scriptures upon this subject, and if it be asked how this control can be exercised without interfering with the free agency of men, or breaking in upon the uniformity of the operations of the laws of nature, I frankly answer that I cannot tell. I know only that according to the Word of God that control is real, and I affirm that if we care to look back over the history of the world, or to go minutely into the tenor of our own past lives, we shall discover that it has been constantly exercised. No one of us here this morning could explain how he came to be in the circumstances in which he is now placed, without taking this divine control into the account. Repeatedly at the critical crossings in our life journeyings we have been, so to say, "shunted" either this way or that by an unseen power, and though we took little thought of it at the moment, certain occurrences in our career so hedged in our way as to lead us on and up to results of which otherwise we had never dreamed. It looked perfectly natural at the time, and yet by these natural means this supernatural control was made effective; for both natural and supernatural are God.

If, again, it should be objected that it seems derogatory to the dignity of God to say that he should concern himself with such minute matters as those which affect our insignificant lives, then the answer is twofold: first, that there can be no perfection without the supervision of details; and second, that apparently small things are often the hinges on which greater and more momentous affairs turn, so that it is impossible to superintend the latter without looking carefully into the former. The choice thus comes to be between no Providence at all, and a Providence which is universal; and even apart from the statements of the Word of God upon the subject, no man who looks intelligently at the history of the world, or at his own personal career, will hesitate long as to which he will accept.

Now if we assent to the doctrine that God's Providence is in and over all events, it will give a new importance in our view to every occurrence. The history of the past will then become to us a part of God's revelation of himself to men, and the incidents of the present will be felt to be the unfolding of that "one increasing purpose" of his which is running through the ages. The newspaper will be read by us as a daily chapter in the unveiling of his plans, and its issue will seem to us to be a part of the unwinding of that roll which shall stretch at last from the beginning to the end of time, — from paradise lost to paradise regained, — and shall be bright with the manifestation of the wisdom and love of the Most High. Nay, more: if we assent to this doctrine, — and there seems to me no alternative between that and atheism, — then the events in our own personal history, painful and pleasant alike, are seen to be "the will of God in Christ Jesus concerning us," and we enter into the assurance of the Apostle when he says, "We know that all things work together for good to them who love God, to them who are the called according to his purpose." I do not say, and Paul does not say, that this result will be brought about irrespective of our own personal agency, but I do say that this, if we are in Christ, will be the result; and for those who really believe that, and are in him, the sting is taken out of trial. As in Paul's case, indeed, the thorn may not be extracted, but the love in the purpose will reconcile us to the pain in the process. To the Christian there is nothing untoward, for everything is of God; and as in the mechanism of a watch, those wheels which seem to run counter to each other are yet working together to produce the movement of the fingers on the dial, so in our lives those things which appear to be contrary are really made to help forward our spiritual growth.

Thus the peace which springs out of this faith is not that of the fatalist who submits to the inevitable, or that of the Stoic who schools himself into insensibility and indifference, but that of one who can say, "He that spared not his own Son, but delivered him up for us all, how shall he not with him also freely give us all things?" It is the resignation of one who, though he cannot see the how, still realizes the fact that "He doeth all things well," and so patiently endures painful things for the sake of the higher good which through them is to be gained. Ah! if we only had more faith in the truth that it is with God we have to do in the losses and crosses of our lives, there would be less of worry and despondency in our hearts. Disappointment would become in our view a stepping-stone to something larger than the hope whose realization we had missed. Loss would become the precursor of a higher gain, and sorrow the forerunner of a pure and lasting joy. If God is arranging all things for our good, why should we ever flee from the post of duty, or fling ourselves in sadness "under the juniper tree"? If even in our bereavements he has been supreme, why should we be rebellious and refuse his consolation? Can we not trust him any further than we can see him or understand his workings? What has he done that we should be so suspicious of him? Nay, having shown his love to us by the giving up of his Son on our behalf, can we ever be suspicious of him after that? Oh, thou afflicted and tossed with tempest but not comforted, lay fast hold of this truth. He with whom thou hast to do in the things which have caused thy sorrow is God who loved thee and gave his Son for thee, and by and by, if thou wilt but cling to him, thou wilt see that he never loved thee more than when he sent this stroke upon thee; for he is thy Father, and

>" A Father's hand will never cause
> His child one needless tear."

But I remark in the fourth place that we have to do with God in the duties of daily life. Our responsibilities in society and business are not to each other merely, or to the laws of the State alone, but to God. We are under obligation to our fellows, indeed; but we are so because God has laid these obligations on us. In the home we owe love to each other, and ought to be characterized there by mutual helpfulness and forbearance. But if we should fail in these respects we are guilty not only of sin against the members of our family, but also of sin against God. There is an Unseen Guest in each of our abodes, who is by us dishonored and disobeyed every time we violate the holy obligations of the household. Ah! if we but remembered that, how much easier it would be to "show piety at home"! In business, too, we have not to do merely with our human customers; buyer and seller alike are dealing with the unseen God. The obligations which the one owes to the other are at the same time obligations which they both owe to God; honesty is not merely what the one is bound to show to the other, but what both alike owe to God.

This used to be recognized in England in the legal form of a bill of lading, which, if I remember rightly, commenced thus: "In the name of God, Amen." And the same truth was acknowledged in the erection in all old European towns of a cross in the middle of the market-place. These things originally meant that God was to be regarded as a party to every bargain, and that men were to buy and sell as constantly under the influence of the love of him who died for them upon the cross. But, alas! I fear that nowadays all this is too sadly forgotten, and the selfish maxim, "Every man for himself," has come to be too largely received and acted upon. They try to salve their consciences by adding, "and God for us all;" but if every man be only for himself, God will be for none of us. Let it not be so, I beseech you, among you. Remember that God is dealing with you in every transaction. Treat every one with whom you are doing business as you would treat the Christ. Then your counting-house will become sacred, and your store will be a training-place for the fellowships of the skies. Do you say that is Utopian? Then I reply that, whether you acknowledge it or not, you are already dealing with God in every transaction; and it is better that you should know it, for it is impossible to outwit him, and he will hold you to a rigid reckoning at last.

I ought now to remark, in the fifth place, that we shall have to do with God in the awards of final judgment. But here your time will not permit me to enlarge. The judgment is absolutely certain; for "it is appointed unto men once to die, and after death the judgment." It is to be universal; for before the judge shall be "gathered all nations." The judge is to be the Omniscient One who is acquainted with the secret things of each man's heart and life, and the righteous one who shall render to every man according to his works. And his awards are to be eternal; for the wicked "shall go away into everlasting punishment, but the righteous into life everlasting." Now when we take all these things into consideration, and remember that we are making now the materials for which these awards are to be given at the last, "what manner of persons ought we to be in all holy conversation and godliness?" The day of judgment will make nothing new. It will only reveal the characters which we are making now, and stamp them with the fixity of eternity. Thus we invest the brief space of our lives here with tremendous importance, for it holds in it the issues of eternity; and it does so because in the whole matter we have to do with God. Oh, will you remember this awful truth, and live every day now so thoroughly with God, and in the fellowship of Christ, that you shall have what the Apostle has called "boldness in the day of judgment"?

We have to do with God. That is the great truth for the day. We are environed on every side with God. We cannot move a step without confronting him. We cannot engage in any work without dealing with him, or, as the Hebrew poet has sublimely put it, "He has beset us before and behind, and laid his hand upon us." It is a solemn thought for the sinner, but it is full of joy to him who has made God his friend; for he can sing, "How precious are thy thoughts unto me, O God! how great is the sum of them! If I should count them, they are more in number than the sand. When I awake I am still with thee." To which of these classes do you belong, my hearer? I leave you to give the answer; but whether you be sinner or saint, here is an appropriate prayer for each of you: "Search me, O God, and know my heart; try me, and know my thoughts, and see if there be any wicked way in me, and lead me in the way everlasting." Amen.

VII.

"I KNOW WHERE THOU DWELLEST."

I know thy works, and where thou dwellest, even where Satan's seat is.— REVELATIONS ii. 13.

PERGAMOS, or Pergamum, the seat of government for the Roman Province of Asia Propria, was situated in Asia Minor, some three miles to the north of the river Caicus, and about twenty miles from the sea. It had been formerly the capital of the kingdom of Mysia, and was at first famed for its wealth, which was said to have had its origin in the fact that Lysimachus, a successor of Alexander, intrusted nine thousand talents to the keeping of one of its rulers, who appropriated the money, declared himself independent, and founded a kingdom whose last monarch bequeathed all his dominions and treasures to the Romans. Among these treasures was an immense library, consisting of two hundred thousand rolls, which Antony gave to Cleopatra, by whom it was added to the great collection at Alexandria, where it was ultimately destroyed by the Caliph Omar.

Side by side with this pre-eminence in wealth and literature, there was in Pergamos an equally conspicuous devotion to idolatry. In a grove hard by the city there was a cluster of famous temples, dedicated to Zeus, Minerva, Apollo, Venus, Bacchus, and Æsculapius, but it was to the last named of these that the deepest homage of the Pergamenes was given. Their city was "temple-keeper" to Æsculapius, even as Ephesus was to Diana; and in their case, as in those of other Asiatic Greeks, idolatry was associated with the worst forms of licentious indulgence. That of itself would be warrant enough for speaking of their city as the place where Satan's seat or throne was; but there may, perhaps, be something still more definite in that description, for the serpent, which among Jews was a familiar name for Satan, was the distinctive symbol of Æsculapius. A living snake was kept, and all but worshipped, in his temple at Pergamos, and the representation of a serpent was stamped upon some of the coins of the city. It is possible, therefore, that there may be some allusion to these things in the language of my text.

Now in this seat of Roman power, this centre of Greek idolatry and culture, this "cathedral city of paganism," as one has called it, a Christian church had come into existence. We know nothing of its early history. We cannot tell when or by whom it was planted. All our information regarding it is derived from this epistle to its members. But from that we may gather the following particulars: namely, that it had been blessed at first with considerable prosperity; that after a time it had been assailed by fierce persecution, and had given the name of Antipas to the roll of "the noble army of martyrs;" and that, after having successfully resisted the intolerance of oppression, it was in danger of being corrupted by the insidious influence of the pleasures and fashions of the city, so that its members needed to be warned against yielding to such allurements.

From the first, the world has sought to vanquish the church in one or other of two ways. It has attempted either to destroy it by persecution, or to corrupt it by patronage. It has tried to exterminate Christians by putting them to death; and when that has failed, it has endeavored to take the aggressiveness out of their Christianity by beguiling them into fashionable sins or tempting them to self-indulgence. If they could not be thrust out of the world, they might be amalgamated with the world. If they would not yield to its persecution, they might be won by its flattery. If they could not be terrified by its violence, they might be courted by its attentions.

Now of these two methods the latter is by far the more insidious, and many who have been proof against the first have fallen ignominiously before the second. Not one of the Pergamenes, so far as we know, renounced Christ through fear of persecution; but when the grandees of the city invited them to their banquets, and showered upon them polite attentions, some of them were overcome, and this letter was written to put them all more thoroughly on their guard. They were in a place whose moral atmosphere was laden with the poison of licentiousness and idolatry. It became them, therefore, to keep up the general tone of their spiritual health, lest they should become infected with these evils; and those among them who had become victims to their influence are earnestly exhorted to repent, lest they should be destroyed with the sword that cometh out of the mouth of him "who walketh in the midst of the candlesticks and holdeth the stars in his right hand."

Many important things are suggested by this brief summary of the history and condition of the church at

Pergamos, but it is not my intention to allude further, except incidentally, to the case of these ancient disciples. My purpose rather is to put before you some thoughts naturally rising out of the words of the text, and calculated to be of service to us, both for warning and encouragement, in our daily life.

Notice, then, in the first place, that it is possible to be a Christian anywhere. Pergamos was the place where Satan's seat was; and yet even in that city there was a Christian church, concerning many of whose members the Lord could say that "they had held fast his name, and had not denied his faith." Christianity is not a thing of locality, but of character. There are plants which will grow in some latitudes, but will die in others. Tropical shrubs will not flourish within the Arctic circle, and the Alpine flora are not found on low-lying plains. But Christianity can live wherever a man can live, for it is a thing of personal character; and as that is a matter of choice, and a man always is what he chooses to be, he may be a Christian if he choose in any circumstances, or in any place. Christianity consists in the loyalty of the heart, and the allegiance of the life to Christ; and these may be maintained anywhere. Obadiah kept his conscience clear even in the household of Ahab. Daniel preserved his integrity to God amid the corruption of the court of Babylon, and Nehemiah maintained his piety in the palace of the Persian emperor. Nor are instances of a similar sort wanting at the other end of the social scale. As Jonathan Edwards said, in words which have become proverbial, "The grace of God can live where neither you nor I could;" and they who work in the streets and lanes of the cities are often cheered by coming in unexpected places on humble Christians who are walking with God as truly as Enoch did.

And what is true of places is equally so of occupations. Unless a man's business or occupation be in and of itself sinful, as pandering to the vices and demoralizing to the characters of his fellows, he may serve Christ in any profession or trade. The Roman army under the empire was a very poor school for morals, and yet all the centurions mentioned in the New Testament seem to have been men with some good thing in their hearts toward the Lord. The sailor is proverbially rough, and yet among our seamen have been found some of the bravest and most earnest Christians of our times. The population of our mining districts is commonly considered to be somewhat regardless, and yet when some dreadful explosion has occurred, and some of the workmen have been buried for days by the collapse of the shaft, we have read such accounts of their prayers and praises during their living grave as have convinced us that they, at least, were genuine disciples of the Lord. Character may take some of its coloring from circumstances; but it is itself independent of them, for it is the choice of that personal will by which a man breasts circumstances and makes them subservient to his own great life purpose.

Now, if this be so, if it be true that a man may be a Christian anywhere, what follows? This, in the first place,—that we must not be prejudiced against a man because of the locality in which we find him, or the work in which he is engaged. Even the Lord Jesus came out of Nazareth, and we know how near Nathanael was to making a fatal mistake regarding him, by ignoring the principle on which I am now insisting. Test a man by what he is, rather than by where he comes from. Let not the bad reputation of the quarter in which he lives, or the evil report of the trade at which he works, keep you from being just to him, or from recognizing the Christ image in him, if it be truly there. The real question is whether he is serving Christ; and if he is, let the difficulties of his situation only commend him all the more strongly to your confidence and assistance.

If it be true that a man may be a Christian anywhere, it follows in the second place that we ought never to excuse ourselves for our lack of Christianity by pleading the force of circumstances, or the nature of our business, or the character of the place in which we reside. How often do we hear one say, "There is no use in trying to be a Christian where I am," and in how many cases have we a repetition of Herod's history when men say, "We are very sorry, yet in our circumstances and where we are, we are under the necessity of acting thus or so." But it is never necessary to do wrong. No circumstances can compel you to sin. He who pleads his situation for declining to become a Christian would not be a Christian even if that were different, for, as I have said, Christianity is a thing of heart and life, and where that life is it will breast circumstances. It is the dead fish that floats helpless down the stream, but the living one makes its way up in spite of the current. What an example the noble Havelock gave in this regard! Men were prejudiced against him because being in the army he was a devoted Christian, and some "candid" friends told him that his piety stood in the way of his promotion. Now hear what he wrote to them on that subject: "Old —— and others used to tell me that it was believed at the Horse Guards and in other quarters that

I professed to 'fear God,' as well as to 'honor the Queen,' and that Lord Hill and others had made up their minds that a man could not be at once a saint and a soldier. Now I dare say such great authorities must be right, notwithstanding the examples of Colonel Gardner and Cromwell and Gustavus Adolphus; but if so, all I can say is, that their bit of red ribbon was very ill bestowed upon me, for I HUMBLY TRUST THAT IN THAT GREAT MATTER I SHOULD NOT CHANGE MY OPINIONS AND PRACTICES, THOUGH IT RAINED GARTERS AND CORONETS AS THE REWARD OF APOSTASY." That was rising above circumstances. That was greater heroism even than he showed at the relief of Lucknow, and that may well animate us, wherever we are, to hold fast our loyalty to the Lord Jesus.

But, passing to another thought, the words of my text suggest the truth that it is harder to be a Christian in some places than in others. We have seen that one may be a Christian anywhere, but in our earnest insistence upon that, we must not allow ourselves to forget that some places and circumstances are more favorable for the development of Christian character than others. Thus there are households in which it seems to be the most natural thing in the world for a child to grow up into the beauty of holiness, and there are others in which everything like loyalty to Christ would meet with the bitterest opposition, and could be maintained only by strenuous exertions. When the English deist visited the good Fénelon, he said, "If I stay here much longer I shall become a Christian in spite of myself." That represents the one sort of surrounding. But there are too many specimens of the other among us to require minute specification here. The boy who is brought up in a rough, irreverent, and immoral neighborhood has far more to contend with if he is to be a Christian than he who resides in a different sort of locality. It is also undeniable that the environments of some professions or trades are more trying to those who are seeking to follow Christ than are those of others. Each, indeed, has its own hardships, and none is entirely free from difficulty; but some have more than others. It was easier, I sometimes think, for our fathers a hundred years ago to cultivate Christian character, especially on its contemplative and devotional side, than it is for us in these days. It is easier for a pastor to manifest some qualities of character than it is for a merchant; or rather, perhaps, I ought to put it thus: A merchant has more to test certain qualities of character in him every day than a pastor has in a month. When the lymphatic Dutchman, who took things always easily, said to his nervous and excitable pastor, who was speaking somewhat testily: "Dominie, restrain your temper," he was met with the pertinent and perfectly true reply, "Restrain my temper, sir! I would have you to understand that I restrain more temper in the course of a single day than you do in a year." That was a difference in temperament. But the same thing holds in occupation and surroundings, and while we must be religiously on our guard against excusing *ourselves* for our shortcomings by our circumstances, we yet must frankly acknowledge in our estimates of others that it is harder to maintain Christian principle in some places than in others.

What then? If that be true, what follows? This, for one thing: the Lord knows that it is true, and he will estimate our work by our opportunity. Read these words once more: "I know thy works and where thou dwellest, even where Satan's seat is." We may be sure, therefore, that if we are in a hard place he will give us strength according to our day, and grace according to our need. He will not fail us nor forsake us. He prayed for Peter when Satan sought to sift him as wheat, and he will not forget to intercede for us when we are in the place "where Satan's seat is," that our faith may not fail. "I know where thou dwellest," so he can always tell where to find us. He can come to us at once, and give us the help we require. None of his communications go astray because they are wrongly addressed. When Paul was to be encouraged he sent Ananias to him with this direction: "Go into the street which is called Straight, and inquire in the house of Judas for one called Saul of Tarsus, for behold he prayeth," which in modern phraseology would be —

> SAUL OF TARSUS,
> Care of JUDAS,
> STRAIGHT STREET,
> DAMASCUS.

And when Cornelius was to be instructed he received this command: "Send men to Joppa, and call for one Simon, whose surname is Peter. He lodgeth with one Simon, a tanner, whose house is by the seashore. He shall tell thee what thou oughtest to do." Or putting it into its modern equivalent, —

> SIMON, whose surname is PETER,
> Care of SIMON THE TANNER,
> SEASHORE COTTAGE,
> JOPPA.

Yes, he knows where we dwell, and all his blessings get into the hands for which they were intended. That which was meant for one is not despatched to another; but each gets his own grace, and the grace is suited to the place in which each one dwells. So we may leave ourselves implicitly in his hands. He knows our circumstances. He can tell what there is in them of extenuation, and what of necessity; and so he will make all just allowance for the one, and give all required assistance in the other.

But as another lesson from the point on which I am here insisting, we ought to learn to be charitable in our judgments of others. While we hold ourselves to a rigid reckoning in all circumstances, let us make all due and loving allowance for the circumstances of others. The flower in the window of the poor man's house in the close and dingy city street may be far from being a perfect specimen of its kind, but that it is there at all is a far greater marvel than it is to find a superb representative of the same species in the rich man's conservatory; and there may be more honor to one man for what of Christianity he has maintained in the face of many obstacles, though it be marred by some more or less serious blemishes, than there is to another, in whom are no such imperfections, but who has had no such difficulties.

But coming now to another thought, let me remark, as suggested by this letter, that the harder the place in which we are, we should be the more earnest by prayer and watchfulness to maintain our Christian character. Where the danger is greatest, the vigilance should be most wary. Where the perils are most insidious the prayers should be most earnest. These are truisms in the Christian life. We are all already convinced of their truth, and we all admit their importance; but as it seems to me, we do not sufficiently act upon them, because we have wrong ideas as to what the most serious things that menace the Christian life really are. Instead, therefore, of insisting here on the duties of prayer and watchfulness, in regard to the importance of which we are already convinced, it may be more profitable to say a word or two on the question, what the hardest place in the Christian life really is.

It is not always that in which there is the greatest external resistance to Christianity. That kind of opposition, indeed, may be to some temperaments very specially trying. But all history shows that the greatest danger to the Christian is not in that which openly assails him. An avowed antagonist he meets as an antagonist. He prepares himself for the encounter, and is rarely taken unawares by such an assailant. But when the ungodly meet him as friends, then he is in real peril. The world's attentions are more deadly to him than its antagonisms, and it is against them that he must be specially on his guard. When Christianity becomes respectable, and its adherents are taken notice of by those who care nothing for their faith, when they are invited to the feasts at which the world's idolaters do homage to their own deities, ah! then, like the Pergamenes, they are in danger of being swept into the doctrines of Balaam and the practices of the Nicolaitanes. These influences break down the boundary between the church and the world, and let the world into the church, thereby destroying its purity and insuring its destruction. My brethren, is there no danger of this in the days and in the place in which we live? In the recoil against some features of what has been called Puritanism, have we not gone into the opposite extreme of seeking to propitiate the world, by doing everything in our power to please it; and must not the upshot of all that be the amalgamation of the church with the world? And that means the corruption both of the church and the world; for if the salt have lost its savor, not only is the salt made useless, but that which is salted therewith is lost. Let us take heed to ourselves, therefore, lest we be deceived by the friendship of the world. The church is in the world, as a boat is in the sea. It can float only by keeping above it, and if we let it become, as I may say, *world-logged*, it will be swamped as surely as a boat will be that is filled with water.

But I hasten to the last thought suggested by this text and the letter in which we find it: this, namely, that the greater the difficulty which we overcome in the maintenance of our Christian characters, the nobler will be our reward. It would be, I have no doubt, a little difficult for one to say, offhand and in a moment, which of the seven promises "to him that overcometh," which we have at the end of these seven epistles, he would prefer; but the longer I think upon the subject, the more am I disposed to put highest this one in the letter to the Pergamenes: "To him that overcometh will I give to eat of the hidden manna, and will give him a white stone, and in the stone a new name written, which no man knoweth saving he that receiveth it." About the former of these blessings there can be no mistake, for the manna is Christ, the Bread of Life, and the meaning of the phrase, "I will give him to eat of the hidden manna" is this: "I will bring the victor into the true Holy of Holies, which is heaven, and will feed him there with that which hitherto had been hidden from his sight. I will bring him into glory; and he shall see my face, and feast on fellowship with myself."

That, however, is the common privilege of all the redeemed, and there is added an individual and distinctive honor. "I will give him a white stone, and in the stone a new name written, which no man knoweth saving he that receiveth it." Now here are three things, each of which is significant, — the white stone, the new name, and the great secret. A white stone was used for different purposes of old, — sometimes for giving a vote for the acquittal of one charged with a crime, sometimes as a token to secure admission to a banquet, and sometimes simply as an expression or manifestation of the love of one friend to another. The last seems to me very clearly to be the meaning here. "I will give him a special evidence of my love."

Then there is the new name written in the stone. Now throughout the Scriptures whenever a new name was given by God to any one, it was connected with some particular crisis in his history, and designed to be specially commemorative of that. Thus the name Abram was changed into Abraham when the Lord established with the patriarch the covenant of circumcision, and first set up a visible church upon the earth, a thing well worthy of such special recognition. So when Jacob received the name Israel, it was in connection with that night-long wrestle with the angel, which left its mark not only on the patriarch's body, but also and more particularly on his character. Now bearing these things in mind, we shall discover in this new name something distinctively commemorative of the personal history and conflicts of the individual on whom it is conferred. And when it is added that "no man knoweth it saving he that receiveth it," we have the further peculiarity that as referring to the most terrible struggles and most sacred experiences of the man, it is a matter of holy confidence between him and the Lord. There are secrets between the Lord Jesus and each of his people even now and here. He is something to me that he is not to any one of you, and he is something to each of you that he is not to me. The sun belongs to all the flowers alike, and yet he is to each something that he is not to any of the rest, giving to each its own distinctive appearance, its crimson tips to the mountain daisy, and its beautiful combination of colors to the violet. Just so, Christ has through my personal history revealed himself in some aspects to me that he has not to you, and through the personal history of each of you, he has revealed himself in some aspects to each of you that he has not to me, and this new name at last will be the gathering up, so to speak, into one mnemonic word, of all that personal revelation which Christ has made to each individually through his history, experiences, and conflicts. Thus in the case of each of us our life on earth is determining the quality of our heaven, and the more faithful we are to Christ in spite of difficulties, and through his grace bestowed upon us, we shall have the more meaning packed for us into this new name, making it all the fuller of significance to ourselves, and all the more mysterious to others. If another were to receive that name it would be to him incomprehensible; but as given to us, it will be to us bright with its summary of our history in the past, and lustrous with its promise of fellowship for the future, giving to each of us something in heaven, which shall be his very own, — which shall be to him the very heaven in heaven, — a confidential sacred secret between each of us and the Lord.

Now if this be so, is there not much in it to nerve us to constant steadfastness in the work of the Lord? There is a conflict, — we cannot get rid of that; but if we hold on, and hold out, we shall be conquerors, and this new name will tell us at the last how much more than conquerors through him who loveth us.

VIII.

THE SILENCE OF JESUS.

And the high priest arose, and said unto him, Answerest thou nothing? what is it which these witness against thee? But Jesus held his peace. — MATTHEW xxvi. 62, 63.

Then he questioned with him in many words; but he answered him nothing. — LUKE xxiii. 9.

When Pilate therefore heard that saying, he was the more afraid; and went again into the judgment hall, and saith unto Jesus, Whence art thou? But Jesus gave him no answer. — JOHN xix. 8, 9.

THE Lord Jesus did not deal with every man in precisely the same way. If you would not misunderstand my meaning, I would say that he was not equally frank with every man, but treated each according to the spirit which he found in each. Thus we read in one place that though "many believed in his name," he did not "commit himself unto them, because he knew all men, and needed not that any should testify of man, for he knew what was in man." You remember, also, how differently he spoke to each of the three who wished to follow him, saying to the first, "Foxes have holes, and birds of the air have nests, but the Son of man hath not where to lay his head;" to the second, "Let the dead bury their dead, but go thou and preach the kingdom of God," and to the third, "No man having put his hand to the plough and looking back is fit for the kingdom of God." Similarly he expounded the meaning of some of his parables to his chosen disciples, while he withheld their interpretation from the multitude. And even in his education of the twelve "he taught them as they were able to bear it," keeping back from them at one time that which he communicated to them at a riper stage of their development. Thus we have the general principle established that when our Lord was on earth the measure of the fulness of his revelation of truth to men was conditioned by their disposition toward himself, and by their general moral character.

Now that principle will satisfactorily account for his communicativeness at some times and his silence at others during his three trials, — first before Caiaphas, next before Herod, and last of all before Pilate, to which I purpose now to direct your attention. Caiaphas was surrounded by the scribes and elders, who had already made up their minds that the Lord was to be somehow got rid of; and therefore when, as a mere matter of form, the High Priest said to him, after the false witnesses had spoken against him, "Answerest thou nothing?" we read that "Jesus held his peace." Whereas, when the same Caiaphas, as the President of the Court before which he was arraigned, put him upon his oath in the usual fashion, "I adjure thee by the living God, that thou tell us whether thou be the Christ the Son of God," there was an immediate, full, and direct response. In the one case there was a mere attempt to get him to commit himself. In the other, there was a judicial inquiry made in the solemnest of all forms, and hence the difference of his demeanor in the one and in the other. So again, when Herod, for the mere gratification of a long existing curiosity, and in the hope of seeing some miracle wrought by him, "questioned with him in many words," "he answered him nothing," because he knew when and how to act upon his own precept: "Give not that which is holy unto the dogs, neither cast ye your pearls before swine, lest they trample them under their feet, and turn again and rend you." The tyrant who gave up the head of John the Baptist rather than offend his paramour, was not the sort of man to be benefited by any words or works of the Master in this testing hour, and so "he answered him nothing." In like manner when, after the sad and hopeless scepticism of his question "What is truth?" Pilate asked him "Whence art thou?" the Lord knew that he could say nothing that would be accepted by a man who was in such a spirit, and so "he gave him no answer." If the Roman governor had waited in reverent candor for a reply to his former inquiry, the probability is that he would not have needed to make the latter, inasmuch as the quality of the answer would have clearly indicated that he who gave it came down from heaven. But to all such questions, now, Pilate had made answers impossible by the manifestation of his settled agnosticism, for if it be impossible to tell what truth is, or if there be no such thing as truth, it is vain to ask whence it comes.

It was not, therefore, from caprice, still less was it from fitful sullenness, that our blessed Master in these trials acted, when he answered some questioners and declined to make response to others; and his whole conduct here, as in all the other scenes of his earthly life, is for our ensample, that we should follow in his steps. There is "a time to be silent," as well as "a time to speak;" and the highest wisdom is often needed to discriminate the one from the other. But oftener, perhaps, than we wot of silence is the true policy. I would not go the length of him who was so continually saying, "Speech is silvern, but silence is golden," and who was breaking silence every time he said it; but it is not always cowardly to hold one's peace; and in determining whether or not we shall do so, we ought to have regard, not so much to our own safety, as to the disposition of those who have put us to the question. We need not gratuitously expose ourselves to ridicule, or make ourselves "martyrs by mistake." When no good end is to be served by our speech, it is generally better to be silent; but if we do resolve to speak let us remember the good rule: —

> " If wisdom's ways you truly seek,
> Five things observe with care:
> *Of* whom you speak, *to* whom you speak,
> . And *how,* and *when,* and *where.*"

But I have not chosen these texts to-day simply to enforce such a lesson as that, valuable as it unquestionably is; for, as I have been meditating on the deportment of the Living and Incarnate Word in these recorded instances, I think I have seen in him a close analogy to the Written Word. The Scriptures, which are so responsive to some, are silent to others. Many get out of them answers which are full and satisfactory to the questions which weigh most heavily upon them, while multitudes of others find nothing in them, and get nothing from them; and the reason is to be sought for in the different disposition and character of each of these two classes. The extent to which the Bible is a revelation to any man is conditioned very largely by the moral character and distinctive principles of the man himself. Or to put it in shorter and simpler form, that which a man gets out of the Bible depends very largely on what he brings to the Bible.

Nor let any one suppose that this is aside from God's usual way of dealing with men. We find precisely the same thing in other departments. Take, for example, that of external Nature, and how familiar is the aphorism that "the eye sees only that which it has the power of seeing"! A landscape which would charm one beholder has little or no attraction for another. A poet sees in a flower "thoughts that do lie too deep for tears;" but there are many like the pedler of whom the same poet has said that —

> "A primrose by a river's brim
> A yellow primrose was to him,
> And it was nothing more."

One observer will see a great deal more in a picture or a statue than another, because of the greater measure of education or of taste that he possesses; and the music which gives exquisite delight to a cultivated ear, is little better than a pleasant noise to him who has no perception of "the concord of sweet sounds." The reader takes out of a book only that in it which he can understand, appreciate, and assimilate. The "Principia" of Newton will be unintelligible to many who yet can drink in with delight the poetry of Cowper, or peruse with eager enjoyment the historical descriptions of Macaulay. We are familiar with such differences as these, rooted as they are in some cases in natural aptitudes, and in others in educational proficiency. But we have the same also in the moral sphere, with this peculiarity, however, — that they are *moral* differences, for which, as caused by the voluntary action of the individuals, they are personally responsible. On all spiritual matters, the man receives only such things as accord with his spiritual nature, as he has chosen to make that for himself by his own predilections and habits. The apostle has laid down the general law here in these words: "The natural man receiveth not the things of the spirit of God, neither can he know them, because they are spiritually discerned;" and all the instances which we may specify are only illustrations of the truth of his assertion. Now, as it seems to me, the most common of the influences which keep men from seeing what the Bible contains, or in the phraseology of my text, which make the Bible silent to their questions, are just those which we find in the particular individuals to whom here "Jesus held his peace;" and therefore we may profitably spend a few moments in the consideration of them.

First of all, then, among the influences in men which make the Bible a silent book to them, we find *prejudice*. The scribes and elders, at the head of whom was Caiaphas, had already determined that Jesus must be put to death. They could not endure the pure white light which he had made to "beat" upon their principles, or the withering condemnation which he had pronounced upon their lives. For long months they had been planning to get him into their power; and now that he had been betrayed into their hands, they had no mind to allow him to escape. It made no matter, therefore, what he should say in reply to the false witnesses whom they had procured to testify against him. They had prejudged his case, and so when they asked him for an answer he "held his peace." Now in the same way, prejudice, whatever be its source, gets nothing out of the Scriptures. If you bring a full pitcher to the spring, you can take no water away from it. If the mind be already made up to reject the Bible, it can get no answers from it to any of its questions. The reader who is animated by that spirit will read only to sustain his prejudice, and will be at no loss to find something which he can pervert to his purpose. The man who is resolved to believe no good of another will either find or make evil in him, and the more difficult that is felt to be the more firmly will he hold by his antagonism. I am not surprised, therefore, at the way in which some men speak of the Sacred Scriptures, for this explains the whole matter. When, for example, such a thinker as John Stuart Mill undoubtedly was, in certain departments, speaks of the discourses of Jesus which are preserved in the gospel by John as "poor stuff,"[1] we read his words at first with a shock of surprise. It seems strange that such a man should pronounce such a judgment on sayings which have been regarded by others as the most sublime and the most suggestive that ever came from human lips. But when we remember that Mill read them with all the prepossessions of one who had been educated without any religion at all, and in utter atheism, our wonder ceases. To one so "set" in his judgments, Jesus had no word to say. He was dumb as he was to Caiaphas and the priests, not because there is nothing in his discourses, but because Mill lacked the spiritual sense for the discernment of what is there. The eye had not the power to see what was in the sayings, and he went away remarking, "There is nothing." Like Nathanael, he said, "Can there any good thing come out of Nazareth?" but unlike the guileless Israelite, he did not divest

[1] See Mill's "Three Essays on Religion," p. 254.

himself of that prejudice when he went to "see," and therefore he heard no voice where so many others, who were to him intellectually but as "babes and sucklings," heard a voice from heaven.

We must not, therefore, allow ourselves to be overawed by the mental greatness of many who have affirmed that Jesus in the Scriptures has given no answer to them. For more than intellect is needed here,— even the docile, candid, guileless spirit, together with the religious sense; and in the absence of these, the mightiest mind will go astray. Here is the law: "If any man be willing to do his will, he shall know of the doctrine whether it be of God, or whether I speak of myself." If there be any one here, therefore, who is anxiously seeking to settle for himself the question who and whence Jesus Christ is, — who is bewildered amid the conflicting testimonies that are borne concerning him, and who is making application to himself for a solution, — let me beseech him first and before all things else to divest himself of prejudice. Dismiss all evil impressions which may have been made upon you by the wicked conduct of some of those who have called themselves by his name. Judge him not by the influence of this church or of that upon human liberty or progress. Reject him not because of the treatment given to science and its votaries by the mediæval hierarchy. But form your estimate by what is said by him and written of him in this Book. Bring a candid, sincere, prayerful spirit to its study, and you will receive from it a full and satisfying answer; but without these qualities in you it will give you no response. It yields its treasures only to the reverent and the humble, and so it comes that the things which are "hidden from the wise and prudent" it reveals "to babes."

Nor ought it to be forgotten here that the same prejudice that makes the Scriptures as a whole a sealed book to so many operates also in the embittering of religious controversy, and the keeping of Christians from coming to agreement regarding the teachings of the Bible. That was a pregnant saying of Archbishop Whately to the effect that it is one thing to seek to be on the side of Scripture, and quite another to seek to have Scripture on our side; and the divisions which have separated, and which still keep apart from each other the different churches of Christendom have their origin largely in the fact that as a general rule their members have been more anxious to have Scripture on their side than to be on the side of Scripture. They have read their own views into the Scriptures, rather than sought to get at the full teaching of the Scriptures. In the homely phrase of John Newton, "Each, on one subject or another, has been trying to light the candle without taking off the extinguisher," and naturally they have not succeeded. But it is one of the most hopeful signs of our times that the exposition of the Scriptures has become so common, and that the desire of interpreters has increasingly come to be to get at the simple meaning of the inspired writers, rather than to make their statements square with some pre-accepted system. This is the true inductive method; and out of that will come a system which shall be distinctively Biblical rather than metaphysical, and which shall gather into itself the fragments of truth that are in every system. But to get at that we must bring unbiassed minds to the investigation, and to secure such minds we must ask that God, by his Holy Spirit, may open our understandings to understand the Scriptures.

But I remark in the second place that habitual indulgence in sin will prevent us from receiving any answers to our inquiries from the Scriptures. For the aggravated sinner, who, when he came to his "narrow place," gave up John the Baptist to death rather than part with Herodias, the Lord Jesus had no answer to his many questions. *His* opportunity was gone. He did not take the tide when it was at the flood, and now he must go unblessed. But we see the same thing still in the fact that hardened sinners find no good thing in the Bible. The truth is that they have so perverted their moral judgment that they do not know good when they see it. The man who is constantly hammering boiler plates soon becomes deaf from the very noise which he and his fellow-workmen make by their hammering. The hand becomes horny and callous by the constant doing of that very thing which at first blistered it and made it bleed. And in the same way the conscience becomes hardened, and the spiritual perception becomes blinded by habitual sin. Thus it comes that the Herods of to-day get no answers from the Christ. Inevitably the habits of a man warp his judgment, and "the god of this world blinds" the eyes, so that a man does not believe that which would condemn himself, and cannot see that which his own sin has hidden. There was terrible power in the retort given by Richard Knill to an Indian officer of dissolute habits, who, at the mess table, was declaring that he could make nothing out of the Bible because there were so many mysteries in it, and to whom the missionary said, "The seventh commandment, sir, is very plain." We may rely upon it, therefore, that wherever the life is wrong, there can be little enjoyment taken in, and little instruction derived from, the Scriptures. Observe, I am not saying that every man who finds nothing in the Bible must be living a grossly immoral life, like that of Herod. I do not think that is true; and just at present I believe that there are many men of excellent habits who, for other reasons, can find little or nothing in that which is to me the Word of God. But what I do say is that when the life is immoral the Scriptures are silent to the man. His conscience is too scared to be moved by their condemnation, and his mind is too blind to perceive their heavenly beauty. If, therefore, there should be any here who want Christ to speak to them, — who desire to know whether he be anything to them or not, and if he be anything, what he is to them, — let me beseech them to put themselves into the requisite condition for getting an answer from him. If you are indulging in secret sin, forswear it; if you are practising evil habits, break away from them; if you are gloating in avarice over the hoards of covetousness, give your riches wings and make them fly in blessing over the land; if you are living in intemperance or lust, abjure it. Get back to the simplicity and docility of childhood. Say like little Samuel, "Speak, Lord, for thy servant heareth;" and then he will give you such a revelation of himself out of the Scriptures as shall make them forever dear to you, and shall lead you to say to him like Thomas, "My Lord and my God!"

But now thirdly I remark that the influence of sceptical philosophy makes the Bible silent to those who are under its power. Pilate did not believe that there was any truth; or if there was any, he did not believe that men could come to its discovery. He belonged to the same class as the elder Pliny, who said,

"The only certainty is that nothing is certain;" and filled as he was with that conviction Christ could say nothing that he would accept, so "he answered him not a word." Thus he was an ancient representative of those modern philosophers, so many of whom are eminent in their several departments and estimable in their lives, who affirm that we can know nothing save through the senses, and that we can have certainty only concerning such things as we can handle and see either with our unassisted senses or with the aid of the scalpel and the microscope; that is to say, we have no certainty save in regard to material things. If you question them as to the future life they affirm that we can know nothing about it. It is not certain that there is no such thing, neither is it certain that there is. We know nothing and can know nothing about it, and there they stand.

Now if I were to argue the matter, I would ask how it comes in this prevailing uncertainty that they are so sure that everything is uncertain in this department? I would urge further that even on their own showing there is a possibility that there is a spiritual realm and life, and that being so, that it is awfully dangerous in them to act as if uncertainty regarding the existence of a future life were all the same as the demonstrated certainty that there is none. For professing to believe simply in ignorance about it, they live exactly as if they were sure that there is nothing of the kind. And to be sure of that, they must know and be sure of everything. I cannot forget here John Foster's argument with the atheist when he says virtually that "the man who affirms that there is no God arrogates to himself the omniscience of the very God whom he denies; for if he do not know everything, then the very thing which he does not know may be that there is a God." So to be certain that there is no certainty possible about the future life, one must have all possible certainties before him, which is tantamount to saying that he is omniscient. Besides, we must not ignore our own spiritual intuitions. There is a world within us, as well as around us, and it is alike unphilosophical and unsafe to exclude that from our consideration on a question like that to which we are referring. True, we cannot gauge its phenomena by the outer senses, as we do those of external things; but they are not the less real for all that, and when they are taken into the account, they point unmistakably — as even Socrates made clear — to a life beyond, of which this is only the vestibule.

But leaving the argument of the matter, I return to the statement that where this sceptical philosophy has taken hold of a man, he finds nothing in the Scriptures, or rather nothing in the Scriptures finds him. For this again is a case of prejudice. He comes to the Scriptures with convictions already formed which are at variance with their principles, and so it is not strange that they have nothing for him; and before he gets any help out of them, or any revelation that will benefit him, he must get rid of the false philosophy which he has accepted. When he comes sincerely desirous to know the truth, and that alone, no matter what happens to his philosophy, then there is hope of his finding something in it; but until then, to him as unto Pilate, Jesus will give no answer.

The sum of the matter, then, is that what we get from Christ or from the Scriptures will depend entirely on the disposition which we bring to him or them; for thus the words of the old psalm are verified, "With the merciful man thou wilt shew thyself merciful; with an upright man thou wilt shew thyself upright; with the pure thou wilt shew thyself pure, and with the froward thou wilt shew thyself froward."

But I cannot conclude without reference to another case, in which Jesus, for a time at least, held his peace. You remember that when the Syro-Phœnician woman came to him pleading for her daughter, we are told that he answered her not a word; but as the record makes apparent, that was only in order that he might bring her faith unto greater strength, and give her a richer blessing in the end. So there may be sincere, earnest, unprejudiced, and agonizing inquirers into the nature and meaning of the Sacred Scriptures, who as yet find nothing satisfactory in them. And to them, with that history in view, I would say, Do not give up the examination. Hold on in the spirit in which you have begun. Doubt not that the answers that you seek will come; and when they do they will lead you to a richer and a stronger faith, while the experience will enable you all the more skilfully and successfully to deal with those who are still in perplexity. See only that you keep the spirit of candor, sincerity, and humility, and then to you also it will be proved that "unto the upright light ariseth in darkness." Above all, cultivate the spirit of prayer, and ever as you sit down to read the Bible ask God to open your eyes to behold the wonderful things which it contains.

IX.

THERE CAME OUT THIS CALF.

And there came out this calf. — EXODUS xxxii. 24.

"OH, Aaron, how could you say that? It would require all the gravity of the most stolid Oriental, one would think, to keep you from losing countenance as you spoke; and an equal measure of self-control more wisely directed might have enabled you to resist the importunity of the tribes, when, with hearts set on mischief, they determined to make to themselves a visible representation of Jehovah."

But Aaron was not the man for a crisis like that. Older than Moses by three years, he was deficient in many of the qualities which were so conspicuous in his younger brother. Ready and eloquent in speech, he seems, like many who have been similarly endowed, to have been pliant and flexible in disposition. His nature was soft and yielding, taking impressions from others rather than making them on others. He had more of the softness of the melted wax than of the hardness of the die. Or to vary the illustration, he floated on the current which others formed, but he rarely, if ever, made a torrent which swept all opposition before it. He excelled in the passive virtues of patience and endurance. Under the stunning blow which deprived him of two of his sons in a moment no hasty word escaped his lips; while on the occasion of the Korahitic rebellion he waited with quiet and becoming dignity until his position had been established, and then he lovingly made intercession for the staying of the plague. But here, when firmness, promptitude, and courage were required, he failed. Out of a timid regard to his own safety he would not oppose the wishes of the people; and so it happened that the spark which determined opposition at the right time might have at once extinguished, became at length a mighty conflagration, in the flames of which some thousands were consumed. Hence his conduct was condemned by Moses, and was at the same time displeasing unto God, for in the account given in Deuteronomy Moses uses these words: "And the Lord was very angry with Aaron to have destroyed him, and I prayed for Aaron also the same time."[1] But "these things happened unto them by way of example, and they were written for our admonition." Let us see, therefore, what we may learn from this dark and humiliating chapter in the history of Aaron.

In the first place, we may see that the sinner always seeks to father his guilt upon somebody else. As Matthew Henry quaintly remarks in his commentary upon this passage: "Sin is a brat that nobody is willing to own." Aaron lays all the blame upon the people. Now it was true that the suggestion first came from them. But Aaron was there in the place of their ruler for the time, and it was his duty, as such, to oppose their evil wishes, and refuse their sinful request. This, however, from whatever motive, he weakly refrained from doing. He uttered no protest; he took no means, so far as we know, to make plain to

[1] Deuteronomy ix. 20.

them the sinfulness of that on the commission of which they were intent; he did not even so much as indicate that he himself could not but condemn their purpose. He simply surrendered without an effort at resistance. Perhaps he was afraid lest in their madness they might put him to death. Indeed, there is a Jewish tradition to the effect that Hur was slain at this time by the people for attempting to resist them in the carrying out of their design. But even if it had been true that Aaron's life would have been actually endangered by resistance, it was his duty to have resisted, and he might have consoled himself with the thought that he never could die in a better cause. But he did not resist; nay, he did more than yield, for he gave his skill, and with that his sanction, to the gratification of their desire. His weakness, thus, as weakness in a magistrate at a critical juncture always is, was worse than wickedness. To talk, therefore, as if the whole blame belonged to the people was simply to juggle with his conscience, while yet in spite of all his efforts to stifle its convictions, it would not be thus silenced. The people *were* set on evil; that was true. But that was not the whole truth; for instead of seeking to prevent them from committing sin, he aided and abetted them in its commission, and so he was a partaker in their guilt.

But so it has been from the beginning. The sinner is always, in his own representation of the case, the victim of some one else. The last thing he will do is to make a full, fair, unequivocal, and unqualified personal confession, "I have sinned." Adam said, "The woman gave unto me, and I did eat." Eve said, "The serpent beguiled me, and I did eat." Herod said virtually, "If I had not committed myself before those who were with me, I would not have consented to John Baptist's execution." And if we may judge of the prodigal in the parable from his modern representatives, who come almost daily to our doors, he must often enough have blamed others for his degradation before he came to the frank acknowledgment that the fault was all his own, — "his companions had robbed him;" "his employers had defrauded him;" "his fellow-workmen had lied about him;" "he had been the victim of a conspiracy," and the like. Many times, I doubt not, he had spoken after that fashion. There needed to be endured by him the misery of the swineherd's life, and the hunger which the husks would not satisfy before he came so fully to himself as to say, "Father, *I* have sinned." Mark, I pray you, where I have put the emphasis, "*I* have sinned." Most of us, I fear, when we are confessing sin, are thinking of the sins of other people, not of our own; or if we are thinking of our own we are doing our best the while to put the guilt of them on others. Let us take care, therefore, lest in exposing Aaron here we are not condemning ourselves, for alas! "the heart is deceitful above all things." That was a very wholesome advice given by an old minister to a young pastor in regard to the management of his church, "When things go wrong blame yourself first." And it would be well if, when we are thinking of our own misdeeds, we were to act upon the same principle, and take the whole guilt of them to ourselves. The very attempt to put it upon others is an evidence that it is ours; for there is profound knowledge of human nature packed up in the French proverb, "He who excuses himself, accuses himself." Let us be honest, therefore, and when we have done wrong, let us frankly admit it, and seek forgiveness where alone that is to be found.

But, in the second place, we may see that the excuses offered by the sinner are often as absurd as they are untrue. As we have seen, Aaron told a part of the truth, but he kept back so much of it as to make his statement, as a whole, false. He admitted so much; but he gave such a coloring to the rest as almost to make it appear that the greater part of the blame was due to the people, and the rest of it to Moses, because of his protracted absence, while between the two he had been made a victim. But now observe how absolutely ridiculous this other statement is: "They gave me their gold, and I cast it into the fire, and there came out this calf." As if the whole matter had been a thing of merely natural evolution, and not of deliberate manufacture! It reminds us of the boy, who, on being reproved by the schoolmaster for blowing his whistle, averred that he was not to blame, for "it whistled itself," or of the blundering servant, who never breaks a dish, but always says, "I was only lifting it, and it broke." Nay, we meet the same thing in much more important places. A moment ago I used the words "natural evolution," because I could not find any better to express my meaning. But they suggest at once a doctrine as absurd as this statement of Aaron. I do not refer, of course, to what I may call Theistic Evolution, which regards evolution as the method adopted by God in the creation of the world, and all the creatures upon it. With that I have no fault to find, save that — so far — I think it has not been proved, and I hold my mind in suspense concerning it, waiting for more light. But I speak now of the

Atheistic or Materialistic form of that doctrine, which tells us that there was first a primordial germ that came, no one can tell how or whence, and that out of that, by slow degrees and a long process of development, under no spiritual superintendence, and simply of itself, there was ultimately evolved this great and glorious universe; and I say that we have in that something infinitely more absurd than this statement of Aaron, "I put their gold into the fire, and there came out this calf." There are others, also, who would have us believe that these Gospels of ours, so distinct from each other in the individuality of their styles, and in the purposes which they were evidently intended to subserve, are the result of what may be called a fortuitous combination of traditions, or a literary chance medley; that some time late in the first century, if not far on in the second, "all who had any sayings of Christ, or about him, brought them and cast them together," and there came out these three most remarkable tractates, which ever since have been the seed-bed of the moral and religious progress of the world. Compared with that, Aaron's history of the Genesis and Exodus of this golden calf is sober sense; and when I take these things into consideration, I own that Aaron's story does not seem to me to be quite so extravagant as it did before. But I allude to these matters only to show that if we allow ourselves to laugh at Aaron, we must not regard his absurdity as entirely antiquated.

I return now to consider his excuse as an excuse for sin. He means Moses to believe that the formation of the calf came about without his personal agency; that it was — shall I say? — an accident, or, if you will, an incident, — something that came without any plan or purpose or exertion of his own; that it was, to use a modern phrase, something "over which he had no control." The nearest thing I can find to it in the Scriptures is the saying of David when Joab's messenger came from Rabbah bringing the news of the death of Uriah the Hittite. David knew what he had done to secure, if possible, that Uriah should be slain. He knew that in his own sight, as well as in God's, he was Uriah's murderer; but thus he salved his conscience: "The sword devoureth one as well as another." As if he had said: "Oh, no! it was not I. It was the sword. It simply came about of itself. When a man goes into battle he must take the risk. Why should I distress myself, therefore, about Uriah more than about any one else who was slain that day? Even if I had not written that letter he might have been slain just the same." It was a plausible subterfuge. It did very well till Nathan came with his touching parable of the ewe lamb, and thrust home its application in the terrible words, "Thou art the man!" and then its efficacy was gone, as David cried out, "*I* have sinned!" He could no longer regard Uriah's death as a mere incident of war. He was convicted there and then as Uriah's murderer, and his prayer became, "Deliver *me* from blood guiltiness, O God, the God of my salvation!"

No, friends, sin is never an accident. It is never a thing that "comes out" of itself. It is a voluntary act, and for every such act the actor is responsible. We cannot do wrong until we choose to do it, and the choosing is a free act of our own. I say a *free* act; that is, a thing from which we might have refrained, if we had pleased. No man, no set of circumstances, can compel us to will; that we always do for ourselves, and for that we are responsible. For an accident, pure and simple, with which our wills have had nothing to do, we are not responsible. But if that which we call an accident has come to pass through our voluntary agency, it is no longer an accident, and we may not take refuge in calling it by that name; while even for things called accidents, if they have happened through our carelessness or neglect of duty, we must be held culpable for such carelessness or neglect. These are distinctions clearly and fully recognized in human law, and they hold equally under the divine. Let us take heed, therefore, lest we deceive ourselves by giving a wrong representation to ourselves of our conduct; but, acting always as in the sight of God, let us do everything in his name, and then we shall be found equal to all emergencies, and be sustained in every crisis.

But the course of thought which we have followed, besides exposing the weakness of some common excuses offered by men for their sins, suggests three practical inferences, with the briefest mention of which I will conclude my discourse. We cannot but learn, in the first place, to be specially watchful over ourselves. The sinner in this case was Aaron, who had been the companion and coadjutor of Moses all through the conflict with Pharaoh in the land of Egypt; who had with Hur stayed up the hands of the great leader during the battle of the people with the Amalekites, and who was to be the first High Priest. If there was one man in the encampment who could be relied upon during the absence of Moses, that man surely was Aaron; and yet he proved unfaithful. What an illustration this of the wisdom of the Apostle's words: "Let him that thinketh he standeth take heed lest he fall." It is easy to stand when we are in no conflict. But when a crisis is upon us that is another matter, and then it is often found that the braggart in the barrack is the coward on the field. Remember Peter, and do not make his rash protestations lest you be put to shame as he was by his fall. Do not boast what you will do, but rather pray that you may be strengthened to do what you already see and know to be right.

Now, for a second lesson, we may learn to be charitable to others when they prove weak in the hour of temptation. This was Aaron who yielded, and Aaron was in the main a good man. *We* cannot estimate aright all the things that need to be taken into account in judging how guilty a man has been in a given case. It is very noticeable here, too, that Moses said nothing to Aaron about his guilt after he had received these trifling excuses. He probably saw that, even in Aaron's own estimation, they were only subterfuges in which he could not rest a moment, and so he left him to his conscience, which he was sure would not let him have peace until he went to God for forgiveness. But while, so far as we see, he said nothing to Aaron, he spoke to God on Aaron's behalf. Remember the words I have already quoted from Deuteronomy, "The Lord was very angry with Aaron to have destroyed him, and I prayed for Aaron also the same time." Let us, therefore, imitate Moses in this regard, and when we hear others speaking in an extravagant and absurd fashion, as they seek to excuse themselves for their sins, let us take it as a hopeful sign that they think they need to appease their consciences with some opiate, and let us go to our closets and remember them upon our knees before our God.

Finally, let sinners be encouraged after they have fallen, to return to God in penitence. This Aaron was afterwards made High Priest, — afterwards, observe, — and so he had obtained forgiveness from on high; yes, and he was all the better fitted for his priesthood because of this experience. You remember the words of the author of the Epistle to the Hebrews, "Every high priest taken from among men is ordained for men in things pertaining to God that he may offer both gifts and sacrifices for sin. Who can have compassion on the ignorant, and on them that are not of the way, for that he himself also is compassed with infirmity." Aaron learned how much he was thus encompassed by this experience. But he learned, also, how freely God can forgive; and so if there are any here who have been sinning and excusing themselves, let them learn to give over all their foolish and vain and utterly ineffectual efforts to explain away their guilt. Let them go to God, through Christ, in frank confession and with earnest prayer, and he will receive them graciously. He will love them freely, and will ultimately enable them to utilize the lesson learned by them through that experience in ministering to the spiritual welfare of others.

X.

THE RESIDUE.

And the residue thereof he maketh a god.— ISAIAH xliv. 17.

RIDICULE, though not in any proper sense of the word a test of truth, is yet a very effective means of exposing error. No doubt it is liable in unskilful or unscrupulous hands to be greatly abused, and when it is used to give point to personal attacks, or to make a man's natural defects for which he is in no way responsible the laughing-stock of the community, it is worthy of all reprobation. But when it deals purely with principles and practices, and shows the grotesque side of an error, or the ludicrous absurdity of an argument, it is then one of the most deadly weapons in the armory of truth. Indeed, when kept within its own proper limits, and employed by a man as eminent for principle as for humor, it is well-nigh irresistible. Even error, when it has the laughers on its side, becomes formidable; but when they are brought over to the cause of truth, they carry, for the time at least, everything before them. No man relishes the putting either of his conduct or of his reasoning into a ridiculous light. Most people, I imagine, would sooner be condemned for a real fault than laughed at for a harmless foible; and some who have faced the cannon on a battle-field without a quiver have flinched before a battery of derision. One can laugh *with* the multitude, and think little or nothing of *that;* but when the multitude is laughing *at him* he wants to hide himself somewhere. Every one who is at all familiar with literature will easily recall instances in which ridicule was made exceedingly effective on the side of truth. Erasmus did good service with it in his "Praise of Folly." Pascal, in his "Provincial Letters," laughed the Jesuits into defeat, and did more for the Jansenists than Jansen himself. Every one who has read Hugh Latimer's paragraph, in which he makes use of the countryman's saying that "Tenterden steeple was the cause of Goodwin sands," or that other in which he describes the devil as the busiest bishop in the land, or the scathing sarcasm of the passage in which John Knox, after a reference to this very chapter, asks which is the greater miracle-worker, the priest who makes the wafer into God, or the mouse whose profane teeth immediately makes it back again into bread, — will have some idea of the havoc which ridicule can do to the cause of an opponent; and in more recent times the "Eclipse of Faith" by Henry Rogers was not more powerful in its serious argumentation than it was in those Socratic passages, wherein, by the method of dialogue, the sceptic was made to turn upon himself the laughter of all the bystanders.

Now it is not strange that a weapon so powerful should be occasionally employed by the prophets. Elijah mocked at the priests of Baal, and the humor of Elisha made the Syrians ridiculous, when, under color of bringing them to himself, he led them into the very capital of their enemies. But no more splendid instance of its use is to be found in the whole compass of literature than that made by Isaiah in the chapter from which my text is taken. Arguing against idolatry, his double thesis is that they who make graven images are vanity, and that the images made by them are worthless; and to prove both propositions he goes into a description of the process by which idols were made, and then shows us the finished figures carted away like other lumber, not able to help themselves, but oppressing even the animals that had to draw them, and so led into a captivity from which they could not save themselves. Then he contrasts all that with the glorious majesty, uncreated might, and wondrous grace of Jehovah, who could say, "I am the Lord, and there is none else; there is no God beside me. I girded thee though thou has not known me. . . . I am the Lord, and there is none else."

That is the argument; but now see how its strength is increased by the description of the idol-maker. It is like one of those progressive cartoons which we occasionally meet with in illustrated papers, and in which we have a whole history condensed into some five or six scenes. First we see him planting an ash-tree; next, after the ash-tree has grown, we behold him hewing it down; next we have him dividing it into different segments; next we have him putting one of these into the fire and sitting down before it to warm himself, while at the same time he is cooking his dinner over it. Then out of the last log he is represented as carving the likeness of a man, and at the end we see him on his knees in reverent worship before his own handiwork. These are the pictures; and then underneath we have this comment: "They have not known nor understood, for he hath shut their eyes that they cannot see, and their hearts that they cannot understand. And none considereth in his heart, neither is there knowledge nor understanding to say I have burned part of it in the fire; yea, also, I have baked bread upon the coals thereof. I have roasted flesh and eaten it, and shall I make the residue thereof an abomination? Shall I fall down to the stock of a tree? He feedeth on ashes. A deceived heart hath turned him aside that he cannot deliver his soul nor say, is there not a lie in my right hand?"

But now let us turn and look at one or two things suggested by the text.

First of all, then, it reminds us that man must have some object of worship. A great German philosopher and theologian resolved the religious sentiment into a sense of dependence; but whether he was right or not in doing that, it is indisputable that the religious sentiment itself is natural to man. So soon as he begins to think he is met by the questions, whence came I? what am I here for? and whither am I going? and he cannot give even an approximate answer to these inquiries without having suggested to him the ideas of God and a hereafter. These may, indeed, be the remnants of a primeval revelation; and some countenance is given to that view by the fact — which all historical investigation is tending to confirm — that the earliest religion was monotheistic; and by the other fact, that even among the most degraded savages are found the ideas of God and of the future life in some form or other. Corruptions of various sorts have gathered round them, showing that the moral development of man, when left to himself, is always downward; but though covered over with the rubbish of ages, these ideas are still there; and so everywhere there are the acknowledgment of superior beings of some sort, and religious rites more or less

crude. This I know has sometimes been controverted;
but our foreign missionaries are all but unanimous
regarding it, and as a specimen of their testimonies, I
quote the last which has come before my eye, in the
recently published autobiography of John G. Paton,
missionary to Tanna and Aniwa, — a book which ought
to be read by all who are interested in knowing something of the stuff of which our foreign missionaries are
made, the hardships which they are called to endure,
and the success by which their patient years of labor
and trial are generally crowned. The following are his
words: "Let me here give my testimony on a matter of
some importance, — that among these islands, if anywhere, men might be found destitute of the faculty of
worship, men absolutely without idols, if such men
exist under the face of the sky. Everything seemed to
favor such a discovery; but the New Hebrides, on the
contrary, are full of gods. The natives, destitute of
the knowledge of the true God, are ceaselessly groping
after him, if perchance they may find him. Not finding him, and not being able to live without some sort
of a god, they have made idols of almost everything, —
trees and groves, rocks and stones, springs and streams,
insects and other beasts, men and departed spirits,
relics, such as hair and finger-nails, the heavenly bodies,
and the volcanoes; in fact, every being and everything within the range of vision or of knowledge has
been appealed to by them as God, clearly proving that
Humanity, however degraded, prompts man to worship
and lean upon some Being or Power outside of himself
and greater than himself, in whom he lives and moves
and has his being, and without the knowledge of whom
his soul cannot find its true rest or its eternal life."
Add to this the witness borne very lately in my

hearing to a circle of ministers by one who has been recently in India, to the effect that the native religions there are all religions of fear, and that the object of the worshippers is to propitiate their divinities and so keep them from sending injuries upon them, and you will see, that, in connection with their worship, there is a kind of sense of sin, and a feeling of the need of something akin to salvation. But however it may be explained, there is at bottom in every man that which impels him to have some object of worship. He cannot do without that.

And so in the second place we have this other fact suggested by the text; namely, that if a man knows not or has forsaken the living and true God, he fashions a god for himself. This is illustrated by all the idolatries of the world. They are the abortive efforts of men to find the true God, and the idols which have been graven, as Isaiah has phrased it in the context, "after the figure of a man according to the beauty of a man," are but the rude expressions of that desire which God has met and satisfied in the incarnation of his Son. But when we speak of men fashioning a god for themselves we are apt to think only of vulgar and material idolatry, as it is in pagan lands, and to forget those "idols in their hearts," to use Ezekiel's phrase, which men have set up even where the Gospel has been proclaimed, and which are as numerous among ourselves as graven images are in India or Japan. That which a man flees to, in such circumstances as the Christian is in when he flees to Christ, is for him an idol. Now how many of these have men fashioned for themselves in the midst of us! Some are seeking satisfaction in fame; some in exalted worldly position;

some in riches, some in pleasure. There are more shrines for the worship of Bacchus in one of our great cities than there were in all ancient Greece. The temples of Venus are as vile, as loathsome, and as debasing in New York to-day as was that infamous one at Paphos, which Herodotus has described. Mammon, too, has its myriad altars, on which reputation, influence, sometimes even life itself, have been sacrificed. But what need I more here? Every man who is not heart and soul and life devoted to the service of the Lord Jesus Christ, has made for himself some idol or idols to which the homage of his soul is given. He may try to divide his allegiance between his idol and the Christ; but he cannot thus serve two masters. Christ must have the whole heart, or he has really none of it. He must reign "without a rival," and "with no partial sway," and wherever that sovereignty is disputed, that which disputes it is an idol which the man has fashioned for himself. My hearer, have you any such idol in your heart? Search and see, and if you have, make your prayer in the words of the well-known hymn, —

> " The dearest idol I have known,
> Whate'er that idol be,
> Help me to tear it from thy throne,
> And worship only thee."

But I find suggested by Isaiah's argument here this other thought, that the idols fashioned by men for themselves cannot deliver them when they call on them. What a withering exclamation that was which Hosea addressed to the men of Israel, "Thy calf, O Samaria, hath cast thee off!" We can easily see and understand how the graven image is impotent to help in time of need, for there is truth beneath the sarcasm of Isaiah's words: "Bel boweth down, Nebo stoopeth; their idols were upon the beasts and upon the cattle; your carriages were heavy laden; they are a burden to the weary beast. They stoop, they bow down together; they could not deliver the burden, but themselves are gone into captivity." They could not help themselves; much less, therefore, could they help others. But what was true of these external images is equally so of those "idols in the heart," of which I have just spoken. The narcotic to which the sufferer betakes himself for comfort becomes at length a task-master and tyrant, whether its name be alcohol or opium or cocaine. "Riches make themselves wings. They fly away as an eagle toward heaven." The thief may steal them, or the fluctuations of the market may shrivel them up, so that the millionnaire of yesterday may be the bankrupt of to-morrow. The most carefully coddled reputation may be lost, and the popular leader of the present hour may be hissed and forsaken before the year is out. Nay, sooner or later there shall come to each of us the hour which shall try every man's god, of what sort it is, when everything that is perishable shall be lost, and only that which is incorruptible shall remain. Alas for us, then, if we have made false gods our confidence! for we shall then be everlastingly without a god. Nay, not merely without a god, but *without God*, and that is hell! Oh, my hearer! think of that, and now, while you may, choose the good part which shall never be taken away from you, — a God — the God — that is able and willing to help you in time of need. Such a God is Jehovah-Jesus. He will confer on you the true riches of holy happiness, which nothing can corrupt, nor aught destroy. He will give you abiding and eternal good. What he is to you at any time, that he always will be. No change in your circumstances will make any alteration in him. He will not fail you in trial, or leave you in uttermost despair. He is "the same yesterday, to-day, and forever." If he is your present delight, that delight will be perpetual. If he is your peace now, that peace will be eternal. If he is your God now he will be your portion forever. *If!* but why should there be any *if* in the case? Let your soul say now unto this Lord, "Thou art my God. Thou wilt guide me with thy counsel, and afterward receive me to glory. Whom have I in heaven but thee? and there is none upon earth that I desire beside thee."

But I cannot conclude without pointing out to you the keen sarcasm lurking under the word "residue" here. See how this man postpones his attention to religion until after other things have been taken care of by him. The first part of his ash-tree is devoted to his own comfort; he makes a fire with it, whereon he baketh bread and roasteth roast, and is satisfied. With the next part of it he feeds the fire until it glows with heat, and as he sits in front of it he says to himself, "Aha! I am warm. I have seen the fire;" and it is only with the "residue" that he makes his graven image. You smile at all this perhaps; but take care lest you be not unconsciously thereby condemning yourself, for it is not such an uncommon thing after all, even in this enlightened age and land, for people to give to God nothing but a "residue." The youth starts out in life with high ambitions. He will go to college; he will be the prize-taker of his class; he will fit himself for standing in the front ranks in later life. All these he succeeds in accomplishing; but thus far there has been no devotion in his heart to God. He enters into active life, toiling and studying all the while with the most self-denying industry; he rises in his profession; he attracts to himself the attention of the people; he is chosen to a position of honor and emolument. And as he sits in his library looking around him at his cherished books, and thinking of his past, he in effect says, "Aha! I have distanced all my competitors. I have gained position and wealth and comfort." But all these years there has been in his heart no thought of God. He may have gone, indeed, to some house of worship, either for the sake of conforming to fashion, or to please his pious wife; but no throb of gratitude has bent his knee to Jehovah, no impulse to live for Christ has quickened his pulse. His religion thus far has been only the worship of himself. At length, however, the beat of the muffled drum is heard approaching; sickness and its attendant weakness come upon him, and when these admonish him that he is not to be on earth forever, he bestirs himself, and says, "Now it is time to seek the Lord." And what is that but just a parallel to this idolater with his ash-tree log, "The *residue* thereof he maketh a god"? Now I do not affirm, I dare not affirm, that if even then a man were to seek God sincerely through Jesus Christ he would not be graciously received, for I serve a master who has said, "Him that cometh unto me I will in no wise cast out." But still, what a poor, paltry spirit that is which would keep the best of life for self, and then come at last with the beggarly "residue," and give that to God? If you cannot die without devotion to Christ, neither can you live to any purpose without it. Religion is just as important and essential all through life as it is at the end of life. If it is of any value at all at any time, it is of the same value at all times. If it is of any importance at the last, it is of supreme and infinite importance from the very first. Therefore, let it have your earliest attention. "Seek first the kingdom of God and his righteousness," and that will make your life, as a whole, one sacrificial offering of praise to him to whom you owe your comfort in time and your happiness in eternity. O ye young people, will you lay these things to heart, and begin early — begin now — to serve the Lord! And if there be any among you of maturer life verging toward old age, and having nothing before you now but a poor "residue" of life, come with that and give it to the Lord. You may well be ashamed of your offering; but yet in his wonderful grace he will accept it, and bless you forevermore.

There are other departments in which the same thing as I have now exposed may be observed, as for example, in our disposal of our time, in our use of our money, and the like. It is too often only a "residue" we give to God. Instead of beginning the day with him, we postpone our converse with him until at the evening's close we have neither strength nor inclination nor time for any devotional reading or for meditation or for prayer. Instead of giving the Lord of the first fruits of our gains, we lavish expenditure on ourselves; and after we have gratified taste and pride and love of ostentation, we then give a part of "the residue" to the service of the Lord. Ah! friends, is that a caricature; or is it not rather a characteristic of much of the religion so called of our times? I leave the question with each of you. It will bear to be well pondered; and if it be that you find that you have been acting after that fashion, let me beseech you to revise the whole plan of your life, to repent, and to give your hearts to the Lord, — your heart, your whole heart; and then all that you do will be worship acceptable, each act in its own department, to God through Christ Jesus.

XI.

THREE ESTIMATES OF ONE CHARACTER.

Saying that he was worthy . . . I am not worthy . . . I have not found so great faith, no, not in Israel. — LUKE vii. 4, 6, 9.

THE history to which these texts belong must be familiar to you all, and as the details connected with it will come up incidentally in the sequel of the discourse, I will not spend a moment now in their recapitulation. We have here three estimates of one and the same character. Each one of these, from the standpoint of the speaker, was strictly true, and all of them were perfectly consistent with each other. Now my purpose is to show you that both of these statements concerning them are correct, and it may be that some valuable lessons for ourselves may be suggested in the process.

In the first place, then, we have the estimate formed of this man by his neighbors. He was a centurion residing in Capernaum, and his servant, who was dear unto him, was lying at the point of death. He heard that Jesus had come to the town, and wishing to obtain a cure for his attendant, he sent the elders of the place to the Lord, that they might request him to come and heal the dying man; and it was while making this appeal for him that they said, "He is worthy for whom thou shouldst do this, for he loveth our nation, and hath built us a synagogue." Now in regard to this testimonial, two or three remarks may be made. For one thing, it must, I think, be conceded that these elders had enjoyed the best opportunities for forming a judgment regarding him. He lived in the midst of them. They saw him, not merely on review days, or on great occasions, but when he was in undress and off his guard. They were not so likely, therefore, to be imposed upon as those were who met him only on formal business. One may get himself up for an emergency, or put a restraint upon himself in certain circles and for special reasons; but he cannot keep up these appearances at home and among his neighbors all the time. There is an *abandon* in his demeanor in familiar intercourse, which altogether unconsciously to himself reveals the sort of man he is; and so those who live closest to him and have known him longest, know him also best. They can tell whether the polish of the public appearance be that of the thin veneer or that of the solid wood, and their judgment is *usually* accurate. Sometimes, indeed, they may err, either from prejudice or from perversity, but commonly they are correct. Those who live in the same house with us, those who are dealing with us every day in the same trade, those who dwell with us in the same street, marking our constant goings out and comings in, are commonly not deceived in the reading of our character. That is the origin of the proverb that "no one is a hero to his valet;" and he who stands successfully the ordeal of close companionship for months, whether in travel by land or voyaging by sea, or in the transaction of daily business, may fairly be pronounced a genuinely good man. On the other hand, when those who are nearest us are those who most condemn us, we have reason to fear that their judgment is just, and that we are worthy of their reprobation.

But these elders had another advantage in coming to a knowledge of this centurion's character. He had been long enough among them to give them opportunity of testing him. He was not a new-comer into the midst of them. They did not form their opinion from an acquaintance of a few days; but they had watched him closely, and had scrutinized him thoroughly. He was an officer of the Roman army, commanding the soldiers who were posted in Capernaum for the purpose of looking after the tribute. As such, therefore, he would be at first an object of aversion to them. But as he continued among them he so bore himself toward them, performing painful duties with delicacy, manifesting the strictest justice in all public affairs, and showing a kindliness of disposition in all ordinary intercourse, that gradually their prejudices melted away, and they forgot that he was a Roman officer, because he was so good a man.

Nay, more, they saw that as he dwelt among them, he became an inquirer into their religion, and a student of their Scriptures, so that by and by he gave up his idolatry, and then after a time became a believer in Jehovah. This drew him more closely to the people, gave him a deeper interest in their nation, and a more practical regard for their worship, which he showed in rearing for them a synagogue at his own expense. Thus, if I have read his history aright, this act of his, on which the elders dwelt with such loving gratitude, was not a mere matter of policy (as it would be if an English official were to build in India a heathen temple), but an honest tribute to the truth which he had found in the Old Testament Scriptures, and a loving offering to the Lord whom he had discovered in them. It would have been a great thing for a Jew to have received such a testimonial from Jews; but that one belonging to the army of their oppressors should have earned from official Jews, like the elders of Capernaum, such a commendation as that which they here give him, — that was something almost unprecedented, and showed that he to whom it was given was indeed a man of more than ordinary worth.

Now I grant that even one's neighbors may sometimes be wrong in their reading of his character. He may offend them, and so be condemned by them, because just from his very goodness his principle will not allow him to take the course which they desire. I grant, too, that when a man is actuated simply and only by the desire to stand well with his neighbors, he is working from a very low motive. I do not forget, either, that the Saviour has said, "Woe unto you when all men speak well of you." Yet all that does not militate against the fact that it is a good thing when a man (like Demetrius) has "a good report of all men," if it can be added, "and of the truth itself." And usually, in the long run, when a man has a good report of the truth, he will have the same also of his neighbors. I say in the long run. There may be ebbings and flowings in the popular estimate, but give them time enough, and even the people, in what we call their sober second thought, will come right. If a man be standing in the right place, then no matter what fluctuations there may be in his reputation, if he only stand still long enough, the people will come round to him, and those who have been nearest to him will be the first to come and the most enthusiastic in their coming. But the same thing is true on the other side. If a man be acting a false part, then whatever may be his temporary success, he is sure to be ultimately found out, and his neighbors will be the first to make the discovery, and the loudest to utter their condemnation.

Tell me, then, what those who are closest to a man think of him after their experience of him for a course of years, or how the members of a community regard a man who has been continuously before them for half a generation, and you tell me with approximate accuracy what the man really is. The *vox populi*, indeed, is not always, if it be ever, the *vox Dei*, and I should be sorry to give countenance to such a sweeping assertion. But still, as a general rule, every man, in the long run, gets just about that amount of appreciation among his fellows to which his worth is entitled. And if one has come to be regarded by his tenants as a grasping landlord; or by his employees as a hard master; or by his customers as a "smart" fellow, ever ready to take any advantage that offers; or by his household as stern, imperious, overbearing, and the like, he has need to look well to it, for they are very likely to be right. It is bad to seek the approbation of others by pandering to their wishes, and even when we do so, we do not get their real approbation after all; but it is certainly no better to deserve their condemnation by our conduct toward them, and it will do us no harm to remember that as one has said, "There are other woes in the Bible than that which says, 'Woe unto you when all men speak well of you.'" Find out, if you can, how your neighbors and those closest to you regard you and speak of you, and if their estimate be unfavorable, it will be well to examine yourself and see that it be not also accurate.

But in the second place let us look at this centurion's estimate of himself. "I am not worthy that thou shouldest enter under my roof." Now it is clear that these are honest words. This man was not feigning humility. There was no hypocrisy in his protestation. It was the consciousness of his unworthiness that impelled him at first to seek the intercession of the Jewish elders on his behalf. And with the conception which before long we shall see that he had of the nature and dignity of Christ, the very last thing that he would have thought of doing with *him* would be to attempt to appear before him as other than he really was. His was a genuine feeling of unworthiness, just like that which is characteristic in greater or less degree of every truly good man among ourselves. The man who thinks himself good is not nearly so good as he thinks he is, while he who is most conscious of his imperfection is a great deal nearer perfection than he supposes. Humility is one of the constant attendants of moral excellence, and the more a man grows in holiness, the more is he disposed to say with this centurion, "I am not worthy that thou shouldest enter under my roof."

Now it becomes an interesting question, why it is that the good man's estimate of himself should thus differ from that formed of him by his neighbors and friends. And in answer to that two things may be advanced. It is owing, doubtless, in some measure to the fact that he knows more about himself than others do. I dare say that there is not one of us who would not shrink from letting others into the innermost secrets of his heart. We feel that if even those to whom we are dearest should know the thoughts that flit across our minds; the imaginations that fill our souls in moments of interval between serious things; the struggles which we have with meanness, or covetousness, or evil desire, or ambition, or envy; the defeats which we encounter in our battlings with self; the trail of sin which is over our very devotions, and the like, they would spurn us from their embrace; and the consciousness of that keeps us from self-conceit. Who does not know something of that experience which Archbishop Trench has packed so beautifully into these expressive lines?

> " Lord, many times I am aweary, quite,
>   Of mine own self, my sin, my vanity;
> Yet be not thou — or I am lost outright —
>   Weary of me.
>
> " And hate against myself I often bear,
>   And enter with myself in fierce debate;
> Take thou my part against myself, nor share
>   In that just hate.
>
> " Best friends might loathe us, if what things perverse
>   We know of our own selves they also knew;
> Lord, Holy One, if thou who knowest worse
>   Shouldst loathe us too!"

Nothing more than such an experience is needed to make plain to us the point on which I have been speaking, and so I pass on to say further that the discrepancy between the good man's estimate of himself and that formed of him by others may be explained by the fact that the better a man is the loftier does his ideal become. His standard rises with his very excellence. We see this illustrated intellectually in the matter of knowledge. The more a man learns, the more he learns of his own ignorance. We are accustomed to say of the conceited young man, who talks as if what he did not know was not worth knowing, that when he is twenty years older he will not know so much; and Paul was speaking truth, though he seems to me to have been just a little satirical, when he said, "If any man think that he knoweth any thing, he knoweth nothing yet as he ought to know." The wiser a man becomes, he is always the more humble and the more modest. Nor is it difficult to understand how this comes about, for the more a man knows he comes just at so many more points into contact with the unknown. Each new acquisition reveals to him some new defect, each new answer to a question starts up some new inquiries; and thus knowledge is not only an increase of light, but also, if I may so express myself, a discovery of new darkness. Or to take the mathematical illustration which Chalmers was so fond of using in this very connection, "The wider the diameter of light, the greater is the circumference of darkness."

But it is quite similar with holiness. The higher one grows in holiness, the loftier holiness seems to him to become; or, exchanging the abstract for the concrete, the liker I become to Christ, the more I see in Christ that I have yet to imitate. That which is highest in me is my appreciation of and longing for that which is still higher. Then from the other side, that which is holiest in me is my consciousness of even the least impurity within me. So, as one grows in grace, he feels the evil of things in himself which in the beginning of his spiritual career he hardly looked upon as sins at all; and that often leads him to use language of self-abasement, when he is far advanced in the Christian life, which he did not use, and could not honestly have used, at its commencement. The deepest conviction of sin is not that of the newly awakened inquirer, but that of the loftiest saint; for to his cleansed eye and to his purged heart sin is a far more repulsive thing than it can possibly be to one who has just discovered himself to be a sinner. So the better a man is, his standard has risen just so much the higher, and he is the more conscious of personal unworthiness.

We have a beautiful instance of all this in the Apostle Paul. In his first epistle to the Corinthians, which was one of the earliest of his letters, he thus writes of himself: "I am the least of the Apostles, that am not meet to be called an Apostle, because I persecuted the church of God." Some five or six years later, during his first imprisonment, he wrote his epistle to the Ephesians, and in that, referring to himself, he says, "Unto me, who am less than the least of all saints, is this grace given, that I should preach among the Gentiles the unsearchable riches of Christ." Then some years later still, in the last letter that he wrote, while he was confronting martyrdom, and knew not the hour when he would be led forth for execution, he wrote, "This is a faithful saying, and worthy of all acceptation, that Christ Jesus came into the world to save sinners, of whom I am chief." Mark not "*was*," but "I *am* chief." Now observe the gradation as he grew in grace, — first, the least of the Apostles; next, less than the least of all saints; and last of all the chief of sinners, — not because he was becoming worse, but rather because he was all the time advancing in holiness. So it always is, and so we have no difficulty at all in explaining how the good man grows in a sense of personal unworthiness the better he becomes in character. So true is this, my brethren, that you may set it down as incontrovertible, that when a man congratulates himself on his personal worth, he is really unworthy. He who is satisfied here has never really eaten, or, in the words of the hymn, —

> " Whoever says I want no more,
> Confesses he has none."

That is a sure, unfailing test. Satisfaction with ourselves is a clear indication that God has no complacency in us, and if this centurion had said, " I am worthy," he would have manifested utter unworthiness.

But we come now to the third estimate of this man's character; that, namely, of the Lord Jesus himself, who said regarding him, "I have not found so great faith, no! not in Israel." When the Saviour appeared nearing his house, the centurion sent friends to meet him, saying, " Lord, trouble not thyself: for I am not worthy that thou shouldst enter under my roof; wherefore neither thought I myself worthy to come unto thee; but say the word [for so the Revisers have it], and my servant shall be healed. For I also am a man set under authority, having under me soldiers, and I say unto one, Go, and he goeth; and to another, Come, and he cometh ; and to my servant, Do this, and he doeth it." His meaning was that just as he himself belonged to a great organization, in which the word of the emperor was supreme, and each in his own rank had to obey the orders of those who were above him, all being under one individual head, so he recognized that the universe was under law to Christ. Diseases would do Christ's bidding, just as he had to obey his general, and his soldiers or his servant had to obey him; and so it was not needed for the healing of his servant that the Lord himself should go into the house, or, indeed, do anything save speak the word that should order the disease away from him.

Now nothing more than that explanation is needed to make evident the centurion's faith. See in what a position he placed Christ. He regarded him as the supreme power in the universe, having all its resources at his command. He saw not only that he was the Messiah, but also that he was God incarnate, and therein lay the superiority of his faith to that of any Israelite. Not any one of the Apostles as yet had reached the lofty altitude on which this Roman soldier stood; not even the eagle-eyed John had thus far perceived all that the words of the centurion expressed, and so he was placed above them all.

It would be wrong, however, to suppose that this faith was a thing of sudden growth. He had already received Jehovah as the only true God. He had been a diligent student, as I believe, of the Old Testament. He had seen therein that constant outlook for something better, which is the characteristic of all the writers under the old dispensation, and he had been led to think that Jesus was indeed "the coming one" to whom the prophets pointed. He must have heard of Jesus, too, before this interview with him. He must have known much of his sayings and doings, and so he was already prepared to be a disciple; but in this supreme moment, by the grace and spirit of God, a great impulse was given to his faith, so that it sprang up from comparative weakness into a strength till then unparalleled, and the expression of that faith drew out the testimony of the Lord to its genuineness and greatness.

But I wish you to notice that this testimony to his faith is virtually also a testimony to his character; for faith is not cherished except by a certain character.

The Pharisees and Scribes had seen more of Christ probably than this centurion had; and yet they had no faith in Christ at all, because their characters were different from his. Faith is thus a moral test. It is a mistake to suppose that every man, or any man, will believe if only the evidence is sufficient. That may be true in mathematical science, but it will not hold in the moral sphere, for there you will sometimes find such perversity that no degree of evidence will produce faith. There is need of the unbiassed disposition, the sincere search for truth, and the earnest willingness to obey the truth when it is found, before there can be faith. And so this testimony borne by Christ to the greatness of the centurion's faith is at the same time an attestation of the excellence of his character as a simple, open-minded, earnest man, honestly seeking and eagerly welcoming the truth.

Then again the faith which is thus rooted in character reacts upon character. As a man believes, so he becomes. If a man believes in Buddha, he will think Buddha; he will live Buddha; he will become Buddha. And equally if he believes in Jesus Christ, he will think Jesus; he will live Jesus; he will reproduce Jesus in his character and conduct. And so the man to whom the Redeemer could and did say, "I have not found so great faith, no, not in Israel," received one of the noblest eulogies that ever came even from his lips, and earned a distinction that is infinitely beyond all Greek and Roman fame.

Such, then, are the three estimates here given of the character of this one man. They were all true from the point of view of their authors, and that is an enviable person yet in whom such testimonies unite.

But the last is the main one after all, carrying all that is valuable in the other two within itself. The real test is, What does the Lord Jesus Christ think of me? For if he approve, it does not much matter what men may say, and if he condemn, the good opinion of my neighbors will not make up for his displeasure. But to secure his approval we must have faith in him, and how does the case stand with us in regard to that? "Dost *thou* believe in the Son of God?" That is the deciding question; for if thou believest in him thou wilt think little of thyself, and the men around thee will take knowledge of thee that, like him, thou goest about doing good. We may have the approbation of Christ, while men regard us with disapproval. But if we regard ourselves with conceit, that is a proof that we have not yet found the true value of Christ, and that he cannot speak well of us. The first and the last of these estimates, namely, those of our neighbors and of our Lord, may for some reason or other be for a time at variance. But the second and third, if we be Christians indeed, never can be dissociated, for satisfaction in Christ implies dissatisfaction with self, and the more we think of Christ and believe in him the less ever will we think of self. Let us look into ourselves, therefore, and see which rules within us, self or Christ; and if it be self, let us seek such faith in the Saviour as shall make us entirely one with him, so that we can say with Paul, "I am crucified with Christ: nevertheless, I live; yet not I, but Christ liveth in me: and the life which I now live in the flesh, I live by the faith of the Son of God, who loved me, and gave himself for me."

XII.

SATAN'S ESTIMATE OF HUMAN NATURE.

And Satan answered the Lord, and said, Skin for skin, yea, all that a man hath, will he give for his life. — JOB ii. 4.

THE book of Job is a poem, dramatic in form, and consisting for the most part of a series of conversations between Job and his friends. We have therefore to be on our guard as to the degree of authority which we give to the statements of the different speakers. For it is a well-understood principle, that in the books of Scripture the inspiration of the writers does not stamp with the divine sanction and approval the statements which they simply report as having been uttered by others. Thus in the book of the Acts of the Apostles, when Luke quotes, apparently word for word, the letter written by Claudius Lysias, the chief captain of Jerusalem, to Felix the governor at Cesarea, it would be ridiculous if we should conclude, from the presence of that epistle in the narrative, that Claudius wrote it by divine inspiration. What the inspiration of Luke does guarantee is, that we have from him an accurate reproduction of the letter which the chief captain sent. Now in the same way, in the case before us, the inspiration of the author of the book of Job is one thing, that of the speakers whose addresses he reports is quite another. His inspiration vouches for the correctness of the report which he gives of what they said; but each of the speakers is responsible for his own utterances.

Hence in seeking to establish some doctrine by divine authority, we must beware how we use citations from the book of Job. Bildad, Zophar, Eliphaz, Elihu, and Job spoke each for himself. The sentiments of each are his own and not those of God; for we find at the close that Jehovah blames them all for serious error in one particular or another. They are all accurately reported. None of them is misrepresented. For so much the inspiration of the author of the book is a voucher. But they were not themselves inspired men, and their utterances must not be ascribed to the Holy Ghost. I am the more particular to set this before you in the clearest possible manner, because Coleridge in his " Confessions of an Inquiring Spirit " brings forward this very book as furnishing what he believes to be an unanswerable argument against the common view of inspiration; I say the common view, for though he specifies the theory of verbal dictation, yet his argument, if sound at all, would be equally strong against the plenary theory, which is that commonly held on the subject. Here are his words: " Say that the book of Job throughout was dictated by an infallible intelligence, then reperuse the book, and still, as you proceed, try to apply the tenet; try if you can even attach any sense or semblance of meaning to the speeches which you are reading. What! were the hollow truisms, the unsufficing half-truths, the false assumptions and malignant insinuations of the supercilious bigots who corruptly defended the truth; were the impressive facts, the piercing outcries, the pathetic appeals, and the close and powerful reasoning with which the poor sufferer, smarting at once from his wounds, and from the oil of vitriol which these orthodox liars for God were dropping into them, impatiently but uprightly and holily controverted this truth, while in will and spirit he clung to it,— were all dictated by an infallible intelligence? Alas! if I may judge from the manner in which both are indiscriminately recited, quoted, appealed to, preached upon, by the *routiniers* of desk and pulpit, I cannot doubt that they think so, or rather perhaps, without thinking, take it for granted that they are so to think." That is a pretty strong indictment; and in so far as it is a protest against indiscriminate quotation from this book as if all the interlocutors were divinely inspired, I find no fault with its vehemence. But I take leave to say that it is a caricature even of the verbal theory of inspiration,— not to speak of the plenary, which more fully commands our assent. For every man of sense, if he allows himself to think a moment on the subject, sees a difference between a correct representation of the sentiments of another, and the indorsement of these sentiments. Now it is the former of these that inspiration secures in the case of the parties to the debate which is here reported and reproduced, but not the latter. If anything were needed to place that beyond dispute, it is the fact that Job's wife is represented as urging him to curse God and die; for we cannot imagine that she was moved by the Holy Ghost to say anything like that. Besides, in at least two of the scenes, Satan is one of the speakers, and obviously he did not speak by inspiration of God. While, therefore, I have announced the words of Satan as my text for this morning, I do so not (as a pulpit *routinier*) out of any deference to their authority, or because I believe that they were " dictated by an infallible intelligence ;" but because I believe that they give a truthful report of Satan's estimate of human nature, and because I wish to show you the falseness of that estimate, despite the air of plausibility with which it is invested. It is commonly supposed, indeed, that for once at least the "father of lies" spoke the truth, when he gave utterance to the sentiment before us; but in this at least, if we take his words unqualifiedly, men give him more credit than he deserves; and perhaps before I conclude, you will agree with me that when he spoke thus he was laboring under somewhat of a delusion.

I need not spend time in discussing the numerous explanations which have been given of the proverbial expression, "Skin for skin." In effect they all amount to this,— that a man will give up everything to save his life; and the insinuation of Satan is, that Job served God from merely selfish considerations, so that if the alternative should be presented, that he must either give up God or give up his life, he would unhesitatingly prefer to keep his life. In all this, however, Satan was only measuring Job and mankind generally by his own bushel; and for the honor of humanity, as well as because I may make it the occasion of presenting to you some important practical suggestions, it may be well to spend a little time in disposing of his assertion.

Now in the outset, we must admit that there is a degree of truth in it. If that had not been the case, it would not have been so dangerous; for a lie pure, simple, and unadulterated does little harm. It needs to have some truth mixed up with it before it can gain currency. As one has pithily said: "A lie always needs a truth for a handle to it, else the hand would cut itself which sought to drive it home upon another. The worst lies therefore are those whose blade is false, but whose handle is true." Now the handle in which the blade of this lie is "hafted," is the fact that there is an instinctive love of life in every human being. Life is sweet, even with all its trials, sorrows, and distresses, and we cling to it to the last. Nay, just as the ivy twines itself most closely round the walls that are most ruined, so sometimes the tendrils of the soul entwine themselves most firmly round the tabernacle when it is nearest decay. No one loves to die merely for the sake of dying. Even the Christian Apostle did not desire " to be unclothed," except as the prerequisite to being "clothed upon" with his house which was from heaven. It needed all the revelation which had been made to him by the Lord Jesus through his death and resurrection to evoke in him the longing to depart which he has so touchingly expressed. And if that were so with him, it is not surprising that others who have not his faith should passionately cling to life. The poor woman who had spent all her living upon physicians is only a type of many who have impoverished themselves in seeking to prolong their days ; and there was a trembling pathos underneath the words of a wealthy man, when he said, " I lost my health in the making of my fortune, and now I am spending my fortune in the effort to get back my health."

Nor must we forget that this love of life is not only an instinctive principle, but also within certain limits to be presently defined a positive duty. The precept, "Thou shalt not kill," refers to myself as well as to my neighbor, and requires me to use all lawful means for the preservation of my own life, as well as of the lives of others. Hence, a contempt for the laws of health, a needless exposure of ourselves to danger, and a neglect to use means for the prolongation of life, are sins, not only against our physical constitution, but also against the moral law. So much apparent foundation, then, there is for Satan's assertion. We instinctively cling to life, and it is our duty to use all proper means for the preservation of our lives. But still for all that the assertion, in its universal form and as it stands, is false. It is not true to the history even of unregenerate men; far less is it true to that of those who have been born again.

It is not true to the history of unregenerate human nature. Even in the unconverted, there are principles — some evil and some good — which, becoming dominant, subordinate to themselves the love of life. The passions of hatred and revenge have stirred up men to deeds which, even at the moment of their commission, they knew would make their lives a forfeiture to the law of the State; and yet, with the certainty of a felon's death before them, they have deliberately braved it. But there are other illustrations of a nobler sort. The love of adventure has drawn many from the comforts and security of home, and led them to risk their lives in its gratification. The poet has immortalized the soldier "seeking the bubble reputation, even in the cannon's mouth;" and history is always enthusiastic over the patriotic warrior who has given his life for the unity and the liberty of the country which he loves. Nay, even in the estimation of those who have not heard, or who hearing have disregarded, the Gospel of Christ, you will find it admitted that there are some things which are of more importance than life. The student of ancient Roman history cannot read without a thrill of emotion the account of the Roman matron who, as she plunged the dagger into her heart, exclaimed, "Of what use is life, now that my honor's gone?" And at the foundation of that code of honor, so called, in which duelling held place, there lay this principle which Satan here had entirely forgotten that men cared for,— namely, that truth and integrity and purity of character ought to be dearer to a man than his life. Observe, I am not now vindicating any such method of asserting that principle as duelling furnished. I am only directing attention to the fact that the principle was there. So, again, the love of knowledge has, in not a few, predominated over the fear of death, which is but the other side of the love of life. Science has had its martyrs as well as religion; and from the day when the elder Pliny perished in the first eruption of Vesuvius down to that of African and Arctic exploration in our own century, there have been many who have been willing to brave hardship, and even to sacrifice life, if only they might add to the sum of human knowledge, and have their names emblazoned among those who have discovered the most cherished secrets of nature.

And in still another department, how many under the impulse of common humanity have forgotten to care for their own lives in their eagerness to save their fellow-men? When has the life-boat lacked volunteers to man her as she put out through the surf to take the exhausted sailors from the battered wreck? And when the fire has gained the mastery over the burning dwelling, and flame and smoke are issuing from many quarters, have we not known some gallant fellow rush in to save a life, alas! only to lose his own? Or, to take another sort of illustration, when fever is doing its deadly work in the tenement houses of the city, and the hospitals are filled to overflowing with its victims, have you ever known the medical men to quail, or from the love of their own lives, to flee from the post of duty? As one has truly said: "There are no men-at-arms who fight more truly and heroically the battles of their country than the hard-pressed medical officers, who, in a time of epidemic, when nine tenths of the world have been three or four hours asleep, pass through the ranks of the fever-smitten before retiring to the short and often broken rest that must refresh them for another day of battle with the grim destroyer." I may not say that in every instance this is done from consciously Christian motives. In many, indeed, I know that such is the case; but in others I have not the same assurance, and so I put it down to the credit of the natural benevolence of the human heart. Now, with such cases in mind, — and they might be indefinitely multiplied, — I am warranted, am I not, in the name of humanity, not to speak now of Christianity, to call Satan's words in the text a libel, and to repudiate his assertion that, as a universal thing, a man will give all that he has for the saving of his life?

But if this be true, even of unrenewed humanity, how much more so is it of those who have imbibed the spirit of the self-sacrificing Christ? Let us, therefore, turn now and see whether the child of God is so utterly selfish as Satan here insinuates that Job was. That which in a man is what we call the ruling passion, rules over the love of life as well as over other principles within him. Now, in every really godly man the ruling passion is love, — the love of God, and the love of his neighbor for God's sake; and that dominates over all things else. In proof of this I point you, first of all, to the case of Job himself. For all so sanguine as Satan was, he did not succeed in prevailing upon the patriarch to renounce his allegiance to Jehovah. With great adroitness and cunning, indeed, he enlisted Job's wife and three friends upon his side; but they did not shake the sick man's confidence in God. Still, through all his troubles, he held by the hand of the Most High, and amidst the accusations which his monitors heaped upon him, he said, "I know that my Redeemer liveth; and though after my skin, worms destroy this body, yet in my flesh shall I see God." And so, in spite of his vain confidence, Satan was disappointed and discomfited. Think, again, of those noble Hebrew youths as they stood before Nebuchadnezzar, with the furnace blazing in their sight, and tell me if they are meaning to give up everything for their lives, as they say, "If it be so, our God whom we serve is able to deliver us from the burning fiery furnace, and he will deliver us; but if not, be it known unto thee that we will not worship the golden image which thou hast set up." Did Daniel give up all he had for his life when, in order to keep a conscience void of offence toward God, he went unfalteringly into the lion's den? Did Peter and John selfishly consider what would become of themselves when, before the council, they said so courageously, "We ought to obey God rather than men"? And where was this cold calculating spirit of self-preservation at any price in Paul when he exclaimed, "None of these things move me; neither count I my life dear unto myself, so that I might finish my course with joy, and the ministry which I have received of the Lord"? "But what shall I more say?" Is not the jubilant shout of praise raised by the noble army of martyrs yonder the most conclusive proof that Satan spoke words of calumny, and not of truth, when he said, concerning the people of God, and Job as one of them, "Skin for skin, yea, all that a man hath will he give for his life"?

And now having, as I trust successfully, vindicated our common humanity from the sweeping accusation which Satan has here brought against it, let me conclude by drawing two practical inferences from the course of thought which we have followed: —

In the first place, then, let me say that we may learn from this subject that one of the greatest dangers which beset the soul may be expected in the very region to which this assertion of the Prince of Darkness makes allusion. In its broad and unqualified form his affirmation is false. Yet we must not shut our eyes to the fact that through that very love of life, to which he here refers, many of his most insidious temptations may be expected to come to us. With this estimate of human nature in his mind, he has kept continually appealing to men's love of life; and it is astonishing in how many instances he has at least partially succeeded. He tried it with Abraham, and so prevailed for a time, even over the Father of the Faithful, that he lied unto the king of Egypt. He tried it with Isaac, and he who had not flinched from his father's sacrificial knife upon Mount Moriah lied to Abimelech to save his life. He tried it with Elijah, and dauntless as the Tishbite usually was, he fled from before the face of Jezebel. He tried it with Peter, and the man of rock quailed for the moment before the maid-servant, lest he should be recognized as the assailant of Malchus. We may expect, therefore, that, pursuing the same tactics, he will make similar approaches to us. Many a man has been kept from giving himself wholly to Christ; and many of those who in the judgment of charity are really his have been seriously entangled by considerations suggested by him, or by his agents, bearing on their personal safety or on their temporal prosperity. He puts the matter thus: "If you become a Christian, you cannot carry on the business in which you are engaged; or you will lose your situation; or you will forfeit the patronage of some worldly friend; or you will entail great suffering on yourself; or bring yourself to penury and want." Or perhaps he puts it thus: "You must live, therefore you cannot give up this work in which you are engaged, however much your conscience may condemn it. You must live." Now, in answer, I might refer you to the well-known story of the first Napoleon. On being informed that an army contractor had cheated the government by supplying the troops with useless articles at a high price, he sent for him to inquire into the matter. "How is this?" said he. "I understand that you have been breaking your contract." "Sire," was the answer, "I must live." "No," replied the monarch, "I do not see the *must*. It is not necessary that you should live; but it is necessary that you should do right." And though perhaps the measuring line which he used with the contractor might in many things reveal his own misdeeds, yet his words were true. There is no absolute necessity that we should live; but while we live it is an absolute duty that we should do right.

But the same truth will come with infinitely greater force from the lips of the Lord Jesus himself. When Satan, still acting on this his favorite theory of human nature, came to him in the wilderness, as he was an hungered, and said, "If thou be the Son of God, command that these stones be made bread," he made reply, "It is written, Man shall not live by bread alone, but by every word that proceedeth out of the mouth of God." And that meant that life consists not in eating bread, but in obeying God. There is a life higher, nobler, and more delightful by far than that which is supported by bread. It is the life of communion with God, the life of the service of God, the life which is hid with Christ in God; and if that can be maintained alone by resisting unto blood, — yea, unto the death of the body, striving against sin, — then let the body die that it may be maintained. That loftier life is indestructible save by our own act. When character dies it is always by suicide. It must be ours forever, unless we barter it away ourselves for some lower and less worthy object. Let us, then, be on our guard against all enticements that would tempt us to make that deplorable exchange. Let us, not, however hardly we may be bestead, or however sorely we may be threatened, sell this birthright for a mess of pottage. Even if we should be at "the point to die," let us show the tempter that Christ and his salvation are of more value in our eyes than all present comforts, or the satisfaction of all physical necessities. Let us make it evident to him that the Word of God, the true, the right, the good, are nobler things to us than the continued existence of our bodily lives; and let us be ready to sacrifice the earthly and the physical for the heavenly and the spiritual, because we love him who died that we might live. Let no one bribe us, either with pieces of silver, or wedges of gold, or Babylonish garments, or peace, or ease, or security, or whatever else, to betray him or to give up his service. The temptation to do that assails us in many ways every day we live. It meets us in the home and on the street; in the store and on the exchange; in the social circle and in the halls of legislation. Wherever we turn, some appeal to our selfishness is made, with the view of getting us to do that which our Lord disapproves; but whenever it is made to us, or in whatever form it presents itself, let us spurn it from us with disdain, lest peradventure the deep condemnation of others, which leaped to our lips as we read the newspaper yesterday morning, should be quoted against ourselves at the last, and we be thus judged out of our own mouths.

But my second and final inference from this subject is that the noblest greatness of which a man is capable consists in falsifying this assertion of Satan. Who so great as the Lord Jesus Christ? And wherein does his greatness consist? Listen to himself: "Whosoever will be greatest among you, let him be your servant, even as the Son of man came not to be ministered unto, but to minister, and to give his life a ransom for many." That is to say, his highest greatness was manifested in giving his life a ransom for many. And was it not even so? How true are the words of the hymn: —

"To toil, to weep, to die for me,
Thou camest, not thyself to please."

Now, since we call ourselves by his name, we ought to be characterized by his unselfishness. There never was a hero to be compared with him who gave himself on Calvary a sacrifice for human sin; and that only is a heroic life which forgets itself — which, if need be, sacrifices itself — for the same cause as that in which he died, and for the furtherance of which he now lives on high. Let us not, therefore, be continually thinking of ourselves, — *our* interests, *our* comforts, *our* lives, *our* safety; let us take a wider range, and seek how we may best honor Jesus, and serve our generation by his will. How grandly Paul had learned that lesson of the cross when he said, "According to my earnest expectation, and my hope, that as always, so now also, Christ shall be magnified in my body, whether it be by life, or by death!" *There* was the true greatness of self-forgetting heroism. Ah, me! how our littlenesses and meannesses are rebuked and put to shame by this noble "imitation of Christ." And if before the life of the servant we are thus abashed, how can we contemplate the cross of the Master without a blush? In the presence of that infinite sacrifice, how paltry do our schemings and expedients for the protection of our interests and lives appear! Brethren, let us reform all this. Let us ask, and ask on until we get, a fresh baptism of the spirit of Christ, that we may have self within us crucified, and that the love wherewith he was animated may fill our hearts. It is not enough to sing, as we often do, the glowing words of Watts, —

> " Were the whole realm of Nature mine,
> That were a present far too small;
> Love so amazing, so divine,
> Demands my soul, my life, my all."

We need to have our whole lives set to that sublime key. We need to have our entire selves hallowed by that lofty consecration. And when they who bear the Master's name shall thus be distinguished by the Master's likeness, then Satan himself will be compelled to acknowledge his error, and to say, "Skin for skin, yea, all that the Christian has, will he give for his Lord."

XIII.

THE WAY AND THE LEADING.

I being in the way, the Lord led me.—GENESIS xxiv. 27.

THE chapter from which these words are taken presents us with a series of charming pictures of Oriental life, which would be only blurred and defaced by any efforts of mine to illustrate them, or even to point out their beauties. First, we have the scene between Abraham and his servant, in which one knows not whether to admire more the uncompromising loyalty of the patriarch to his God, or the intelligent and unswerving fidelity of the steward to his master. Then comes the quiet eventide by the well of Nahor, with the good Eliezer upon his knees, offering that simple, direct, matter-of-fact prayer, which showed that he knew, from long familiarity with God, how to approach him in supplication. Next we have Rebekah, with the courtesy of true heart-kindness, watering the camels of the stranger, and showing therein the very traits of character which fitted her to be the wife of Isaac. Then we are introduced into the home of Bethuel, where, while yet the traveller stands fasting at the table which has been spread for his refreshment, we hear him tell his errand, with the simple naïveté of earnestness and truth, and when he has finished speaking he is referred to Rebekah, who makes no objection to return with him to Canaan. Next we have the departure of Rebekah from her father's house, accompanied by the faithful Deborah, and followed by the tearful benedictions of her kinsfolk, "Thou art our sister; be thou the mother of thousands of millions, and let thy seed possess the gate of those which hate them." And last of all we have another eventide scene, this time beside the encampment by the well Lahai-roi. Isaac has gone out into the fields to meditate. Yonder in the distance, having alighted from her camel when she was told who he was, Rebekah comes to meet him; and in that holy hour, without the agency of priest or sheik, but with the sanction and approval of Him whose hand had been so visible through all the negotiations, the marriage bond is sealed between them under the twinkling lustre of the silent stars. "And Isaac brought her into his mother Sarah's tent, and she became his wife."

Said I not truly that we have here a series of delightful pictures of Oriental life? But we value the history, not for its artless beauty so much as for its practical suggestiveness. It might be used to illustrate the power of home influence, inasmuch as the faith of Abraham reappears with exquisite simplicity in his servant. Or we might employ it to exalt the sanctity and emphasize the importance of marriage; for though at first sight it seems that Isaac and Rebekah had less to do with this old courtship than any of the other parties named, albeit they were the two principally concerned; yet the care taken by Abraham, as he put his servant under oath, and the holy fidelity manifested by Eliezer, may well instruct those among us who, unmindful of the important issues that hang upon the conjugal relationship, treat the whole matter as a joke, or are well content if they can only secure by it a handsome dowry. Not without its significance, too, in this old history, is the dignity that it gives to domestic service. On the one hand we have Abraham's steward making his master's interest his own, and on the other we have Rebekah's nurse leaving with her the home of her childhood, and going with her to begin that career of confidential companionship with her and her children that ended more than eighty years after, when she was buried at Bethel beneath the oak called, because of the sorrow at the funeral, "allon-bachuth," the oak of weeping.

But I do not mean now to discourse at length on any of these topics. For at least thirty years I have never read this chapter without feeling that, beautiful as all other things in it are, the words which I have chosen as my text are its brightest gem. They have been with me in all seasons of depression or perplexity. When I have been weary they have been as a staff to support me. When I have been faint, they have been as a cordial to revive me. When I have been in darkness, they have been to me as a guiding star. And I can never forget how often during those anxious days I spent, now just twenty-one years ago, upon the wintry Atlantic, after I had left my home, my country, and my church, and before I knew a single person in the congregation of which here I was to be the pastor, I threw myself upon this expression, "I being in the way, the Lord led me," and was comforted in the assurance, which has been fully verified, that he who guided Abraham's servant in the minutest matters, would conduct me rightly.

Without further preface, then, let me bring before you these two things, — the way and the leading. It is only when we are in a certain way that we have a right to expect that God will lead us, and even in that way there is only one kind of leading that we are warranted to look for. Let me try to illustrate these two things.

And first as to the way. This servant was evidently in the way of duty. He was not there on a mere pleasure trip, or of his own motive and choice. He had accepted a commission from his master, and thus far he had faithfully followed the instructions which he had received. He had not hesitated a moment until he had reached the early Mesopotamian home of Abraham, and now the problem was how he was to find out the descendants of Nahor, and secure an entrance into their household. Nor in solving that was he unmindful of the use of means, for, knowing the customs of the country, he had halted at the well, where at that hour it was most likely that he would meet with some of those connected with the place. It was not, therefore, until he had done all that he could that he awaited the guidance of Jehovah.

Now in all this there is much to direct us, for it holds true universally that the way to get more light is to follow fully that which we already possess. This applies to intellectual doubt; and in these days, when so many are perplexed as to what the truth is in reference to many things which are considered to be of great doctrinal importance, it is well to remember that the path to peace lies through the performance of those duties in regard to which we are already certain. The first thing, therefore, which the inquiring spirit has to do is to consider and answer faithfully these questions: "Am I acting up to the convictions which I have? Have I done everything which I hold to be right? Is my conduct abreast of my conscience, or am I living below even that standard which I have accepted? When the case is so stated, it may sometimes appear that the perplexed one is not so eager to receive more light for the attainment of something that yet lies beyond him, as he is to get an excuse for neglecting obligations which he feels that he has ignored. And if that be true, his earliest care should be to remedy such a practical inconsistency, for it is only through the fullest use of that which is known, that we pass to certainty as to those things of which we are still in doubt. And in every case we may say that God leads the doubter into faith through the way of obedience to those principles which he has already received.

Amid all a man's perplexities there are some things which he must hold as certain, and when he is making the best of these he is putting himself into a position to welcome the first glimpses of new light. Sometimes an evil life has led to a shipwreck of the faith; but always a conduct that is up to the level of conviction clarifies the spiritual perception, for has not Jesus said, "If any man be willing to do his will, he shall know of the doctrine whether it be of God, or whether I speak of myself." So if there be any young man before me who is sunk in the miry pit of doubt, let him hold fast by those things which are yet certain to him, and faithfully and earnestly act up to them, for it is by these that God will ultimately lift him out and set his feet upon the rock of faith.

But the same thing is true in reference to conduct. When in our daily lives we are brought to a stand, and see no outlet, then if we are where we are, because we have been faithfully and conscientiously doing what we believed to be right, let us stand still and pray and wait, sure that God will open up our way. But if we have brought ourselves into the difficulty by our own wilfulness or waywardness, or through the seeking of our own pleasure, and not at all because of any moral obligation that was pressing upon us to be there, then let us retrace our steps, and do what our consciences and the Word of God unite in declaring to be right, and we shall find that our perplexity will soon come to an end. It makes all the difference in the world as to matters of conduct, whether we are simply seeking our own gain, our own pleasure, our own honor, or whether we are striving to meet the obligations which God has laid upon us. In the former case we have no right to expect God's guidance; in the latter we may be sure that it will not be withheld. And that accounts for the common experience among all Christians, that so long as they look at their conduct as between them and God, they have rarely any difficulty in coming to a decision regarding what they should do, but as soon as they cumber the question with considerations of personal interest, or of the good opinion of others, perplexity begins. Cultivate, then, the habit of walking in the way of duty, and you will find it a way of light. It is, for the most part, when you want an excuse for evading what you know to be duty that anxiety begins. If you desire to keep a good conscience, and at the same time have all the world's good things,— to serve God and mammon, to be on both sides at once,— then you will be in constant bewilderment, you will be forever balancing probabilities, and never at rest; and what is more, not even God himself can give you rest while you pursue that course, for it is only when you are in the way of duty that he will lead you. How simple all this looks! Would to God that we might all follow this plain maxim, and so have perfect peace.

But again, this servant was in the way of faith. He had a firm childlike and sincere belief in God. He did not think of Jehovah as of one far off, who took no interest whatever in human affairs. He did not consider that *he* was too insignificant for the governor of the universe to care for. But he had the conviction that the Lord was very near him, even at his side, and he spoke to him with the open-heartedness and confidence of a little child with his mother. His faith thus was no mere make-believe. God was to him a real personal being, as interested in the success of his mission as he was himself, and able to help him in his present emergency. Now we do not wonder that such an one was guided. And we may, perhaps, find the secret of our harassments and worries from day to day, in the fact that to the most of us God is little better than an abstraction, — a far away grandee, who has so much else to do that he has no opportunity to care for us. I almost shudder to use these words, and yet in faithfulness I have been compelled to employ them, that you may see how repulsive is that idea of God, which, though we have never dared to formulate it in words, is the truthful utterance of our conduct. We have an abhorrence of the atheism of him who sees no God in the universe, and is forever glorifying law. We have a horror too of the pantheism of him with whom God is nothing better than a fine name for the universe itself. But alas! we are little better ourselves, for though we admit the existence of God, we do not acknowledge practically, at least, his nearness to us individually, and his care over our personal concerns. When we pray to him, it is as to one "far, far away;" and only in the great and apparently important crises in our lives do we think it needful to consult him. So he leaves us to ourselves, and we are care-worn, anxious, and perplexed. Brethren, I am thoroughly convinced that unbelief is at the root of our worry, and that if we had only the same faith as this Oriental servant, and the same consciousness of the nearness of God to us, and his interest in us, as he had, we should be very seldom in difficulty; and when we were, we should be willing to wait peacefully and trustfully for his guidance.

And why should we not have these things? Do you say to me that this man in these old days of ignorance had no such sense of the order of Nature as that which our modern philosophers have given to us, and that therefore it was easier for him to realize that God was with him than it is for us now? But how hollow such an objection is! The regular order of Nature is maintained by the constant presence and agency of God, for what are called laws are just the methods of his operation according as men have observed and classified them. How then can it be easier to recognize his existence and nearness without a knowledge of the constancy and regularity of these operations than it is with it? You have but to put that question to see the absurdity of the supposition. So far from leading us to think of God as at a distance, it seems to me that the discoveries of modern times have brought him nearer to us, if I may so express it, than ever, for if the force that works according to law be the power of God, then every appeal we make to that force, whether through steam or electricity or whatever else, is an appeal to God, and so we come to feel that he is encircling us with his omnipresence, and serving us daily by his omnipotence. Science rightly understood thus helps my faith, and reveals to me a God at hand.

Do you say again that this servant had known much of God's dealings with Abraham, and therefore was the better able to believe that he would help him when he was in Abraham's service? Then I ask in reply, What were the revelations that he received through Abraham compared with those which we have received through Christ? The Gospel, no doubt, was preached to the Father of the Faithful, and we have the highest authority for the assertion that he saw Christ's day and was glad; but his light was only a glimmering in comparison with the fuller radiance of ours, and now we can say, "He that spared not his own Son, but delivered him up for us all, how shall he not with him also freely give us all things?" That is the inference from the atonement as bearing on our daily life; and when we enter into that, when we believe that, we are in the way of being led through every maze of perplexity. By his rod Moses parted the sea, and conquered Amalek, and smote the rock; and in the cross of Christ, when used as Paul has used it in the words I have quoted, we too have a wonder-working staff which will clear a way for us in every difficulty.

Lastly, here, this servant was in the way of prayer. That follows from what I have just said of his faith; but it is sufficiently important to require separate remark. For there is a plain, direct, earnest purpose in his supplication which strikes every reader most forcibly. To some, indeed, it might almost seem as if there were presumption in his petition: for he specifies the way in which he wishes his prayer to be answered, saying, "Let it come to pass, that the damsel to whom I shall say, 'Let down thy pitcher, I pray thee, that I may drink,' and she shall say, 'Drink, and I shall give thy camels drink also,' let the same be she that thou hast appointed for thy servant Isaac; and thereby shall I know that thou hast shewed kindness unto my master."

Now, of course, we should never think of advising any one to pray after that fashion, and you may ask how we account for such a prayer being presented and answered *then*. The reply is to be found in the fact that a child speaks after the manner of a child, and must be answered in a style which he can understand. This servant, as compared with the weakest Christian, was but as a child is to a full-grown man. He prayed after the fashion of a child; he sought a visible token; and condescending to his weakness, God gave him the token which he sought. His request, therefore, differs entirely from the famous prayer of the sceptic, in which he proposed to settle whether there was a God or not according as he received or did not receive a certain prescribed outward sign. That was a tempting of God; but this was a trusting of him. It differs, too, from those superstitious practices in accordance with which people have tried to forecast the future by hap-hazard openings of the Sacred Scriptures; for these were a turning of the Bible into a lottery-box, while this was an application to God. The sign sought in this prayer, therefore, takes its place beside that which Jonathan gave to his armor-bearer, in the day when God delivered into his hands the garrison of the Philistines. The request for it was born of childlike confidence in God, and not of suspicion of God; and therefore, being a real application to him, it was answered by him.

But while we may well hesitate to present our petitions in precisely such a form as this, we may be encouraged from the answer which even this prayer received to go to God in every perplexity. This is the true way to attain the peace and guidance which we desire. For what says Paul? "Be careful for nothing; but in everything by prayer and supplication, with thanksgiving, let your requests be made known unto God. And the peace of God, which passeth all understanding, shall keep your hearts and minds through Christ Jesus." This servant went to the very root of his anxiety, and spoke about nothing else. He did not profess an interest in other matters, which he did not at the moment feel, but he confined himself to that which was pressing upon him. He did not ask for blessings a long way ahead, but said, "Give me good speed this day;" and having unburdened his heart, he waited for God's answer.

Now so it should be with us. When a man is in earnest he will take the shortest way; and instead of going about it and about it, he will come directly to that which is causing him distress, and seek relief. But often when we pray we use the vaguest generalities, and make such indefinite requests that it would be difficult for us when we rise from our knees to tell precisely what we have asked. We go into our closets in the morning, and far from forecasting any of the occupations of the day, we content ourselves with using some stereotyped phrases, and go away without having expressed any particular desire, and having no definite expectation of special blessing in our hearts. Now in all this we are depriving ourselves of a great privilege; and what is more, we are not in the way of being led by the Lord. Why should we not think for a little of what is before us? It is, I am aware, impossible for us quite to anticipate all that in any day we shall have to encounter; but all of us know something of the engagements which we have to meet on the day on which we have entered. Why, then, should we not take time in our morning devotions to go over these in detail, and ask for the guidance which we specially need for each of them. This would make our prayers continually fresh and living things; while at the same time it would impel us throughout the day to be continually on the outlook for the direction which we have asked, and it would send us back to the mercy seat at night with a song of thanksgiving for the blessings which we have received. When we begin to talk with God about our daily life we shall begin also to keep that life for him; and we may be sure that it is only when we are waiting on him in prayer that he will lead us in the right path.

But now I must say a word or two in conclusion about the leading of God when we are in the way. And here, after the thoughts which I have already expressed, it is only necessary that I should give prominence to the fact that this leading is to be looked for by us in and through God's ordinary providence. We are so familiar with the old history which this Book relates, of the pillar of cloud by day and of fire by night, by which the Israelites were conducted through the wilderness for forty years, that when we think of being guided by God we are apt to imagine that he is to make his presence known to us through some visible miracle or by some audible voice. We forget that the miracle is and must be unusual, and that if, in our daily lives, such manifestations were to be common, the very purpose for which miracles were performed at all would be defeated. But though we thus shut out miracle, we do not shut out God; and such a history as this, in which there is nothing miraculous, helps us to understand how, even in and through the commonest incidents of life, God leads those who are in the way. For this is not a solitary instance. We see the same thing in the story of the birth of Moses, in the histories of Ruth, of Nehemiah, and of Esther; in none of which is there the record of anything supernatural, while it is impossible for any one to read them without feeling that God was in them all from first to last.

Now, God is to-day as really in the casual meetings which we have with men upon our doorsteps, in the streets, in our stores, on the railroad cars, or on board ship, as he was here in this interview between Eliezer and Rebekah at the well. He who met the woman of Samaria when she went out to do such a common thing as to draw water at the well, is all the time meeting us; and if we ask him to guide us, he will through casual and ordinary occurrences lead us to the right destination. This, to me, is one of the most striking and one of the most comforting lessons which can be learned from the record which has been before us this morning. We need no Urim and Thummim; we may not seek for dreams and visions and voices; we must not long for signs and wonders; for now, though all these are withdrawn, we have still that overruling and omnipresent providence, of which one has truthfully and suggestively said, "This is, in fact, the great miracle of providence, that no miracles are needed to accomplish its purposes." Through natural law and commonplace incidents God is leading his people to-day as really as he led the Israelites through the desert of

Sinai by the pillar of cloud. We may not have been conscious of it at the moment, and each step we took we may have thought that we could not take another; but still as we moved forward the path opened, and we could always advance a little farther, until now when we look back we can discover that God has been leading us all the time, and we are precisely where he would have us to be. Ay, and when we look back we can see by what casual interviews with other people — as little remarkable as this meeting at the well of Nahor was — God has changed the whole color and complexion of our lives. If each of us here to-day were only required to tell fully out how he came first to be here in this great centre of commerce and influence, I am sure we should find that it was by some common and simple occurrence — no more noteworthy at the time than is the meeting of two strangers at an Eastern well — that we were first led to think of and ultimately to determine on coming hither. But if all that is true of the past, it is just as true of the present. God is in the incidents of to-day, to guide us, just as truly as he was in these; and perhaps the mere bringing up of this history at this time may be like the very hand of the great Father held down for some one here to grasp. Do not despair. Do not imagine that God has forgotten you. If you are in the way of duty, of faith, and of prayer, be sure that somehow through the common incidents of a common day he will guide your feet into the right path.

Ah, what new significance this gives to every occurrence in our histories! How near this brings God to us! When we talk of his omnipresence, we have but a vague idea of his proximity to us; but when we think of him as working in and through the minutest events of our daily lives for our direction, that is another matter, and we begin to realize the meaning of the Master's words, "Lo, I am with you alway!" How sacred, too, in this aspect of them, do the events of our lives become! They are new revelations of God to us, and we too, like these old patriarchs, have our Hebrons and Bethels and Peniels and Moriahs. Let us go this morning in this faith, and we shall feel our hearts lightened, and our pace quickened, as we sing, "A good man's steps are ordered of the Lord." And if haply there should be one here in deep perplexity, let me exhort him to follow to the last limit that which he now knows to be right, and then to entreat the Lord with earnestness and wait patiently the issue. "Wait on the Lord, be of good courage, and he shall strengthen thine heart."

"Lead, kindly Light, amid th' encircling gloom, —
Lead thou me on.
The night is dark, and I am far from home, —
Lead thou me on.
Keep thou my feet; I do not ask to see
The distant scene; one step enough for me.

"So long thy power has blest me, sure it still
Will lead me on,
O'er moor and fen, o'er crag and torrent, till
The night is gone,
And with the morn those angel faces smile
Which I have loved long since, and lost awhile."

XIV.

THE HOLY SPIRIT AS A FACTOR IN OUR PRAYERS.

For we know not what we should pray for as we ought, but the Spirit himself maketh intercession for us with groanings which cannot be uttered. — ROMANS viii. 26.

It is not without serious misgivings that I venture to speak to you from these words. They take us into "the deep things of God," and it is but a little way down into these that our tiny plummets can descend. Nevertheless, during these recent days I have had some profitable thoughts on the Holy Spirit as a factor in our prayers, and I desire to make you sharers with me in them; but like the groanings to which the text refers, these thoughts themselves are largely unutterable, and I shall be content if I can only set you to meditation on the subject for yourselves, that in the silence of your own closets you may go more fully into it than any words of mine can take you.

The passage to which the text belongs is that in which Paul unfolds to his readers the various offices of the Holy Spirit toward believers. He tells them that he descends into their souls as the Spirit of life in Christ Jesus, uniting them to him and making them partakers of his life; that in the power of this new life they are freed from the law of sin and death, and enabled to walk not after the flesh, but after the Spirit; that he leads them as their guide; that he teaches them to cry to God, "Abba, Father," and so witnesses with their own spirits that they are the children of God; and that his work in them is the first fruits of their full and final redemption, a foretaste of its quality and a pledge of its certainty. Then he adds, "Likewise also" (or after the same manner also) "the Spirit helpeth our infirmity." This is a general statement referring to the weakness that is characteristic of our spiritual life as a whole; and the meaning is, that in our lack of strength, no matter in what department that may be experienced by us, the Holy Spirit is our Helper.

Then as a particular illustration of the kind of help he gives, Paul specifies the nature of the assistance which he renders to us in prayer. For we do need help in that exercise, inasmuch as "we know not what we should pray for as we ought;" and he gives us help by "making intercession for us with groanings which cannot be uttered." This intercession must be carefully distinguished in our thoughts from that of Christ our great heavenly High Priest. The intercession of Christ is carried on in heaven according to these words in a subsequent portion of this chapter: "It is Christ that died; yea, rather that is risen again, who is even at the right hand of God, who also maketh intercession for us." But the intercession of the Spirit is on earth, as the result and accompaniment of his dwelling within us, and is carried on in connection with our own supplications. If it be asked how the Spirit in us makes intercession for us, the answer of the text is, "with groanings that cannot be uttered;" and if again an explanation of that answer be requested, we may give the response in the words of the venerable Charles Hodge: "He excites in us those desires which, though never uttered except in sighs, or which, though too big for utterance, are known and heard of God." Or we may give the explanation more fully in the language of Alford: " The Holy Spirit of God dwelling in us, knowing our wants better than we, himself pleads in our prayers, raising us to higher and holier desires than we can express in words, which can only find utterance in sighings and aspirations." And at the close of his exposition of the section he adds: " As these pleadings of the Spirit are heard and answered, even when inarticulate, we may extend the same comforting assurance to the imperfect and mistaken verbal utterances in our prayers, which are not themselves answered to our hurt, but the answer is given to the voice of the Spirit which speaks through them, which we *would* express but cannot."

So much by way of explanation of the text where it stands. Now let us take it up with special reference to ourselves, and as involving in it the " comforting assurance " which, in the sentence just quoted from him, Alford says may be warrantably included in it.

First of all let us note the description here given of our infirmity in prayer: " We know not what we should pray for as we ought." This clause comprehends, as you clearly see, both the matter and the manner of our prayers; both what we should ask, and how we should ask it. And which of us is not conscious that the statement of the Apostle here is true? When James and John came to the Master during his earthly ministry, and desired that they should sit the one on his right hand, and the other on his left, in his kingdom, he said to them, " Ye know not what ye ask." And when we come to read the conversation which he had with them at the time, we discover that they had no right ideas either of the nature of his kingdom, or of the principle on which the honors of that kingdom were to be bestowed, or of what would be involved in the granting of their request in the kingdom such as it was to be. But, really, when we examine the matter carefully, it is just as true of each of us, in the simplest petition that we present, that "we know not what we ask." We may have a definite object in view, and we may think it good and most desirable; but we cannot trace it through all its bearings, we cannot see how the attainment of it would affect us if it were to be bestowed upon us, nor can we tell what may be required of us in the way of discipline and trial before it can be granted. We cannot tell whether the bestowment of it would be a blessing or the reverse; neither can we see by what means God may be pleased to answer our cry. In our shortsightedness, we may ask for things that would be anything but for our good; and so very often we find "profit by losing of our prayers." The imperfect sanctification of our hearts may let us fix our desires on improper objects; and, besides, the very limitation of our faculties as finite beings makes it impossible for us to tell whether what we desire would be a blessing or a curse to us.

Then we know not how to pray as we ought. True, the Lord Jesus has given us a model here, and has said, "After this manner pray ye." But you have only to take up that prayer which he so prefaced, and which is so frequently on our lips, and ponder it word by word and clause by clause, to see how difficult, how indeed impossible it is for us, without the aid of the Holy Spirit, to offer our supplications after its manner. Take these words in it, — "Thy will be done in earth as it is in heaven,"— and which of us can soar to the height which they attain, or encircle the wide domain which they comprehend? Or if you think of the union of faith and humility, of freedom and reverence, of earnestness and submission, that are required if we would pray aright, you will see how impossible it is for us to be sure that our approaches to the Hearer of Prayer are altogether such as can be acceptable to him. Truly Paul is right when he says, "We know not what we should pray for as we ought."

Now some may be ready to say in response to all this, that if these things be so, the natural inference is that we should not pray at all; and if there were no helper provided for our infirmity, perhaps that logic might be allowed. But that is not the way in which Paul reasons. Rather he bids us pray on, in the sure confidence that the Holy Spirit in us will make all that is wrong in our petitions and in our manner of presenting them right in the sight of God, and that the result will be our reception of blessings manifold and gracious from his benignant hand.

This leads me to the consideration of the great truth that the Holy Spirit "helpeth" our prayers; and that requires us to answer the question how and in what respects he maketh intercession for us according to the will of God.

Now here in the first place it is pertinent to say, especially with Alford's inference from our text in mind, that the Holy Spirit rectifies our prayers. We ask what we desire; but through his intercession, that is transmuted into what we need, and we get that from God. He knows "the things of our spirits," because he dwells within us; and knowing these he goes beneath our wishes to our necessities, and presents them to God.

We cannot tell how this is done, but we have the assurance that it is done; for we always get what we need, and not always what we ask. Let me take an illustration. When Peter saw the glory of Godhead streaming through the miracle of the great draught of fishes, he fell at Jesus' knees and said, "Depart from me, for I am a sinful man, O Lord." Now that cry had in it all the impulsiveness, rashness, and inconsiderateness that were so characteristic of Peter. It might have been affirmed of him then, as it was afterwards on the Mount of Transfiguration, that he knew not what he said. It was his way of expressing the self-abasement which Job felt when he said: "I have heard of thee by the hearing of the ear, but now mine eye seeth thee. Wherefore I abhor myself, and repent in dust and ashes." Or that which Isaiah uttered when he exclaimed, "Woe is me, for I am undone, because I am a man of unclean lips, and I dwell in the midst of a people of unclean lips; for mine eyes have seen the King, the Lord of hosts." What he needed, therefore, was not that Jesus should depart from him, but rather that he should have fully revealed to him the gentleness and forgivingness of Jesus; and so the Lord, meeting his necessity rather than granting his request, said, "Fear not: from henceforth thou shalt catch men." Now what the Lord did in that case with Peter's request, before he gave any response to it, that the Holy Ghost does with our unintelligent and impulsive prayers, before they ascend into the ears of him whose name and whose memorial have been in all ages, "the Hearer of Prayer."

But if that be really the case, so far from being discouraged from praying by the fact that we know not what we should pray for as we ought, we are the rather encouraged to offer up petitions for all that we desire;

because we know that our errors of ignorance, or impulsiveness, or excitement, will be rectified by Him who dwelleth in us and maketh there intercession for us, according to the will of God. Speak, therefore, with the utmost freedom when you are upon your knees. Be genuine; ask for things that are real to you; express the desires you feel, and leave it to the Holy Spirit in you to put all right before the Lord. Say what you feel, and be sure that he will rectify all that is amiss.

Then, again, if we have rightly represented the case, you will see how it comes that our prayers are not always answered in the way in which we desired and asked that they should be. No real prayer, I believe, is ever unanswered. But yet we ask for many things which we do not get, the reason being that in response to the intercession of the Holy Spirit, God has given us something better,— even that which we really needed; and the reception of that will remove the desire which we foolishly or ignorantly cherished for something else. It would have been a terrible thing for Peter if the Saviour had taken him at his word, and departed from him, as he did from the Gadarenes; but instead he gave him such a revelation of himself as made him content — oh, how much more than content, delighted — to be continually by his side. So while we do not always get what we ask, we do receive, in response to the rectifying intercession of the Spirit in us, that which makes us no longer desire what we formerly requested. I need not stay to show the bearing of all this on much that is said in these days concerning prayer; but if you will intelligently receive this presentation of the case, you will be saved from the error of those who are far on the way toward making prayer a *fetich*, and who seem to think that God has bound himself by a pledge to give us always precisely that for which we ask.

But passing to another thought, I remark that the Holy Spirit helps our prayers by interpreting them. We do not see or know all that is implied in the words we are using, even when we are praying for things agreeable to God's will; this is especially the case when, as so frequently, we use the words of Holy Scripture, and turn God's promises into petitions. I cannot better express this truth than in the following sentences which I take from a letter in the memoir of an old friend that has just recently been published: —

"When we pray, 'Thy kingdom come,' who knows what all is meant by that petition as Christ did when he put it into the prayer for all ages? Or what two that join in praying agree, — agree they must to some extent, according to the rubric, 'If two of you shall agree,' etc., — but what two agree, not only in meaning all that Christ meant, and that the inspired words themselves mean, but also agree in meaning exactly the same thing? — some inclining more to millenarian views, and some more to the common opinion. And then the amount of misconception, or at least of imperfect intellectual conception, in the views of all of us, it would be impossible to calculate or analyze. It is quite impossible that the prayer should be answered according to our variety of views, with all their falsehood and imperfection. But then if the prayer be sincere, and the feeling true, and the worshipper praying in the Spirit and through Christ, and that not in the words that man's wisdom teacheth, then these words have not only come to us inspired, but they return from us inspired as well, — 'the Holy Ghost interpreting them into their full significance in the presence of the throne;' . . . so that our prayer — 'Thy kingdom come, thy will be done in earth,' or whatever else it be — is heard not according to the meaning *we* put, but according to the meaning *he* puts upon it, and this in virtue of his intercession, one function of which is, I should say, interpretation."[1]

These are weighty words, and I should only mar their effect by attempting to say anything of my own on the subject to which they refer. May I beg you to ponder well the thoughts which they express?

But now, finally, the Spirit helps us in prayer by giving significance to that which we find to be unutterable. The deepest experiences of the soul cannot be formulated in human speech. That which we can put most fluently into words is in the main superficial. The shallow water makes the loudest noise as it flows over the stony bed of the river; but the deep pool is silent. When the heart is most thoroughly stirred, its emotions cannot be spoken "trippingly on the tongue." The highest joys are beyond our expression, and the sorest griefs are those which strike us dumb. We have not advanced far in spiritual experience if we have not discovered that the deepest worship " is that of silence, which of all acts of worship and means of grace brings us nearest to God, nearest to the Unseen and Eternal Real." Some of us have felt that at the communion table, when in "expressive silence" we sat "musing the praise" we could not speak. Some of us, too, have felt it in the depths of a severe trial. You remember those lines of Whittier in his letter of condolence to **Joseph Sturge** on the death of his sister: —

> " With silence only as their benediction,
>   God's angels come,
>   Where, in the shadow of a great affliction,
>   The soul sits dumb; "

[1] Memoirs of Wm. B. Robertson, D.D., of Irvine, by James Brown, D.D., pp. 378, 379.

and you have not had much suffering of any kind in the world if you have not at some time or other been dumb under that shadow. You cannot say anything then to your nearest and dearest earthly companion. You cannot say anything to God. You think you cannot pray. Ah, but you mistake! That silence is the unutterable sighing to which my text refers; and it is made by the Holy Spirit articulate petition in the ear of God. For here comes in the truth contained in these lines of the Danish hymn: —

> "What in the heart lies deepest ever,
> Unbreathed by mortal lip abroad,
> And heard by ear of mortal never,
> Takes voice before the throne of God.
> The silence of our spirits tells
> Its tale aloud where Jesus dwells."

And the result is the coming of blessings upon us which throw a flood of light upon the words of Paul, when, extolling the riches of God's grace, he says that "he is able to do exceeding abundantly above all that we ask or *think*, according to the power that worketh in us." Mark that last clause, — "according to the power that worketh in us;" for it clearly refers to this same intercession of the Holy Spirit which he specifies in my text. Be not unjust to yourselves, then, when either in your joys or your sorrows you get to a place where you cannot speak, even to God, either in praise or prayer. If you are a real child of his, that silence is the truest devotion, and the Holy Spirit will make it so expressive unto God that he will shower his richest blessings on your head.

But I can go no further. What I have said will, I am sure, be helpful to those who receive it; and if any do not now appreciate it, they may, perhaps, recall it with thankfulness when the dumbness either of elevation or depression comes upon them. I conclude with the following hymn from the heart and pen of him from whose letter I have already quoted : —

When joys are joys that words transcend ;
    When griefs have shut the heart ;
When we, who at the altar bend,
    Can only pray in part ;
When angels, both of joy and grief,
    Strike priests at prayer-time dumb, —
'T is then, with thy divine relief,
    Thou Comforter dost come.

When we with words of Scripture pray,
    And do not, cannot know
The meaning full of what we say
    In praying Scripture so, —
By thee, in meaning full, before
    The throne, the prayer is brought,
Whence we receive exceeding more
    Than we have asked or thought.

When joys are joys unspeakable,
    That rise all thoughts above,
And earnest souls with rapture fill
    In the silent heavens of love,
As babe soft mother's arms upraise,
    Thou Dove on thy white wings
Dost bear us up, on God to gaze ! —
    Far down the angel sings.

And when our griefs deep buried lie
    Beneath all utterance dumb,
Into that silent agony
    Thou with thy help dost come.
Then, with the unutterable groans,
    Is intercession given,
That makes, above all trumpet tones,
    Our silence heard in heaven.

Oh, Holy Ghost, the Comforter,
  All speed to help us make.
Our hearts with griefs they cannot bear,
  With very joys they break;
Blind yearnings after God, dumb cries
  That ne'er their aim could reach,
Did'st thou not give their blindness eyes,
  And make their silence speech.

XV.

VISIONS.

And a vision appeared to Paul in the night. There stood a man of Macedonia and prayed him, saying, Come over into Macedonia and help us. — ACTS xvi. 9.

MANY years ago I preached from this text, in its relation to the Missionary Enterprise. That is, indeed, the natural, obvious, and direct bearing of the whole narrative on the practical Christian life of to-day. This man of Macedonia speaks still for the heathen world, and Paul, to whom his appeal was made, is the representative of the Church of Christ. Evermore, if we have ears to hear, we may hear coming from all quarters of the globe the cry of benighted and miserable humanity for help. Would that there were more Pauls among us to respond as he did! And there would be, if there were more among us "constrained," as he was, by the love of Christ, to live not unto ourselves, but unto him who died for us and rose again. In these two things the cry of the heathen, "Come, help," and the command of the Master, "Go, preach," we have the great motive principles for the prosecution of the work of missions both at home and in foreign lands; and we are no true successors of the Great Apostle if we do not give our prayers, our gifts, our energies, our lives, to that transcendently important cause.

I could not, indeed I have felt as if I dared not, take this text, without putting that statement in the very forefront of my discourse; but it is not my present purpose to preach a missionary sermon. I desire rather to look at this vision from quite another point of view. — lower, indeed, and less commanding in its range, but yet giving us a glimpse, at least, of matters which are weighty enough to deserve our serious attention. It is not expressly said that this vision given to Paul was supernatural; but that it was so, is certainly the most natural inference from the words of the historian in the tenth verse, "Immediately we endeavoured to go into Macedonia, assuredly gathering that the Lord had called us to preach the Gospel unto them." We cannot, therefore, place quite on a level with that anything of a similar nature that may come to ourselves. But yet within certain limits we may speak of those beckonings toward future labors in life, or achievements in character, which may be given to us in God's ordinary Providence, which become our ideals for the time, and after which we strive with all the earnestness and enthusiasm of our souls as visions not unlike that which was here given to Paul. It may, therefore, be profitable to see what we may learn concerning them from this incident in the life of the Apostle of the Gentiles.

Most of us in this lower sense have had at some time or other our visions. Such have been the dreams of our youth, which, like those of Joseph, may have exposed us at the time to the ridicule of those around us, but which, at a later date, kept us from despondency, nerved us for effort, and perhaps also prevented us from yielding to the lowest kinds of temptations,— which, at any rate, have allured us on until, in some degree at least, they have been fulfilled. Take two or three illustrations.

There is a boy just seven years old, lying under the bright summer's sun on the bank of a rivulet in Worcestershire, England, and looking wistfully out upon the lands of his ancestors, which had passed into the hands of strangers. As he looks, his vision comes to him. Poor, orphaned, almost friendless as he is, he sees himself the Lord of the Manor, dwelling in the home of his fathers, and possessing their estates. Threescore and ten years after, on that very spot, he told how, as he was lying there that day, there rose in his mind a scheme which, through all the turns of his eventful career, was never abandoned. "He would recover the estate which had belonged to his fathers." This purpose, formed in infancy and poverty, grew stronger as his intellect expanded and as his fortune rose. He pursued his plan with that calm but indomitable force of will which was the most striking peculiarity of his character. When under a tropical sun he ruled fifty millions of Asiatics, his hopes amidst all the cares of war, finance, and legislation still pointed to his ancestral hall. And when his long public life, so singularly checkered with good and evil, with glory and obloquy, had at length closed forever, it was to "that home" that he retired to die.[1] His name was Warren Hastings.

Look again. This time it is a Highland glen, hemmed in by steep and lofty hills, one of Nature's loneliest solitudes, where no sounds are heard but the bleating of the sheep on the mountain sides, and the brawling of the brook over its rocky bed in the hollow. On a huge bowlder by the margin of the stream there sits a man, with heavy countenance, absorbed in thought, — so absorbed that he has not observed the

[1] Macaulay's Essay on Warren Hastings.

approach of a company of gentlemen, his fellow guests at the ducal castle in the neighborhood. They rally him on his love for being alone, and ask him what he is thinking of so deeply. He gravely answers, for his vision had come to him also, that he was planning a system of drainage for the city of Paris, to be carried out when he should be emperor of the French, and their only response is a shout of mocking laughter. But in later years they spoke of it with quite another feeling, for his name was Louis Napoleon.

Look once more, — this time into a little store in the Strand, London. The proprietor is in the act of going out; but he turns upon the threshold and addresses a little boy who is within, "Andrew, won't you come with me?" "Where are you going, Father?" "I am going to St. Paul's to see a new statue, which has been erected in the cathedral." "I'll go with you." So they took their way along the crowded street, and ere long were under the vast dome with which the genius of Wren is forever associated. By and by they stood before the new statue. It was that to the memory of the great philanthropist, John Howard. The boy asked who he was, and what he had done; and his father told him briefly of Howard's work in the prisons, not only of Great Britain, but of Europe generally, and as he listened *his vision came to him*. He, too, would be a philanthropist. He became a minister of the Gospel, and did good service both in the pulpit and in more general work among the English non-conformists; but all through life his vision never left him, and to-day, in the village of Reedham and elsewhere, there are orphan asylums, an asylum for idiots, a hospital for incurables, and other kindred institutions, which owe their origin to the patient and persistent energy of that one benevolent man, in obedience to the vision of his youth. His name was Andrew Reed.

I could multiply similar illustrations indefinitely; but these must suffice, throwing you in, as they must needs do, upon your own cherished visions, and giving their confirmation also to my statement. Young man, you see your vision now, — wealth, honor, usefulness, power, pre-eminence, holiness, — I know not what, but it is there; and you have yours, young woman, too, whether of frivolous social gayety and a leading place in the pleasures of the city, or of practical Christian beneficence and the development of agencies for the advancement of the highest interests of your less fortunate sisters. I know not, but you have them, and you see them once again, as I now refer thus to them. Now concerning these visions, we may learn two things from the case of Paul in my text.

The first is that they commonly take their color from the character, history, and habits of the individual before they come to him. Recollect that this vision given to Paul was miraculous; and yet in this case, as in so many others, the supernatural was grafted on the natural. This Macedonian was inviting Paul to preach to Gentiles. But that was the very thing which the Apostle most desired to do. He had been himself brought up in a Gentile city; he knew the characteristics of the Greeks. He had already had great success in Antioch, and in his missionary journeys through Cyprus, and up in Central Asia Minor to Iconium, Lystra, and Derbe; and so this vision was in the line of the Apostle's own aspirations. I can hardly think of such an appeal being made, in such a way, to the Apostle James. It is possible, of course, but in my view not very probable. He was a Jew of the Jews. He would not oppose Paul's work among the Gentiles, indeed, and used his influence at the council of Jerusalem to get a working agreement carried out between the two parties in the church. But he was not specially attracted to the Gentiles, and there was little in him to which the appeal of a Macedonian could address itself. Therefore it did not come to him; but it was sent to Paul, whose training and travels had prepared him to receive and act upon it. Now if that be true in regard to a vision that was miraculously given, then it is *a fortiori* true in regard to those which come to us in God's ordinary Providence. It is to the heart already ambitious that the visions of conquest and imperial honor come. Out of the mercenary spirit grows the dream of wealth, and to a soul that has heard with sympathy "the still sad music of humanity," comes most powerfully home the cry of the wretched for relief. Just as the landscape shapes itself differently according to the disposition of the spectator, seeming to one enfolded in melancholy and to another bright and jubilant with gladness, so the vision is as is the soul that sees it. That which would have attraction for one, has none for another; and those only fix themselves upon a man, and will not let him go until he has fulfilled them, which are particularly in harmony with his disposition and history. What a man is, therefore, has a great deal to do with determining the sort of visions which will be forceful, or if you will forgive the word, fateful in his life.

For now I go on to remark, as the second thing suggested by this history, that visions of the kind of which I have been speaking very largely dominate the lives of those who have received them. Paul immediately set out for Europe after he had seen this Macedonian and heard his cry. His reception at Philippi, indeed, might tempt him to think that he had made a mistake, and his experiences at Thessalonica, Berea, and Athens might have daunted a less courageous man; but this vision held him up, and he went on and on, until in Corinth a great door and effectual was opened unto him. Now, as we must never forget, his vision was from God, and he had a right to believe that in following its direction he was doing that which his Lord would have him do. But even in those cases with which we are mainly dealing now, a similar effect is produced. A man is ruled by his ideals. They may be rooted in his disposition, character, habits, history; but after they have become fixed they are *supreme in* him and *over* him. Let his vision be accepted by him as such, and then it holds him to itself. Thenceforth the fulfilment of it becomes the one great object of his life, concerning which he says, "This one thing I do."

Now if these things be so, if our ideals dominate our lives, and if our ideals are themselves rooted in our character, habits, and history, what a powerful motive have we in these considerations for giving good heed to the character which we acquire, the habits which we form, and the history which we make. We become what we believe. We *are* what we choose to make ourselves, and we must make ourselves either after the ideal of Christ, or after that of the world in which we find our most agreeable environment. Which are you doing? Which have you done? The question is of immense importance, involving in it not only your

earthly career, but also your eternal destiny. If it be
that the vision which has heretofore allured you be
one of mere worldly ambition, involving in it only
temporal aggrandizement or earthly glory, let me entreat you to revise the whole plan of your life, and to
exchange an earthly ideal for a heavenly; and as the
ideal grows out of, or is grafted upon the character,
let me beseech you further to seek for that regeneration,
that new birth, which shall make you a new man, and
give you for your vision the attainment of "the mark
for the prize of the high calling of God in Christ
Jesus."

Here then is the order in which I would have you
range your objects of desire: First, regeneration, that
you may have in you that new nature which will be
attracted by all that is pure and noble and of good
report, as these are set before you in Christ; next, the
vision of the attainment by you of all these things in
Christ as the grand ideal of your career; and next, the
unification, the focusing of yourself on the continuous
effort to make that ideal real in your own character and
conduct. That will make your life sublime, indeed,
for by the power of the Holy Ghost it will make it
holy, and make you meet to be a partaker of the inheritance of the saints in light.

Not all the visions which have fascinated men have
been fulfilled in them. Not every Hastings who has
dreamed in youth of regaining the acres of his ancestors
has succeeded in acquiring them; and frequently the
visions that have seemed so alluring have been but like
the mirage of the desert, which has dissolved into
nothingness just as the traveller thought he was coming
up to its refreshing waters. But this vision which
Christ gives to every one to whom his Gospel is faith-

fully proclaimed is no mirage. It is possible to gain that which it holds before us, and when we do gain it, we shall not be disappointed with it, but it shall be better to us even than we anticipated. We may have to go through tribulation to reach it, for we can stand upon no summit unless we have climbed up to it. There are Anakim to be conquered before the possession of every promised land. So the path to the attainment by us of the Christ-ideal may lead through affliction and trial and conflict and sorrow; but if we hold on and hold out we *shall* attain it, and no man shall take it from us. Oh! let this vision take hold upon you now, and begin forthwith to act upon it. I send you on no mere perhaps, for in this field ye *shall* reap if you faint not. I allure you to no disappointment; I make no promises which my Master will not keep; I raise no hopes which he will not satisfy. Behold him yonder on his throne in the attitude of alluring love. Listen to his words, as in your vision he speaks to you and says, "Follow me." "Be thou faithful unto death, and I will give thee a crown of life." "To him that overcometh will I grant to sit with me on my throne, even as I also overcame and am set down with my father on his throne."

Suffer me now in conclusion to gather up and preserve for you, as pointedly as I may, a few important principles worthy of being constantly remembered by you on this whole matter of ideals.

First, it is bad to have no ideal in life, for then your life will be little better than mere existence. It needs an ideal to give concentration and purpose and plan to our existence before it can be life indeed. What the lens does with the sunlight, that a vision of the sort

I have been speaking of does with life. It gathers it up into one burning spot, which kindles every inflammable thing which it touches into flame. The plan of the architect, followed by the builder, turns heaps of loose stones into one great structure; and even so the vision of each soul makes the life of that soul a unit, designed for one purpose, and devoted to one end. He who has no ideal has no earnestness, and will never produce anything great. As it was in the case of Reuben, his character is the prophecy of his career, and it might be said to him also, "Unstable as water, thou shalt not excel." So it is bad to have no ideal.

But it is worse to have a bad ideal. You remember the words of our Lord, "If the light that is in thee be darkness, how great is that darkness?" The most diabolical thing that Milton puts into the mouth of Satan is this: "Evil, be thou my good." But there are men who seem to have adopted the same principle. He who has no ideal is not a good man, but his wickedness is of a *negative* sort. He does not commit it of set and deliberate purpose, but because he has not gathered himself up to consider what he ought to have done. He is like an abandoned ship without any one to steer her, and so he is driven hither and thither by the winds of passion or the waves of impulse. But the man with a bad ideal is a *positively* bad man, going deliberately after that which he has made the object of his life, and caring for nothing else if only he can attain it. By the concentration of soul, the energy of earnestness, and the directness of aim which the having of an ideal produces in any man, he who has a bad one is just so much worse than he who has none at all. Therefore let us look well to the sort of ideal we select.

But still further, thirdly, it is a sad thing when

a man has overtaken his ideal. You remember the sigh of the artist when, as he looked on his greatest work, he said, "Alas! I can do no better! I have overtaken my ideal." When that is true of any one, there is an immediate relaxation of effort, and an entire cessation of watchfulness. The object is gained, and so he sits down and rests in self-congratulation and conceit. But there is no such thing as remaining at rest in this life. Character never continueth in one stay. If we cease to cultivate it, and to watch over it, then it begins to deteriorate, and we fall away back toward that from which we came. When I lived in Liverpool my house was not far from several large works in which marine engines were made, and from which sea-going steamers were supplied with engineers. I knew the managers well, and in conversation with them learned a great many matters of interest. I found among the rest that commonly there were from four to six engineers for every ship, and that they were advanced from the sixth on to the first, in the order of seniority or merit, and as vacancies occurred; but the suggestive thing was this, — that so long as they were climbing up toward the top of the ladder, they could all be trusted to be sober, steady, earnest, and active in their work; but when they became chiefs, then there was danger. They had attained their ideal. Now they might relax their efforts, and be less watchful of their habits, and those who yielded to that danger fell. Now is there nothing like that among ourselves; and have we not, some of us at least, fallen before the same seductive influence? Let us see to it, therefore, that we adopt an ideal that we shall never lose by overtaking, and that is to be found alone in the character and example of our Lord Jesus Christ, which is absolute perfection. Do as we may, we never can lose that by reaching it. The farther we advance toward it, the more it opens up for us to enter upon; the higher we rise after it in holiness the higher his example seems to soar above us; the better we become, the more plainly do we see new excellencies in him to be attained. For holiness clears the spiritual perception, and they who have reached the greatest purity are always those who are longing and striving most for the attainment of yet closer conformity to the image of Christ. Oh! that the vision of the Christ might so fill our souls to-day, that henceforth the one aim of each of our lives might be to attain to "the measure of the stature of the perfect man in him"!

XVI.

THE PROVINCE OF FEELING IN RELIGIOUS EXPERIENCE.

Oh, that I were as in months past; as in the days when God preserved me. — JOB xxix. 2, 3.

ALAS! poor Job! He was, indeed, terribly afflicted. He had lost all his property, and been bereaved of all his children; his wife had tempted him to curse God, and his friends, who had come to sympathize with him, had remained to pronounce condemnation on him. Naturally enough, therefore, he had for the time being come to think that God had forsaken him. But, natural though it was, this opinion was not true. So we judge of this outcry of misery from his heart. For God was as really with him then as ever he had been, and he himself was as good a man as ever he had been. Nay, more, he had as much of God's grace as ever he had been favored with, only that had gone meanwhile into another direction than the emotional. The stimulant which would exhilarate, perhaps intoxicate, a man in health, may only just suffice to float him through a dangerous and depressing illness; and much in the same way the grace which in one set of circumstances would lift one up to exuberant joy may in another be no more than enough, if indeed it be enough, to keep him from sinking into depression or despair. So Job was allowing his feelings to mislead him. He was judging of God's attitude toward him by his emotions, and as these had fallen below zero, he concluded that God had forsaken him. But he was not the last, by any means, who has fallen into that mistake; and therefore this explanation of his case may fitly form the starting-point this morning for an attempt to define and illustrate the proper province of feeling in religious experience. Without further reference, therefore, to my text let me enter at once on this important and interesting though somewhat delicate and difficult subject.

First of all, then, let me remark that feeling follows intelligent conviction and belief of the truth of something that immediately concerns us as individuals. To take the illustration of Dr. McCosh, in his admirable work on "The Emotions": "Four persons of very much the same age and temperament are travelling in the same vehicle. At a particular stopping-place it is announced to them that a certain individual has just died suddenly and unexpectedly. One of the company looks perfectly stolid; a second comprehends what has taken place, but is in no way affected; the third looks and evidently feels sad; the fourth is overwhelmed with grief, which finds expression in tears, sobs, and exclamations. Whence the difference between the four individuals before us? In one respect they are all alike. An announcement has been made to them. The first is a foreigner, and has not understood the communication; the second had never met with the deceased, and could have no special regard for him; the third had often met with him in social intercourse and business transactions, and had been led to cherish a great esteem for him; the fourth was the brother of the departed, and was bound to him by a thousand ties, earlier and later."[1] From this imaginary case, which every one feels is perfectly true to nature, it is evident that feeling follows faith in that which is clearly understood, and that it is strong or weak in proportion as that which is believed affects us personally in a nearer or more remote degree. Now, applying these principles to the Gospel, we find that feeling is the effect of faith in the clearly understood statements of the Word of God concerning sin and salvation, as affecting us as individuals. It is not first the feeling and then the faith; but it is first intelligence, then faith, then direct and immediate personal interest in that which is believed, and then feeling. But if this be a correct analysis, you will see at a glance how far wrong those are who make the absence of feeling in them an excuse for not coming to Christ, as well as those who are constantly sighing and crying for more feeling of love to Christ as an evidence of the genuineness of their religion. Their error does not simply consist in putting too high a value upon feeling, but also in putting it into the wrong place. Even if the sinner had feeling, that would not commend him to Christ; for if it did, it would be something in himself which divided with Christ the glory of his salvation, and we know that no countenance is given in Scripture to anything of that kind. Again, if the feeling of love to Christ is to be regarded as the only ground of assurance, that also is giving to feeling a value which does not of right belong to it, since, so far as the ground of assurance is within the heart, it consists of the character as a whole viewed as the fruit of the Spirit, while the emotion of love to Jesus is only one feature of that character.

[1] McCosh on the Emotions, p. 1.

But that which I wish principally to insist on here, is that those who are sighing and crying directly for feeling, are beginning at the wrong end. They are, to use a common expression, putting the cart before the horse. They are calling for an effect without caring about the cause which is to produce it. Feeling *follows* faith in the statements of the Word of God concerning sin and salvation, as clearly understood by me in their application to me individually. If, therefore, I want feeling, I must turn my attention to these statements. If I want to feel my need of salvation, I must give good heed to what is said in the Bible about sin. I must endeavor to fathom its terrible significance. I must realize that in all its depth it is true of me; and then feeling will come of itself, such feeling as will make me cry, "What must I do to be saved?" If again I want to have love to Jesus, I must seek to understand and believe all that is said in the Scriptures concerning his person and character and sacrifice on my behalf. I must endeavor to realize what I should have been and become if he had not undertaken for me, and in the proportion in which I succeed in doing that, love and gratitude will take possession of my heart. If I want to be joyful, I must attend to, understand, and believe the tidings of salvation that are to make me joyful. And so with every Christian emotion. It is not to be sought directly as an end; but it will come through our understanding of, and belief in, those statements that are adapted and designed to produce it, each in its own order; first the intelligence, then the faith, then the feeling.

These things being so, you are already prepared to accept my second remark, to the effect that there can be no religion, in the Christian sense of that word, without feeling. That must be evident from the truth already established that feeling follows faith. For if there be no feeling there has been no faith, and where there is no faith there is no religion, for "without faith it is impossible to please God." The emotional is just as truly a part of our nature as the intellectual or the moral, and as regeneration affects the whole nature, it must transfigure the emotional portion of it as really as the others. The new birth does not uproot or lop off any part of our humanity; it only takes the sin out of it all. It does not eradicate our feelings, but it christianizes them. We still fear and love and hope and rejoice; but the things which we fear, the objects which we love, the good which we hope for, and the matters over which we rejoice, are different, — are, indeed, entirely the opposite of those which we feared, loved, hoped for, and rejoiced over before. All that we admit; but, after all, that is only a part of the great transformation which the Scriptures call regeneration.

Therefore I go on in the third place to note that feeling is not the whole of religion. That which the Holy Ghost produces in us through faith in Jesus Christ, is a whole new nature, and as we have just seen, that nature includes the intellectual, the moral, and the volitional, as well as the emotional. Or if you will have it in another form, religion is character, and emotion is only one element of character. The important question, therefore, is *not* what or how does a man feel, but what *is* he? As the man is, so are his feelings. If he be a new man, then just as his mind will be occupied with new thoughts, and his conscience will own a new Lord, and his will will obey a new master, and his conduct will serve his generation by the will of God, so his feelings will follow in their appropriate exercise. Mark I said again will *follow*. So the first duty, I reiterate it, is to have the *man* right, and that is to be secured by the giving of his heart to Christ to be renewed and sanctified by his Spirit. Leave the feelings out of the account for the moment, while you give yourself to Christ; and then, having done that, you will discover that they are a part of that self whom you have consecrated to the Lord. But they are not the whole of that self, and therefore they are not the whole of religion. Religion is right thinking and right acting, as well as right feeling toward God and our fellow-men for Christ's sake. The feeling stands midway between the thinking and the acting, passing the one on, as it were, to the other; but it cannot be made a substitute for either, and only in the combination of the three have we the genuine holy character which is the outcome of regeneration.

But now I advance another step, and remark in the fourth place that the feeling which does not lead to action, but terminates simply and only on itself, is always dangerous. The feeling which does not spring from intelligent faith is fanaticism; on the other hand, that which does not lead to action is sentimentalism, and it is difficult to say which of the two is the more pernicious. But for the present I have to do only with the latter, and on the first blush of the matter it may surprise you when I allege that feeling which does not lead to action has a hardening influence on the heart. As Bishop Butler has put it in a very suggestive passage in his Analogy, "From our very faculty of habits, passive impressions, by being repeated, grow weaker."

We have a familiar illustration of that fact in the effect produced upon one by the constant reading of sensational novels. That, as every one knows, is a species of literary dram-drinking. To have the same effect produced, the dose must be constantly increased, until at length a point is reached when, no matter how large the dose, the old excitement is no longer felt. Nor is this the worst of it. For the oftener one weeps over the tale of fictitious misery, the less disposed he is to be moved by real suffering; and so we can very well understand how the French executioner, whose heart was so hard as to care nothing whatever for the victims of his guillotine, yet wept profusely over the sorrows of Werther.

Now precisely the same law holds in religious matters. If emotion comes to be regarded as the whole of religion, and if it does not stimulate to holy activity, then by and by the emotion itself will disappear, and the heart will be hardened into utter impenetrability. The hearer who is intensely moved by one discourse, but goes away straightway forgetting all his impressions, and is not brought to immediate and decided Christian activity, will be less moved by the next, and less by the next, until at length he becomes "past feeling," and gives himself over to work all manner of iniquity with greediness. Hence, as Butler says again, "Going over the theory of virtue in one's thoughts, talking well, and drawing fine pictures of it, — this is so far from necessarily or certainly conducing to form a habit of it in him who thus employs himself, that it may harden the mind in a contrary course, and render it gradually more insensible; that is, form a habit of insensibility to all moral considerations." All this comes of giving exclusive attention to the matter of feeling; and so to escape from that danger it is necessary that we should set ourselves strenuously to reduce our feelings to actions. The emotion must be made a motive principle, else the result will be most pernicious. If one is moved to love, let him seek some means of manifesting that love; if to compassion, let him give his compassion an outward form in beneficence; if to fear, let him exert himself to guard against the danger of which he is afraid; if to penitence, let him forsake the sin for which he feels regret; if to admiration, let him stir himself up to imitate, so far as he may, that which he admires. The tears which are "idle" will ultimately exhaust the fountain out of which they flow, and the feelings that are not fruitful in good works will by and by paralyze the heart, and render it entirely unimpressible; for all such abuse must end in impotence.

But now to complete the presentation of the subject I must add, in the fifth place, that the feeling which leads to action is just for that reason less a matter of consciousness as feeling. It becomes transmuted into conduct; and just as steam makes less noise when it is driving machinery than when it is being blown off, so the oftener feeling is transmuted into action the less does one come to be aware of the feeling that is in the action. For here, too, the law of habit comes into operation. In reading a book we have to go through a great many separate acts; first we have to take cognizance of the individual letters, then of the separate words into which they form themselves, then of the clauses, then of the sentence, then of the bearing of the sentence on the object which the author has in view; but such is the force of habit that most of us now in reading are conscious only of the last of all these, though they must all have been gone through in every case. Now the same is true of actions, for in each of these there is first a perception of duty, then an emotion of desire, or something analogous to that, then a volition, then the action; but habit has obliterated the consciousness of all save the volition and the action. Still they are all there, and if we should judge entirely of the action by the simple test of feeling, we should come to an entirely wrong decision regarding it. We saw a few minutes ago that passive emotions decay in vividness by repetition, and now we see that practical habits strengthen by exercise; so that we come to the conclusion thus expressed by Butler, that active habits may be gradually forming and strengthening by a course of acting upon such and such motives and excitements, whilst these motives and excitements are by proportionate degrees "growing less sensible, that is, are continually less and less sensibly felt." Or to put it more simply, a man may be advancing in moral excellence by that very course which deadens his consciousness to his emotions. When holiness, therefore, becomes a habit, we are less sensible of feeling, not because the feeling is not there, but because its operation has become automatic through the habit which we have acquired of turning it into action.

The same truth may be made apparent in another way. Thus you are not so conscious of your affection for the members of your family when you are at work daily for their support, as when you are sitting by the fireside in the winter evening with them all around you; but it is *there* all the same, forming one of the strongest motives for your business energy and enterprise. So you are not so conscious of your love to Jesus when you are battling with temptation, as when you are at his table of privilege; but your very conflict and victory have sprung out of that love, since but for it they had not been.

Now, narrowing into a conclusion, let me say that if the principles which to-day I have enunciated be true, as I think you must all admit they are, then mere feeling must be a very unsafe and unsatisfactory test of the genuineness of our interest in religion. The more habitual acts of holiness become, there must, as we have seen, be the less consciousness of emotion connected with them. The feeling that becomes a motive power does thereby so wholesomely spend itself, that there is nothing of it left for the mere luxury of enjoyment in itself. So it may be that the very absence of feeling may be a proof of progress rather than an evidence of indifference. *May be*, I have said, for we are not warranted to say universally it is. The true test is not the feeling but the life, not the emotion but the conduct, according to that law of Christ, "By their fruits ye shall know them." If, therefore, the life be Christlike, rooted in faith in Jesus, and devoted to obedience to him, then the feeling which prompted that obedience has stiffened into a principle, and so its absence in our consciousness as emotion will not be a sign of indifference. If again there be neither obedience in the life nor feeling in the heart, then the absence of feeling in such a case is an evidence of insensibility. If, once more, there be a gush of emotion which has no influence on the life, and which is indulged in for the sake of enjoyment in the emotion itself, then the feeling is the merest sentimentalism, and is not only worthless as an evidence of piety, but positively injurious as tending to produce spiritual insensibility.

This, however, is not all. Feeling is affected by so many other things that it is not safe to give it much importance as a test of our Christianity. For it is influenced greatly by the state of the bodily health, and oftentimes the spiritual adviser is called in when really it is the medical attendant who is required. Again, it is affected by the intellectual calibre of the man. He who is represented in the parable by the stony ground, — the thin layer of earth on the top of a rock, — the man, that is, who has little intellect and a stony heart, — strange as it may seem, shoots suddenly up into emotion; but, alas! as quickly settles down into withered and hopeless apathy. And to mention only one other case: the man who is environed on every side by trial, as Job was here, is very apt to have his emotion tinctured by his trial. Certain diseases, as we know, are always attended with certain peculiar effects upon the feelings. Now if all these things are true, how foolish it is in us to take our feelings as the only test or evidence of the genuineness of our piety. The child on board ship thinks that the sky is moving to and fro; but that is stationary, and it is the ship that is continually rolling. So the assurance that rests on mere feeling will be constantly unstable, and the man will imagine that God is changing toward him when the alteration is simply and only in himself. The true ground of assurance is that expressed by Paul, "I know whom I have believed," — the knowledge which we have of Christ; and they are blessed who have learned in this matter to turn away from the study of their own frames and feelings to the contemplation of the Lord.

But if the element of feeling must ever be an uncertain test of the genuineness of our religion, the absence of it ought to be no hindrance to any one's coming to Christ in simple faith for salvation. He who puts off his coming on the ground that he has no feeling, is thereby seeking something that will commend him to Christ. He is trying to get up something that will have some merit in it; and so he is seeking to be in part, at least, his own savior. But there can be no salvation *that* way. The sinner who would be saved must give up trust in everything but Christ. He must have no confidence in prayers, or tears, or anything, or any person, but Christ. And then, when he thus trusts Christ, the feeling will come in its own proper place to do its own proper work; for it will come as love to the Lord who died for him and rose again, and it will constrain him to live only and always to the Saviour who has redeemed him at the cost of his own precious blood. Let no one, therefore, be deterred from coming to Christ because he has no feeling; but let each unconverted one here come to Christ as he is, and Christ will make him what he ought to be.

XVII.

THE PLACE AND POWER OF INDIVIDUALITY IN CHRISTIAN LIFE AND WORK.

I — yet not I. — 1 Cor. xv. 10, and Gal. ii. 20.

This expression, used twice by the Apostle Paul, and each time in a passage referring to his personal experience, may for that reason, as I believe, be regarded by us as characteristic of the manner in which he was accustomed to think and speak concerning himself and his work. He did not ignore his own individuality. He knew himself. He had a clear and correct apprehension of the qualities of character, idiosyncrasies of disposition, and powers of mind by which he was distinguished from all other men. He knew what he could do, and what he could not do. He understood his own peculiarities, aptitudes, abilities, and limitations. He estimated these, also, at their true value, and put them in their proper place. He did not reckon them as of supreme importance, for he is careful to say, "I live, yet not I, but Christ liveth in me;" and "I laboured, yet not I, but the grace of God which was with me." But neither did he regard them as of no account, for he distinctly specifies in the one case that the life which he describes was his life, "I live;" and in the other, that the labors which he performed were his works, "I laboured." There was that about his life as a Christian man, and his labors as a Christian Apostle, which was clearly traceable to his own personality; but the energizing influence which gave holiness to the one, and efficacy to the other, came from the grace and spirit of God, who wrought in him and through him and with him. The "*I*" was regenerated by Christ, yet so that it remained the "*I;*" and the labors were made effectual by the grace of God, yet so that they were conditioned and shaped by the "*I.*" His life was different from that of every one else because it was *his* life; but it was holy because it was Christ that lived in him. His labors were distinct from those of others because he could say, "I laboured;" but they were so abundant and so fruitful because he could say, "I laboured, yet not I, but the grace of God which was with me." Fitly, therefore, may we take our two texts — which, indeed, are not so much two as one — as suggesting for our consideration at this time *the place and power of individuality in Christian life and work.*

We begin at the foundation by remarking, in the first place, that there is a distinct individuality in every man which knows itself as "*I*" and "*me.*" It is no part of my present purpose to enter into a full metaphysical inquiry how we come to the consciousness of our own existence as distinct personalities. The famous argument of the great French philosopher, "I think, therefore I am," does not help us much, for, as you see, the "I," whose existence is inferred in the conclusion, has been already postulated in the premise; if I know that I think, I already know that "I" am the "I" who thinks. We cannot get at it, therefore, by a process of reasoning. So others have viewed it as an intuition, and others still as a conviction which comes to us naturally and irresistibly in connection with certain experiences. Perhaps Tennyson has given us the true genesis of the matter in his beautiful lines in "In Memoriam;" —

> " The baby new to earth and sky,
> What time his tender palm is prest
> Against the circle of the breast,
> Has never thought that this is I.

> " But as he grows he gathers much,
> And learns the use of ' I ' and ' me,
> And finds I am not what I see,
> And other than the things I touch

> " So rounds he to a separate mind,
> From whence clear memory may begin,
> As through the frame that bounds him in
> His isolation grows defined."

More akin to the object which we have in view, however, is it to get at the constituent elements of the "self" that is in each of us. The germ of the whole, as it seems to me, is in the consciousness or experience of causation. I can and do produce certain effects on things outside of me by the exercise of a power inherent in me; and that in which that power inheres, and by which it is put forth, is the "me" within me. Allied with this causation is free-will, which sits behind causation and directs it at its pleasure. Then, as the result of free-will, is responsibility. The "I can" leads up to "I ought," and so consciousness develops into conscience. That is more or less the same in every man. But all this while I am exercising those powers of perception, memory, judgment, and the like, which we call intellectual, which are different in degree in different persons, and which thus give to each his distinctive mental character. Then come in temperamental peculiarities — however these may be explained — which give their hue to all the rest, just as the stained glass in the window gives its own tint to the light which passes through it. To these must be added the influence of education, environment, experience, and the like, and the whole combine to form in a man that which we call his individuality. Now, as I have said, that is different and distinct in each. No one is precisely and in every respect the double of another. There is a generic likeness between man and man which stamps all as human; but there is also a specific difference in each which makes him recognizable as himself. Just as the features of the face in one man are different from those of all other men, so there are marks of individuality in the character of each. One is impulsive, impetuous, explosive; another is calm, judicial, deliberate, and well ballasted. One is severely logical; another is intensely intuitional. One is poetic; another is prosaic. One is pre-eminently endowed with mental ability; another is possessed of only average intellect; and a third, perhaps, has less of mind than the common run of men. Nay, even among those who are of outstanding greatness there are other distinctions, as between Shakspeare and Milton, or between Bacon and Butler; and the same is true of men at every point in the scale. But I need not dwell on this department of the subject, for the truth on which I am insisting is universally admitted.

I go on to remark, therefore, in the second place, that when the Spirit of God regenerates a man, he does not destroy this individuality. Regeneration is not a change in the peculiarities by which a man is distinguished, but rather the purification and consecration of these, and of the man himself as a whole, to a new service. No doubt it is said that "if any man be in Christ," or in the phraseology of my text,—for it comes to the same thing,—if Christ be living in any man, he is a new creature; and we know that again and again Paul calls the regenerated man a "new man." Now, there is a deeply important sense in which that is true; but there is another, no less important in its own place, in which it is also true that the man is the same man. The change which is wrought in regeneration is spiritual, affecting his character and life toward God, and turning all his energies, powers, and peculiarities into a new, because a holy direction; but it does not directly and immediately, at least, change these energies, powers, and peculiarities themselves. Physically speaking, the man looks just as he did before. Perhaps a more placid and more happy expression comes into his face; and if he has been addicted to evil habits, the dissipated and bloated appearance gradually passes away from his countenance as the result of his altered life. But he is easily recognizable as himself, and no one would mistake him for somebody else.

Now, precisely the same thing is true intellectually. As the result of his new interest in the word of God, there may come a quickening of his intelligence, so that he may become at length more vigorous mentally. Or from the new value which he has come to put upon himself, as a man redeemed by the blood of Christ, he may be impelled to assiduous self-culture, in order that he may make himself the best possible offering to his Lord, and that may give new brightness to his intellect. But these are indirect results of his having been regenerated, and not a part of his regeneration. The act of the Holy Spirit in quickening a soul into newness of life is not such as would change a half-witted man — for example, like Dr. Calamy's poor Joseph — into the intellectual peer of a Newton or an Edwards.

We all recognize that; but the same thing is equally true of the qualities of what we call the temperament or disposition of a man. He who was impulsive before his regeneration will remain impulsive; and though the Spirit of God may enable him to restrain that quality from running to a sinful extreme, yet it will still characterize his religious life. The man who was of melancholy temperament before he was regenerated will have his piety after regeneration shaded and sometimes clouded by its influence; just as the cheerful man will manifest after his conversion a peculiarly cheerful Christianity. John did not lose his Johannine qualities when he became a disciple, and Peter was Peter to the end. The same natural qualities which distinguished Paul as a persecutor came out in Paul the Apostle; and the differences between such men as Luther and Calvin were rooted in the original idiosyncrasies of the men, and such as would have distinguished them from each other if they had never been regenerated. The individuality of a man, therefore, furnishes the mould into which the new life of the Holy Spirit runs, and gives to that life its character and shape. What a great annual regeneration we see every spring-time in the world of Nature when the earth renews her verdure, and the trees put on their foliage, and the birds resume their songs. But the new life does not make them all alike; each flower and tree and bird retains its own individuality. All the trees do not take the leaves of the oak, royal as that is; neither do all the flowers assume the appearance of the rose, beautiful though that may be; while the birds do not unite in the one song of the lark, ecstatic and inspiring though that is. But we have birch and maple and beech and chestnut in the wood; we have lily and violet and daisy and pink among the flowers; and the notes of the thrush and the bullfinch and the blackbird fill the morning hour with music. Thus the new life in flower and tree and bird reveals itself through the distinctive peculiarities of each, and thereby are secured the wondrous harmony of colors in the landscape, and the marvellous yet attractive medley of the chorus of the grove. So it is also with regenerated men. The new life lifts up into itself the individuality of each believer, and uses that as a means of manifesting the grace of God. Thus it comes that in the Church of Christ we have not the dull monotony of uniformity, but the living beauty of variety.

It is but a corollary from what I have just said, when I go on to remark, in the third place, that when the Spirit of God works through a man, he uses the individuality of the man in all its features. Precisely as the Holy Spirit respects human individuality in regeneration, he employs it in the work which he seeks to perform through the instrumentality of the renewed man. He makes it largely determine the kind of service which the man is to render to his generation and to the church, and it colors and qualifies that service itself. For illustration of this we need not go beyond the limits of the Word of God itself. Thus take the case of inspiration, and you will see how truly each of the sacred writers might have said, "I, yet not I, but the Spirit of God in me." Indeed that was substantially what David *did* say when he affirmed, "The Spirit of the Lord spake by me, and his word was in my tongue." I grant indeed that the result of inspiration was to secure the accurate transmission of God's message to men, while in sanctification the Spirit of God does not secure, here at least, perfect holiness of life in the believer, and in Christian activity he does not lead the believer, here at least, to the performance of a perfect work. But if the individuality was not disturbed but used in inspiration, the result being such as I have described, we are warranted in concluding, *a fortiori*, that it is not disturbed while the Spirit works in man to will and to do of his good pleasure. Now we have clear evidence of the existence both of the Divine and human elements in the Scriptures. That God and not men merely was the author of these books is apparent from the character of the revelation made in them; from the predictions which they contain and which have been so marvellously fulfilled; from the unity which pervades them, so that, though many men were engaged in producing them, and though the time of their production extended over nearly two thousand years, we distinctly perceive "one increasing purpose" running through them from first to last; and especially from the Christ who is in the centre of them all and whose light irradiates each particular part. But the distinctively human element is no less conspicuous in each of the several portions of which they are composed. The Egyptian training which came to be a part of the individuality of Moses fitted him for the reception of the plan and the superintendence of the erection of the tabernacle, and it comes out as clearly also in the exactitude of the statutes which his books contain. The lyric tension of David's poetic soul, so responsive in its vibrations to joy or sorrow, to penitence or praise, is distinctively different from the cool calculating philosophy of Solomon, which took time to shape itself into epigrammatic and aphorismal proverbs. No one could mistake the style of Isaiah with its lofty grandeur and magnificent cadence for that of his plain, homely country brother and contemporary,

Amos, with his frequent allusions to the life of a herdsman, and a gatherer of sycamore fruit. Ezekiel, like a priest as he was, put much of his prophecy into the description of a restored Temple; and Daniel saw visions of composite figures like those which we now know were common among the Babylonian sculptures of his day, and which therefore he must have often seen. Thus like the watermark in the paper which is the signature of its maker, the individuality of style which is woven into each of these Old Testament books is the signature of its human authorship, — the "I," which in this case also is as we have seen accompanied by the "yet not I, but the Spirit of God." But the same is true of the Apostles and evangelists. No one can peruse Mark's Gospel attentively without perceiving his keen eye for minute matters of look and gesture, and his eager energy as manifested by the constantly recurring "straightway." The very youngest reader feels, even if he cannot explain, the difference between the Gospel by John and the Epistle to the Romans; and the plainest and least educated man can tell the distinction between the practical pungency of the Epistle of James and the weird majesty of the Book of Revelation. Clearly therefore the inspiring Spirit used the individualities of the writers in giving us the Scriptures.

But what is thus so markedly true in the matter of inspiration is equally conspicuous in the lower departments of spiritual effort. The idiosyncrasy of the man points out to him the work which he is to undertake, and colors and qualifies his performance of that work. Peter's personal feelings and peculiarities designated him for labor among the Jews, and so the Spirit "wrought in him to the Apostleship of the circumcision." Paul again as a Hebrew of the Hebrews, yet at the same time a native Hellenist and a Roman citizen, was specially fitted for a universal Apostleship; and so the Spirit in him "was mighty toward the Gentiles." So also we account for the specialty in the service performed at different times in the history of the church by such different men as Athanasius, Augustine, Bernard, Wycliffe, Tindal, Luther, Calvin, Knox, Wesley, Whitefield, and a host of others.

These were all men possessed of marked individuality, and easily distinguishable from each other and from other men. Each was different from each of the rest, yet Christ was in them all and his grace was with them all; and it was through that in each which constituted what logicians would call his differentia that his special work was accomplished by the grace of God. No one of them could have done the others' work, and each was fitted by his individuality for his own. So in departments lowlier still, the man with an organizing faculty finds his sphere as a superintendent in some mission school; just as the woman with much motherhood within her, an aptness to interest and instruct and develop the little ones, sees and seizes her opportunity as the teacher of an infant class. Thus, whatever our distinctive idiosyncrasies may be, we may be sure that we have them, not that we may repress and destroy them altogether, but that they may be employed by the Spirit of God for the accomplishing through us of a work which no one but ourselves can perform. In the orchestra each instrument has its own office, and if one be silenced, none of the others can fully supply its place; and so in the service of our common Lord, by works of faith and labors of love each of us has his own note to sound, and it ought to be our endeavor to give the Spirit of God free play, through each of our characteristics, for the sounding of that note.

But now, advancing another step, I remark in the fourth place that the actual result in all cases is to be traced to the operation of the Spirit of God through our individuality. The man is the instrument, but the Spirit is the hand that works with it; and the glory is due not to the instrument, but to him who uses it and gives it efficacy. He knows what agent to employ for any special purpose, just as the skilled artificer knows which of his tools to take for the accomplishment of that which he has presently in view; and he knows also how to use it for the gaining of his end. In a large manufactory there are multitudes of separate machines for different purposes. On one floor you may find, as I did a day or two ago in a printing establishment in this city, a whole array of printing-presses; on another a large number of folding-machines; on yet another sewing-machines, and cutting-machines, and what not,—each adapted for its separate work, but all moved by the same engine. The power comes from the same source, and that after all does all the work. Now of course men are not machines; but the analogy may help us to understand how, though there may be in each of us distinct aptitudes and abilities fitting us for different kinds of service, yet the Spirit of God may be in all of us, the energizing and operative principle. We ourselves, separated from that Spirit, could do nothing. He might work without us, but he has chosen to work through us and with us. Still, though that is the case, the work is done by him; and so, no matter what our success may be, we must say with Paul, "I laboured, yet not I, but the grace of God which was with me." This is one of the commonplaces of our faith; yet perhaps it has become so commonplace to us that it ceases to produce its appropriate result. For if we considered it fully we should never be surprised at the results flowing from the agency of any man, since these are all due to God; and we should never be dismayed by the magnitude of any undertaking to which we are fairly called, since it is to be accomplished not by us, but by God. We often marvel at the fruits of the labors of a single individual, and marvellous they would be if they were attributable to him; but who can limit the Holy One of Israel, and why should we be surprised at the greatness of anything done by him? If we had faith in him, our wonder would cease; "for is anything too hard for the Lord?" Then on the other hand, if we had this faith we should not be found so frequently faltering before difficult duty. When Theresa, whom the Spaniards call a saint, started out to build a hospital with nothing but three halfpence, and they wondered at her rashness, she replied, "Theresa and three halfpence are nothing, but God and three halfpence are sufficient;" and she carried it through. Ah, do we really believe the words, " Lo, I am with you alway, even unto the end of the world;" and " Greater is he that is in you than he that is in the world"? If we did, we should oftener see that wonderful antithesis which the world does not understand,— the loftiest courage in closest alliance with the deepest humility; the " I " doing and daring everything because of its consciousness of the " not I," but Christ living in it; the individual rising above himself because he has fully surrendered himself to the Spirit of God to be inhabited and energized by him.

To sum up, then, let us distil the essence of our discourse into these two lessons. First, respect your own individuality. Be content to be yourself; but let that self be purified, energized, and inhabited by the Lord Jesus Christ. Do not attempt to force yourself into the mould of the experience of another. Be not concerned if your Christian experience should be different from that of others. Come to Christ in your own way, only see to it that it is *Christ* you come to; live your own life, but be sure it is a Christian life; do your own work, but take good heed that it is Christian work. David in Saul's armor was not more encumbered than you would be were you to force yourselves into the individuality of another. Stand then on your right to be yourself. As one has well said, "No really great man does his work by imposing his maxims on his disciples. He evokes their life." He awakens them to be themselves. This is what Christ does for his disciples. He gets at the inner fountain of their being and then lets the streams of his influence flow thence through their individuality. Let him do so with you.

Then in the second place give God all the glory for what you are and have done. It is he that worketh in you to will and to do, and the language of your hearts ought ever to be, "Not unto us, O Lord, not unto us, but unto thy name give glory, for thy mercy and for thy truth's sake." He is the noblest preacher who is distinctively himself, imitating no other's manner and copying no other's style, while yet he preaches not himself, but Christ; and that is the highest type of Christian who is himself, while yet Christ is seen and felt to be living in that self, and working through it. This will secure originality of enterprise as well as success of effort, and lead to the same result in our case as in Paul's, when after his conversion it is recorded of those around him that "**they glorified God in him.**"

XVIII.

THE READINESS OF THE GOSPEL OF PEACE.

And your feet shod with the preparation of the Gospel of peace. — EPHESIANS vi. 15.

THE great Apostle was much given to the use of illustrations. Like his divine Master, he clearly saw the analogy between things external and things internal and spiritual, and employed the one for the purpose of making the other more easily intelligible. By the relation of the members of the body to each other, and to the body as a whole, he illustrated the unity of the church as the body of Christ, and the duty of its members to him and to each other. The athletic games of the Greeks were made by him to illuminate the Christian life, and the manner in which its duties are to be discharged; and in the passage from which my text is taken, the different pieces of the armor of a Roman soldier are employed to illustrate the spiritual furniture of the good soldier of Jesus Christ for the conflict which he has continually to wage. Nor, when you think of it, could it be said to be unnatural for him to take spiritual lessons from such a quarter; for he had come both frequently and intimately into intercourse with the soldiers of the imperial army. They were familiar figures in the streets of Tarsus and Jerusalem, where most of his early days were spent. He could not but meet them often in such colonies as the Pisidian Antioch, Troas, and Philippi. He had been accompanied and guarded by them on that famous midnight journey from Jerusalem to Cesarea. A band of them had been his fellow voyagers in the corn ship which was wrecked upon the coast of Malta, and at the very time when he was dictating this letter a soldier of the Prætorian guard was chained to his right arm. It was no wonder therefore that he should have become familiar with the different pieces of armor worn by them, or that he should find in them much that suggested spiritual analogies and lessons for the prosecution of the Christian life. In fact, he came to regard the soldier as a parabolic picture of the Christian man, and he has in these verses made a spiritual use of everything about him. It would be deeply interesting to take up the whole description; but to do that as it should be done would take not one discourse, but many, and therefore we must make a selection. I take to-day the shoes, or sandals, both because there is among us much ignorance of the meaning of the Apostle's reference to them, and because, when rightly understood, that reference may be very helpful to us in our daily experience.

The allusion of Paul in the text is not, as some have supposed, to the greaves, which were a kind of military legging, but to the *caligæ*, or sandals, which were worn by the ancient warriors, and the soles of which were thickly studded with hobnails.[1] Now what precisely corresponds to these sandals in the armor of the Christian man? Not the Gospel of peace itself, as some commentators have supposed, nor as others would explain the phrase, the foundation or firm base of the

[1] Eadie, on Ephesians *in loco*.

Gospel of peace. It is true, indeed, that the word here rendered "preparation" is used in the Septuagint to mean foundation; but such a sense is altogether out of harmony with the metaphor here employed. The Apostle is not speaking in this place of the ground on which the Christian soldier stands, but of the sandals which he wears, and these only can be "the preparation" spoken of. But what is meant by "preparation"? When you ask a chemist what a particular bottle contains, he will sometimes reply, "It is a preparation of this or that;" and so we are apt to say that the preparation of the Gospel of peace is some special modification of the Gospel. But neither is that the particular shade of meaning which the word expresses. It signifies the state of preparation which is wrought out in a man through the possession of the peace which the Gospel confers upon believers. It would be less ambiguous if we were to read it, "the preparedness," or "the readiness" of the Gospel of peace, and the illustration of the Apostle may be thus paraphrased: "Like as soldiers have their feet shod with sandals, armed with iron, as a preparation or defence against the roughness, and a security against the slipperiness or miriness of the roads, so do ye arm yourselves against the slippery temptations of your Christian course by having in you that readiness for every emergency which is the result of unfeigned acceptance of the Gospel of peace."[1] Or, putting it in a yet more definite form, the feet are the instruments, and therefore the appropriate symbols of motion; and the Christian soldier whose career is a march and a battle, and a battle and a march, must always keep himself in marching order. He must be ready for either marching or fighting at a moment's

[1] Bloomfield, Greek Testament on the passage.

notice, and he is to get that readiness from the Gospel of peace. For "the possession of peace with God creates blessed serenity of heart, and confers upon the mind peculiar and continuous celerity of action and motion. There is nothing to disconcert or perplex it, or to divide and retard its energies."[1]

Such, expressed as briefly and clearly as possible, is the true meaning of the text. Let us now see what, as Christians, those things are for which we ought to be always ready, and how the Gospel of peace gives us readiness for them. Now, as regards the first of these two questions, the true answer is that we ought to be ready for anything which we are called to face as the people of God still living in the world. But that is too general a statement to give us anything like a proper sense of the full gravity of the case; and if we would get that we must descend, in some degree at least, to particulars.

First of all, then, we must be ready for *service.* The believer is not saved by his works; but he is saved that he may work, and the genuineness of his new life is to be manifested by service. Like David, he is to "serve his generation by the will of God." Everything which he does is to be done out of regard to God, and the particular sphere of labor which he is to fill is to be defined for him by the circumstances and necessities of the generation to which he belongs. We are not required to do precisely the same things as our fathers did, but cherishing the same principles as our fathers cherished, we are to apply these to the new needs of our own times; and so the Christian service is kept from being stereotyped, and there is always need for

[1] Eadie, on Ephesians *in loco*.

inventiveness in the finding of new ways of applying Christianity to meet the new necessities. The Gospel is suited to every age in the world's history; but the methods which are adopted for bringing it to bear upon men must vary with the state and condition of the men with whom we have to deal. For example, the service of one generation of the people of God in this country, and in one department, was the mitigation of the hardships incidental to slavery; that of the next was the emancipation of the slaves themselves, and the destruction of slavery as an institution; and that of the next is the education and elevation of the freedmen, that they may worthily perform the duties of citizens among us. Now the possession of peace with God, much more the assurance of the possession of the peace of God within us, will give us readiness for the performance of the service which is required of us by the will of God, and defined for us by the necessities of our own generation. For where there is peace there is whole-souledness: there is nothing to disturb the attention, divide the heart, or divert the mind; and so he who possesses it can give himself wholly to that, to which he gives himself at all. He can and will say of it, "This one thing I do." Whatever he is in, he is in altogether; and so his service is that of a whole man. He never thinks of serving two masters. The peace which he enjoys unifies his heart, while the fact that he has got it as a free gift from God so fills him with love to God that he seeks to make his work the very best which he can do. The possession of this peace will keep him also from being fastidious about the place in which he serves. For in a heart that is filled with the peace of the Gospel there will be no room for any mean and petty jealousies of other people, and the man who is thus blessed will not be so anxious to get the first place, as to do that which most needs to be done. It is said by some one that if an angel were sent to earth on the business of God, he would be equally ready to till the ground or to sit upon a throne, because his one desire would be to do God's will; and similarly, the man who has peace with God will accept with equal readiness the meanest or the most prominent position, because his desire will be to work for God, and do first that which needs to be first attended to. You see, therefore, how true it is that peace is power, and how that power is spent in the service which we render to our God.

But in the second place the Christian must be always ready for sacrifice, and the possession of the peace of God will give him that readiness. When the Lord Jesus laid down the conditions of discipleship he said, "If any man willeth to come after me, let him deny" or renounce "himself, and take up his cross, and follow me;" and in the parallel passage in Luke the words are, "Let him take up his cross daily." Now that virtually means that the Christian must be ready to follow Christ at whatever cost, — even, if need be, at the cost of life itself. He is not to go out of his way seeking for a cross, for that would be to make himself a "martyr by mistake;" but if, while moving on his appointed path of duty, he is confronted with a cross, then he is to take up that and humbly and bravely bear the suffering and sacrifice which it imposes, for Christ's sake. Then, as he never can tell when precisely he will be met by such a cross, he must hold himself always in readiness for it.

Many of you must have seen the beautiful and suggestive device by which the Christian's true feeling as to what may be before him has been symbolized. In the centre of the picture is a magnificent ox. On the one side there is an altar with a fire upon it, and everything prepared for sacrifice, and on the other there is a plough with a yoke all arranged for being put on the neck of the patient animal; while beneath there is the motto in Latin, signifying "Ready for either." So the Christian must aim at being always ready, either for the plough of service or for the altar of sacrifice. That was the case with Paul when he said: "And now behold I go bound in the Spirit unto Jerusalem, not knowing the things that shall befall me there, save that the Holy Ghost witnesseth in every city, saying that bonds and afflictions abide me. But none of these things move me, neither count I my life dear unto myself, so that I might finish my course with joy, and the ministry which I have received of the Lord Jesus to testify the Gospel of the grace of God." And again: "What mean ye to weep and to break mine heart? for I am ready, not to be bound only, but also to die at Jerusalem for the name of the Lord Jesus." And the secret of all this was that he had in his heart the peace with God which springs out of the willing acceptance of the Gospel, and of the Saviour whom it reveals. You cannot terrify the man who is at peace with God; for when you do your worst upon him, you but open the death door through which he passes into the presence chamber of his Lord, to share his glory and his happiness for evermore. You know the sublime thunder psalm of the "sweet singer of Israel." It is the twenty-ninth in the Psalter, and describes the coming up of a terrific storm from the Mediterranean to

Jerusalem, as seen by a spectator on Mount Zion. First it is seen over the waters of the Mediterranean, — "The voice of the Lord is upon the waters;" next the storm is breaking the cedars of Lebanon; then it shakes the wilderness of Kadesh. And as it gradually comes up and up toward the Holy City, and rolls out its awful reverberations immediately overhead, there comes this assurance of safety: "The Lord will give strength unto his people; the Lord will bless his people with peace." It is the very climax of sublimity; but it is also an external figure of the spiritual calmness of the man, who, amid the mutterings and thunderings of his earthly enemies, has within his heart the peace of God. Having God with him, he can sustain no loss or damage, and every sacrifice which he is called to make is cheerfully offered; for the Lord is able to give him more than others take away. Men did not give him his peace, and they cannot take it away; and so long as that is true, everything is well with him, and he is ready for anything.

But passing on to another point, let me say in the third place here, that the Christian should be always ready for sorrow, and that the Gospel of peace will give him that readiness. The believer does not escape sorrow in the world. He knows neither in what form nor at what time it will come upon him. But it will come in some form or other, sooner or later in his experience. It may be caused by the loss through bereavement of those who are nearest and dearest to him, or through the estrangement of friends from him, or through reverse of fortune and the coming on him of great adversity; but it surely will come, and he ought to be ready for its coming. But where shall he get that readiness? Not from philosophy; that may make a Stoic of him, and lead him to submit, somewhat haughtily, to the inevitable, but it will give him neither the resignation nor the consolation of the Christian. Pride will not give it to him, for that will only wrap him in the mantle of seclusion, and make him discontented and irritable with God and all around him. But the Gospel of peace will give it to him, for that assures him that everything that comes to him is under the supervision and control of God. That reveals to him that God is his Father, and that in all his dealings with his people he dealeth with them as with children, and therefore in the tenderest love and the highest wisdom. That lets him see through the cross into the heart of God, and leads him to reason that he who spared not his own Son, but delivered him up for us all, being himself unchangeable, still loves us, even when he permits trouble to come upon us; and lifting the veil that hides the future from view, that tells him that "our light afflictions, which are but for a moment, work out for us a far more exceeding and eternal weight of glory." So the Lord is his comforter under every sorrow; and knowing the riches of his consolation, he is ready for sorrow, whensoever God is pleased to send it on him. Look at Job and see how he bore himself when one terrible affliction came upon him after another with the greatest suddenness and severity, and as you hear him say, "The Lord gave and the Lord hath taken away, blessed be the name of the Lord," you have an illustration of the power which the possession of peace with God has in the preparing of the heart for sorrow. Let us see, therefore, that we acquaint ourselves with God, and be at peace with him, that so we may be able to sing with the sacred poet:

"God is our refuge and strength, a very present help in trouble. Therefore will not we fear, though the earth be removed, and though the mountains be carried into the midst of the sea; though the waters thereof roar and be troubled, though the mountains shake with the swelling thereof."

But I remark in the last place, that the Christian should be ready for death, and that the Gospel of peace will give him that readiness. You know the solemn exhortation of the Lord himself, — "Be ye also ready, for in such an hour as ye think not the Son of man cometh." That which we most of all need in the prospect of our leaving the world is readiness to go. Nay, that readiness, rightly understood, is all we need. This is most impressively taught us, singularly enough, by the great dramatist, in one of his most thrilling tragedies, albeit many of its readers have never felt the full force of his words, or even marked the words themselves until they have been pointed out to them. When Horatio seeks to dissuade Hamlet from his last conflict, and offers to apologize to his adversary for his non-appearance, the prince replies: "Not a whit; we defy augury. There's a special providence in the falling of a sparrow. If it be now, 't is not to come; if it be not to come, it will be now; if it be not now, yet it will come: *the readiness is all.*" Ah, yes! the readiness is all. And in what does that readiness consist? Not in any special occupation at the moment, — for it matters not what the Christian may be doing when the summons comes, — but in the habitual character of the soul; not in the performance of any rite, such as the observance of the supper, or the reception of extreme unction; no, but in the faith which rests on Jesus

Christ, and in the possession of that peace which he bestows. This it was which upheld Paul, when, in the near anticipation of death, he said: "I am now ready to be offered, and the time of my departure is at hand. I have fought a good fight. I have finished my course; I have kept the faith. Henceforth there is laid up for me a crown of righteousness which the Lord, the righteous Judge, shall give me at that day, and not to me only, but unto all them also that love his appearing." What doth hinder, my brethren, that we should have this peace of heart now? It will make life sweeter, more useful, more blessed, as long as we are to live upon the earth, and it will make death only the gate into the palace of the king, with whom we shall reign in glory everlastingly.

XIX.

THE INTERPRETING INFLUENCE OF TIME.

Jesus answered and said unto him, What I do thou knowest not now, but thou shalt understand hereafter. — JOHN xiii. 7 (Revised Version).

THESE words belong to one of the most familiar narratives in the Gospel history. The disciples were sitting with their Master at the table at which the Lord's supper was instituted. He had just informed them that one of them should betray him, and though for a few moments that announcement filled them with consternation and sorrow, yet the impression was only temporary, for very soon they were engaged in a most unseemly and ill-timed discussion as to which of them should be accounted the greatest. This was not the first occasion on which that question had been debated among them, and ever as it came up they had been severely, yea, somewhat sternly, reproved by their Lord for allowing it to arise. But this time, with Gethsemane and Calvary so immediately before him, he dealt in a peculiarly tender manner with their fault. He met it with an acted parable, wherein he set before them the object of his mission into the world, and the sacrifice which his coming into it involved, and then repeated in another form the sentiment which he had expressed before in these words, "He that will be greatest among you let him be your servant, even as the Son of man came not to be ministered unto, but to minister and to give himself a ransom for many."

The acted parable was on this wise. Rising from the table round which they were assembled, and while they were at supper, he laid aside his upper garment, girt himself with a towel, filled a basin with water, and washed their feet. Then when he had finished he enforced the moral of his procedure by the words, "Know ye what I have done unto you? Ye call me Master and Lord, and ye say well, for so I am. If I then, your Lord and Master, have washed your feet, ye also ought to wash one another's feet."

Now while this parable in action was being carried out, the Lord came to Peter with the intention of washing his feet, and that impulsive Apostle interposed with the objection so well meant, but so greatly mistaken, "Lord, dost thou wash my feet?" This was at once set aside by the reply, "What I do thou knowest not now, but thou shalt understand hereafter;" and then after a little further conversation Peter submitted to the will of his Lord. Thus the words of the text have special and primary reference to the meaning of the washing of his disciples' feet by our Lord, and they have their original fulfilment in the explanation of that act furnished by our Saviour himself, and which he begins by saying, "Know ye," or understand ye, — for the word is the same as that which the Revisers have translated "understand" in the text, and is altogether different from that in the clause, "thou *knowest* not now," — understand ye, "what I have done unto you?" The "hereafter" of the text, therefore, is the "hereafter" of a few minutes. There was in it, as it was originally used by the Lord Jesus, no direct allusion to the future life, though the principle applies, with even greater force, to the hereafter that is beyond the grave; and my purpose this morning is to set clearly before you the meaning of the principle itself, the area which it covers, and the influence which it should exert upon us in our daily lives.

First let us look at the principle itself. Briefly expressed, it is that the difficulties of the present are often explained by the lapse of time, so that what may be hard to unravel to-day may be easily disentangled after a few months, or it may be years, have gone. The topic of the morning, therefore, may be announced as the interpreting power of time.

There is something in the very fact that an event is past which enables us to understand it better than we did when it was happening. We all recognize that there is truth as well as beauty in the Laureate's lines, —

> " Or that the past will always win
> A glory from its being far;
> And orb into the perfect star
> We saw not when we moved therein."

When we are in the midst of any movement, we are too close upon it to judge of it aright, and so we either overestimate its importance, or fail to recognize its full significance. But after it has done its work, it is put, so to say, into its right perspective, and we see it correctly. While it was going on it was unfinished, but now that it is past it is completed, and we can thereby understand it better. The proverb that "fools should not see things that are only half done " has put this view of the case in a compact and portable form, which carries conviction into every mind; and if we but remembered it more frequently we might be saved from many an unnecessary perplexity and many a sorrowful experience.

But while this interpreting result may be produced by the lapse of time taken merely by itself, it is intensified by what that passing of the present into the past may bring, almost always, indeed, does bring, along with it. Thus, for one thing, it brings a growth in the individual's own intelligence, which helps him to an explanation of what before was difficult. Your little child puts a question to you, which you find it impossible to answer, not because the whole difficulty is not plain to you, for you have got for yourself the right solution, but because he has not yet the intelligence to take in that solution. You cannot put it into his vocabulary, and you must wait until by his mental growth that vocabulary has increased before you can hope to make the matter clear to him. So you tell him to defer the question, and then when some time has elapsed, and his education has developed him into sufficient intelligence, he gets the solution for himself, and does not need to ask any one concerning it. Which of us has not had this verified in his own studies? While you were yet, let me suppose, in your teens, you took up a work, which you heard your elders speak of with the highest appreciation, and began to read it for yourself. It was, say, the "In Memoriam" of Tennyson; but in that stage of your career you could make little or nothing of it, and you laid it aside, with the feeling that it had been extravagantly overpraised. After some years, however, you chanced to hear a lecturer refer to the same poem in terms of highest commendation, and you resolved to make another attempt at its perusal. This time you saw a great deal in what before you

thought to be meaningless or obscure; but still there
was much that was dark, and it was only after years
more had elapsed that you grew into the understanding
of it all, and felt that there was no extravagance in
the statement that it is one of the finest contributions
which have been made to the literature of the English
language in this nineteenth century of the Christian era.
Thus one measures his mental growth by the degree in
which he rises toward the mastery of some thoughtful
work which has taxed his ability to the utmost.

Still again time carries in it the educating influence
of experience, and that contributes to the better understanding of what was obscure in the past. A man sees
only what he has the power to see, and the power to
see depends a good deal on the environment of the seer.
Standing in the daylight one cannot ordinarily observe
the stars; but if you put me at the bottom of a deep
mine-shaft I will clearly descry the planet that is passing at the moment overhead, even though on the surface
of the earth it be bright as noonday and all the stars
invisible. Now few things clarify the spiritual perception like experience. In early youth one finds it difficult to understand many of the Psalms; but in maturer
life, after he has had trial of disappointment, or personal affliction, or the treachery of professed friends,
or the ingratitude of those whom he has benefited, he
does not require a commentator to make them clear to
him; or rather, God himself, through his own experience, has been their true interpreter, and he is willing
to wait for his explanation of the rest. Dr. Duff found
the key to the vindication of what are called "the
imprecatory psalms" in the horrors of the Indian
Mutiny, and one begins to understand why he has been
afflicted when he finds that his own trials have put into

his heart sympathy for the sufferings of others, and charity for their faults.

Finally, here we must remember that the lapse of time gives opportunity to the individual for the enjoyment of the teachings of God the Holy Spirit. These disciples did not fully comprehend the Lord's meaning in the washing of their feet until after they had received the Holy Ghost. He was promised to them "that he might guide them into all truth," and "bring all things to their remembrance whatsoever Christ had said unto them," and his ministry extends to all who love the Saviour and keep his commandments. He carries on his operations not only by direct suggestions, but also through the words of men and the dispensations of Providence, and the result of all is that believers under his instructions grow in acuteness of spiritual perception, and come to understand much which was before incomprehensible. In proof of this, one has only to look at the contrast between intelligent men of the world and simple-minded believers in their judgment of spiritual things. When the celebrated statesman, William Pitt, accompanied his friend Wilberforce to hear Richard Cecil preach, he declared that he could not understand what the minister would be at, though his companion affirmed that it was clear to the intelligence of many in the audience who had not a tithe of his ability, because they were taught of the Spirit. When the Holy Ghost begins to instruct a man we may look for great proficiency, for we may say of him with Elihu, "Who teacheth like him?" He worketh in and with and through all other agencies; and so if we put together all that we have enumerated, the mere lapse of time itself, the opportunity which it furnishes for mental growth, for diversified experience, and for that teaching of the Spirit which not only utilizes all of these, but is directly communicated to the believing soul, we may clearly comprehend how true it may become that what one of God's children knows not now, he shall understand hereafter.

But now, in the second place, let us look at the area which this principle covers. It applies first to the mysteries that are found in Scripture. We need not be surprised to find mysteries in God's revelation to men; for men are finite. They cannot understand the infinite, and therefore their knowledge, whether communicated by God or not, must be imperfect. But imperfect knowledge is just another name for mystery, and so we must expect to find that in connection with every communication made by God to men. If we do not find it, indeed, we may fairly conclude that the communication has not come from God at all. But as the years revolve, the mystery may diminish, and may finally disappear, or at least cease to trouble us. Thus we all know that the things which disturbed us many years ago in our Bible study are not the same as those by which we are now perplexed. The old ones have been either solved or shelved, and others, about much higher and more momentous things, have taken their places, to be in their turn pushed aside by mysteries arising out of or connected with still higher themes. This explains why it is that elderly Christians find it so hard to put themselves back to the standpoint occupied by young people, or to speak words of wisdom to them about their difficulties. It is so long since they felt the same perplexities, that they have forgotten how they extricated themselves from them; and because they are no longer perplexities to themselves, they cannot understand how they should disturb any one else. But the principle beneath my text might teach them to advise their distressed friends to let the subject that is disturbing them alone for a time, and turn their minds into another channel, in the hope that what they know not now, they shall understand hereafter.

Thus, to take the subject of inspiration, which is disturbing so many minds at present, it may be pertinent to say that it is not the earliest question that should be taken up by the Biblical inquirer. In truth, it ought rather to be the last result of an inductive examination into the nature and origin of the Sacred Scriptures. Let the perplexed one take up first the Gospel narratives, and after having satisfied himself about their authenticity and genuineness, let him seek to settle for himself the question, "Who is this Jesus who is called the Christ?" If after candid examination he is led to the conclusion that he is a man and nothing more, then he may turn away and think no more either about him or his words or his works. But if he is compelled to believe that in Jesus Christ *the Word*, who was God, is *incarnate*, then faith in him is clearly due to him, and obedience to him ought to be absolute and implicit. Let him thus believe him and obey him for a time, and then he will find his former difficulties no longer pressing upon him. He may not be able — judging from my own experience, he will not be able — to formulate in words a theory of inspiration which will fit all the facts, or which will be satisfactory either to himself or others; but he will practically regard the Holy Scriptures as his standard of faith and conduct. He will believe what Christ says just because it is he who says it. He will obey what he commands just because it is he who commands it; and that will keep him so busy, and make him so happy, that he will neither have the time nor the heart to occupy himself with that which has now become to him a question of subordinate interest.

So it will be also with other subjects, such as election, foreordination, and the like. The key for the unlocking of mystery is put into the hand of obedience. There is a sense in which it is true that we must know in order to do; but there is another, in which it is also true that we must do in order to know, and here lies the comfort in the Saviour's words, "If any man be willing to do his will, he shall know of the doctrine whether it be of God." So let the perplexed among us turn away meanwhile from the obscure, the difficult, the mysterious, and study Christ, and by following that course they will discover that what they know not now they will understand by and by.

But the principle in the text applies also to the dispensations of God's providence. There are great anomalies constantly occurring in the world around us. We must believe in the all-controlling providence of God. The only alternatives to that are that things happen by chance, or that they have been fixed by hard, impersonal, remorseless fate. But a rational being cannot rest in either of these for a moment. Still if all things are working out the will of God, and if God is wise and just and good, how comes it that he allows such things to happen as we read of daily in our newspapers? That is an anomaly, a seeming inconsistency, a mystery. We cannot explain it, but neither must we allow it to paralyze our piety. It is a case for the application of the principle before us. We can let it alone, and wait and trust. God's ways are past finding out; but God himself we know, for he has revealed himself to us at and through the cross of Calvary, and we have such confidence in his love that we can trust it, even when we cannot see how it can be consistent with much that is happening daily in the administration of his providence.

But most of us, probably, are more distressed by God's dealings with ourselves than with the anomalies occurring in his government of the world at large. Why does he send affliction upon us? And how comes it that the affliction which he sends takes the form that it assumes? Have we not all at times been distressed with questions like these; and was our distress not caused because we had forgotten the words of this morning's text? The author of the Epistle to the Hebrews has said, "No chastening for the present seemeth to be joyous, but grievous. Nevertheless afterward it yieldeth the peaceable fruit of righteousness unto them which are exercised thereby." Now the trouble has been that we overlooked that important word "*afterward.*" We wanted to have the whole explanation at the time when the chastening was upon us, and because we could not get that then we aggravated our trial by our own futile attempts to get a solution for ourselves. But when we have been content to wait, the peaceable fruit has rewarded our patience. It is better, therefore, to bow before God and bear the rod, while we pray for the working out of his purpose in us, than it is to chafe and fret our spirits in the impotent attempt to find out that which in his own time he will reveal to us, without any effort of our own at all. There are few of us past middle age who cannot attest the truth of my declaration when I say that in the "afterward" of our trials we have had their interpretation. I think at this moment of a specially heavy affliction, through which now seven and twenty years ago God made me to pass, when in the short space of ten days he took two of my children from my arms; and as I look back upon it now, I am at no loss to understand it, for it put sympathy into my heart, and pathos into my speech, so that I might be the better able to succor and to sympathize with all who might be similarly afflicted. I knew not then, I dreamed not then, of the work that was in store for me here so far away from my native land; but often since has God given me to see that through that dark discipline of trial he was fitting me for this ministry and service. I am sure that many of you could give similar testimony concerning your own trials, so true it is that what we did not know at the time we have come to understand very thoroughly afterwards.

But now, finally, what may we learn from this subject in our daily life? It may well, in the first place, teach us patience. It repeats to us the caution of Paul, that we "should judge nothing before the time." It bids us wait God's time, and tells us that whatever it may be that is disturbing us,—

> "God is his own interpreter,
> And he will make it plain."

And so it encourages us to combine hope with our patience. It puts the light ahead, and tells us to steer by that. In this way it makes the patience easier. There is an explanation coming, therefore we may be the better upheld as we wait for it. "For if we hope for that we see not, then do we with patience wait for it." Keep the hope steady, and the patience will not fail; but if you let go the hope, the patience will go too. Therefore though the interpretation of a trial may be long in coming, do not sink into fretfulness, far less into despair. "Though it tarry, wait for it. It will surely come; it will not tarry;" and when it comes, you will find that it has been worth waiting for.

Throughout my discourse, as you must have perceived, I have dealt with the text as relating to the hereafter of time.

But true as it is in that, its original application, it is even more so of the hereafter of eternity. The dark things which time has left unillumined will be brightened in eternity. What troubled us here will cease to perplex us there; for we shall have no sin dwelling in us to dim our spiritual vision, and we shall be face to face with God, "in whose light we shall see light." I say not, indeed, that there shall be no mysteries there, for that would be a mistake. Mystery, as we have seen, is imperfect knowledge, and as man is finite his knowledge must be always imperfect, and so there must always be some mysteries left for his solution. There will always be in heaven the eternal approximation of the finite toward the infinite; but the finite will never attain to the full knowledge possessed by the infinite, and in the unbridged gulf between them mystery will ever dwell. But then in heaven no perplexity will be felt regarding it, for there our confidence in God will be perfect, and we shall be content to let him interpret himself to us, *as* he will and *when* he will; and that constantly increasing revelation of himself and interpretation of himself to us will constitute one of the great charms of the celestial life, and keep it from being the dull monotonous thing which many seem to think it is to be. Why should we not seek to have here and now this growing knowledge of God and of his ways, this absolute trust in his perfect wisdom and love, this patient waiting for the unfolding of his purpose, and so have therein heaven itself begun on earth?

XX.

PRAISE.

Sing praises to God, sing praises! sing praises unto our King, sing praises! — PSALMS xlvii. 6.

THE psalm from which these words are taken was evidently composed for the celebration of a victory gained by God's ancient people, through his gracious assistance over some confederated nations. In this way God had, as it were, chosen Israel's inheritance anew, and proved himself to be king over all the earth. Hence all nations, as well as that of Israel, are called to praise Jehovah, who had in this signal manner displayed his lordship over them. The ode had its origin, doubtless, in some historical occasion, though it is now impossible fully to determine what that occasion was; but we may describe its general purport in the words of Perowne, who calls it "a hymn of triumph, in which the singer calls upon all nations of the earth to praise Jehovah as their king, and joyfully anticipates the time when they shall all become one body with the people of the God of Abraham," and adds, "In this sense the psalm may be called Messianic, a prophecy of the final triumph of God's kingdom on the earth." This view is corroborated and confirmed by the peculiar structure of verse fifth, — "God is gone up with a shout, the Lord with the sound of a trumpet," — which, whatever may have suggested it at first, it is now impossible for us to read without thinking of the ascension of Christ into glory after his triumph over his and our enemies in his resurrection from the dead. Accordingly, it is by most commentators interpreted as having a prophetic reference to that great event; and so the command "sing praises," which immediately follows, is a call to offer praise to him who died for our sins, rose again for our justification, and is now "exalted at the right hand of God, a Prince and a Saviour, to give repentance unto Israel, and the remission of sins."

Accordingly, it is not out of place to turn your thoughts on this communion morning to the uses of praise. No doubt the special object of the Lord's supper is to show forth the death of Christ; but that death would have been without meaning and value to us if it had not been followed by his resurrection and ascension, and therefore we cannot commemorate it either fully or intelligently without taking into account the light which they have shed upon it, and we cannot do that without offering praise to him as our risen and reigning Lord. Nor can we forget that part of the exercises at the first observance of the Lord's supper, a part, too, which we ourselves sacredly follow on every occasion when we gather round the table of the Lord, was the singing of a hymn. It is every way appropriate, therefore, that we should here and now meditate a little on the great objects which are to be gained by the singing of praises to Jehovah-Jesus, our Redeeming God.

Praise may be specifically defined as the expression of gratitude to God, more particularly for his grace in redemption, in words of rhythmic cadence and poetic fervor sung to appropriate music. The great prerequisite in offering it is sincerity. First and before all things else we must have the melody of the heart. We must ourselves have experienced the deliverance which we celebrate; we must understand the words which we use, and feel the gratitude which we sing. If we do that, then we shall give to God of our best, and the music will be only the fitting vocal expression of our deepest emotions. But presuming that all these things are secured, let me proceed to enumerate to you a few of the results which may ordinarily be expected from our singing of praises to our God and Father in Christ Jesus.

First of all, then, we ought to sing praises, because to do so honors God. The richest spoils that the Israelites brought with them out of Egypt were poetry and music; and the first use to which they turned them, after their emancipation, was to glorify him who had not only brought them safely through the Red Sea, but had also submerged their enemies beneath its refluent waves. Praise was born that day when Moses sang his grateful song, and was answered in responsive chorus by Miriam and her sisters. That was the national anthem of the Jews, and the prelude and prophecy of the song of the redeemed both on earth and in heaven. It told of deliverance, and glorified the deliverer. So let us "shew forth the praises of him who hath called us from darkness into his marvellous light," and when we receive any special blessing from his hand, let us signalize it by special praise. The hymnology of the Church is the register of its spiritual life. As that rises it rises, and every time of peculiar revival has been marked by some great outburst of praise. This is as true of the individual as it is of the Church. He who has obtained the great salvation, or who has just been favored with some fresh baptism of the Holy Spirit, cannot refrain from praising God. He feels that if he "should hold his peace the stones would immediately cry out;" and so to relieve himself of his pent-up feelings, and more especially to give glory to God, he calls upon his soul to bless and magnify the name of him who hath crowned him with his tender mercies and loving kindness. For the honor of God, then, and to show forth his glory, let us learn to sing praises.

Secondly, let us sing praises, for to do so gives relief to the soul in sadness. How many illustrations we have of this effect of song in the Psalms of David! Some of the sweetest of these lyrics were born in sadness. They begin in a minor key with a plaintive *miserere*, and rise step by step up a ladder of music to ecstatic hallelujah. In the closing strophe the faith which prompted the song at the first comes forth like a daisy emerging at daylight from the grass, and opening its petals to the morning sun. The night had made it bend its head, and covered it with dew-drops, and now, as it lifts itself to greet the dawn, the tears of the darkness become the diamonds that encircle its crimson-pointed coronet. And the experience of David in writing and singing such songs at first has often been repeated in those who have used them. As the inscriptions painfully graven by the God-fearing prisoner on the walls of his chamber in the Tower of London remained to cheer and comfort and direct the sad ones who were incarcerated there in later days, so these psalms have been a comfort to God's people in every age since they were chanted first. They have been the means of inspiring many a despairing one with hope, and many a timid one with courage. They have been the stairway up which many a forlorn one has climbed from the depths of sadness to the heights of spiritual joy in communion with God. Christian sufferers everywhere in times of danger and crisis have turned to them without disappointment, for the steps which David hewed for himself up the steep hillside of life remain unto this present, and are as serviceable for us as for him. Other portions of Scripture bid us trust in the Lord forever; but these odes show us how to trust, and when we remember that he who sang, "Cast thy burden on the Lord and he shall sustain thee," was at the very moment fleeing, homeless, crownless, all but friendless, from the violence of a son who had become a traitor and a rebel, we can well understand that the cable which could bear so great a strain with him, will hold with us in every uttermost emergency. When you are in sorrow or despondency, therefore, do not cease your singing; for if you continue your praise, he to whom you offer it will ere long enable you to say, "Why art thou cast down, O my soul, and why art thou disquieted within me? hope thou in God, for I shall yet praise him, who is the health of my countenance and my God."

Thirdly, sing praises, for to do so braces the soul for conflict. The Lord Jesus himself, in whom the prince of this world had nothing, sang a hymn just before he went forth to his final duel with the arch enemy and his dreadful anguish in Gethsemane. He knew what was before him, and he went forth to meet it singing praises. So in later days those who have been called to resist unto blood striving against sin, have braced themselves for the encounter by the music of a psalm. Luther knew this power of sacred song, for in his times of sorest darkness he was accustomed to say, "Come and let us sing the forty-sixth psalm;" and the battle hymn of Gustavus Adolphus was as potent a factor in securing the final triumph of Protestantism as the "Feste Burg" of the Reformer was in rousing enthusiasm at its beginning. The Covenanters of Scotland advanced to the charge at Drumclog under the inspiration of praise, for —

> " The glens and the rocks with the wild music rung,
> As they chanted a psalm and rushed on."

There was no withstanding an energy so heaven-derived as that, and when we shall meet our spiritual foes in the same fashion we, too, shall be "more than conquerors." Every war has its own watchword of song; and many are the stories told by those who fought on either side in our great civil strife of the effects produced upon them by the striking up of a patriotic song which would be taken up by regiment after regiment, all along the lines, until their hearts thrilled with the enthusiasm out of which heroism was born. But the same thing is true in our holy war with sin, Satan, the world, and the flesh; and we would win more victories over the lust of the eye, the lust of the flesh, and the pride of life, if we fought more frequently with a song for a weapon.

Fourthly, sing praises, for to do so robs temptation of its power. In eastern lands men charm serpents and make them harmless by the influence of music, and one of the best ways to foil Satan is with a sacred song. As the harp of David soothed the soul of Saul, so that the evil spirit departed from him, and as the minstrel's music prepared the spirit of Elisha for receiving the inspiration of the Holy Ghost, so we may at once drive away evil, and attract holiness by the use of praise. You remember Trench's beautiful sonnet on the contrast between Ulysses and Orpheus, in the devices which they severally employed to neutralize the power of the Sirens' charm, but for the sake of the lesson which it teaches I will repeat it here, —

> "Ulysses, sailing by the Sirens' isle,
> Sealed first his comrades' ears, then bade them fast
> Bind him with many a fetter to the mast,
> Lest those sweet voices should their souls beguile,
> And to their ruin flatter them the while
> Their homeward bark was sailing swiftly past;
> And thus the peril they behind them cast,
> Though chased by these weird voices many a mile.
> But yet a nobler cunning Orpheus used:
> No fetter he put on, nor stopped his ear,
> But ever, as he passed, sang high and clear
> The blisses of the gods, their holy joys,
> And with diviner melody confused
> And marred earth's sweetest music to a noise."

He who has Jesus in his soul has a greater than Orpheus on board with him, and by giving expressive utterance in song to the happiness which Christ imparts, or better yet, by allowing the Christ that is in him to sing out his own song of purity and peace and joy, he will so fill his ear with heaven's own music as to make himself indifferent to the voice of all earthly charmers, charm they ever so wisely.

Fifthly, sing praises, for to do so publishes the Gospel to others. Many who have fled from a sermon have been caught by a song. The little child just come home from the Sunday-school, and singing the hymn which she has learned there, has not unfrequently been the means of the conversion of an ungodly father or a graceless mother. And sometimes the nail driven by the preacher has been riveted by the hymn that followed the discourse. I have read of one, who, going out of curiosity to worship with some Methodists in an Irish barn, felt his conscience sorely disturbed by the minister's appeals, yet he was able to resist all these; but when at the close of the sermon the whole congregation, at the call of the preacher, took up and sang through the hymn beginning, "Come ye sinners, poor and wretched," that, by the grace of God's Spirit, broke him down. Sing on, then, the old, old story of Jesus and his love, and by the song you will become a preacher as you virtually say, "All that fear God, come, hear, I'll tell what he did for my soul."

Sing praises, finally, because to do so will prepare you for heaven. There preaching will be unnecessary in the presence of him who is the living truth; there sacraments will have no place, for the glorious realities of which these were the symbols will be fully enjoyed; there prayer will be unnecessary, for in the presence of the Lord there will be nothing left for us to desire, since we shall have fulness of joy and pleasures for evermore. But there praise will be unceasing and ecstatic; so that is the one ordinance that is common both to earth and heaven, and therefore in that we have the best foretaste and preparative for heaven. Let us, therefore, value it highly, and engage in it often, so that we may be at length the fitter for joining in what Milton calls "that undisturbed song of pure concent, aye sung before the sapphire throne, with saintly shout and solemn jubilee": "Worthy is the Lamb that was slain to receive power and riches and wisdom and strength and honour and glory and blessing." "Sing praises to God, sing praises! Sing praises unto our King! Sing praises!"

XXI.

THE IRREPRESSIBLE IN CHRISTIAN TESTIMONY.

We cannot but speak. — ACTS iv. 20.

THE words are those of Peter and John before the Jewish Council when they were examined concerning the healing of the lame man at the Beautiful Gate of the Temple. The members of the Sanhedrim, unable to deny that a notable miracle had been performed by the Apostles in the name of Jesus Christ of Nazareth, came to the conclusion to dismiss them from the bar; but with the view of preventing the diffusion of the Gospel which the prisoners proclaimed, they sought to exact from them a promise that they would not "speak at all nor teach in the name of Jesus," and it was in answer to that demand that they said, "Whether it be right in the sight of God to hearken unto you more than unto God, judge ye, for we cannot but speak the things which we have seen and heard." It was a right ringing reply, carrying within it an assertion of the doctrine of liberty of conscience and of the right of free speech, which has been the watchword in many a memorable struggle since their days.

But though there is much in that aspect of the words to stir our pulses, and although it needs an effort on our part to forbear from entering on an enumeration of the historic triumphs which these principles have won through the courage of Christian confessors and martyrs during the past eighteen centuries, my purpose this morning is to confine your attention to the four words, "We cannot but speak," which I have read as my text. They are a declaration of the fact that the two Apostles could not restrain themselves from the utterance of their testimony to the sayings and doings of the Lord Jesus. Necessity was laid upon them to speak these things. But that necessity was not an external compulsion. Nobody forced them to speak. They were not terrified into their utterances, still less were they bribed by any material considerations to make their statement; but they were moved by an inner and irresistible impulse. They could not hold back that which in them was forcing itself into expression. The utterance of the things which they had seen and heard in their intercourse with the Lord was in their hearts, as the word of God was in Jeremiah's, "as a burning fire shut up in their bones, and they were weary with forbearing, and they could not stay." Like Paul in Corinth, "they were pressed in spirit." There was that in them that would not allow them to keep silence. For their own relief, as well as for the good of others, they had to speak. Now it is of this phase of experience that I am at present to treat, — the irrepressible in Christian testimony.

And first of all let us seek for an explanation of this irresistible impulse. We are familiar with it in other departments, and our knowledge of it there may help us to the analysis of it here. Sometimes this constraining impulse to a certain course is to be traced to that subtle thing which we call genius, so that in spite of all obstacles that may be in his way the man at length finds vent for what is in him, and rises to eminence. It is thus, for example, with the poet and the artist, the musician and the engineer. Pope tells us that as a child, —

"He lisped in numbers, for the numbers came;"

and these early effusions were the indications of what he was afterwards to become. No matter though John Leech's father designed him for a medical man, and had him actually started in the way to that profession; his heart was in those sketches, the earliest of which made Flaxman say of him when he was only six years old, "That boy will be an artist. He will be nothing less or else." You might have put Mozart or Mendelssohn anywhere you chose; but you could not have prevented them from becoming musicians. Faraday's home-made electrical machine, when he was a book-binder's apprentice, was the prophecy of his future greatness in electro-magnetism; and the clay engines and Liliputian mills set up by the boy George Stephenson in the small streams running into Dewley Bog, were the precursors of the snorting locomotive. Thus the sphere of each of these men, and of many others like them, was determined for them by their innate proclivities, and professionally, at least, they might all have said that "they could not but" become what they ultimately were.

In others this irrepressibility is the result of emotion. We are all familiar with the manifestation of this quality in the matter of temper, for we speak of the explosiveness of anger, and of the loss of self-command in consequence of some special provocation. But the same thing is seen in the matter of love; and the mother for her child, or the friend for his friend, or the philanthropist in the cause of suffering humanity, are all alike self-forgetting, and incapable either of being restrained by others, or of holding back themselves when circumstances require their exertion.

So, too, there is an uncontrollable element in sorrow, and the feelings in such cases are so strong that they "cannot but" make vent for themselves in tears.

But strongest of all, perhaps, in their power to compel their external expression are the dictates of conscience, when that faculty is enlightened by the truth and quickened by the Spirit of God. Examples of this are abundant throughout the history of the Church. Each member of "the noble army of martyrs" is a case in point, and some have given utterance to their sense of the necessity which was thus laid upon them in sayings which, like that in my text, "the world will not willingly let die." Thus we have such words as those of Polycarp, "Eighty and six years have I served him, and he has never done me wrong; why should I deny him now?" Those of Luther, "Here I stand. I can do no otherwise. Retract I cannot, God help me. Amen." Those of Knox, "I am in the place where I am demanded of my conscience to speak the truth, and therefore the truth I speak, impugn it whoso list." Those of Bunyan, "If I were out of prison to-day I would preach the Gospel again to-morrow by the help of God;" and those of the Scottish Covenanter, as he lay weltering in his blood, "Though every hair of my head were a man, I would die all those deaths for Christ and his cause."

Now when we turn to the case of the Apostles in the text, we find at the root of that irrepressible impulse to testify to Christ, the greater number of those influences which I have specified. There was in them the deep, earnest emotion of love to Christ, and love to their fellow-men for Christ's sake, the eager desire to secure the highest welfare of those with whom they came into contact, and the loyal response of their consciences to the command of their ascended Lord; and though we may not claim for them that which men call genius, yet in the operations within them of the Spirit of God, we have something which corresponded to it, while it vastly transcended it both in the purity of its nature and the intensity of its quality.

Thus the analogy of other men in other departments helps us to understand "the cannot but " of Peter and John here; for we discover in the Apostles the combination of all these different influences, each of which in itself has been mighty enough to produce a similar effect in different individuals in the history of the world.

But now having analyzed and accounted for this peculiarity in the two Apostles, we shall find in that itself the explanation of many other things about them. Thus to begin with, it fully accounts for their earnestness. It is the irrepressible in a man that makes him earnest. He who speaks because he must say something will never rise to any measure of intensity in his utterance; but when there is in him something which compels itself to be said, then he cannot help being in earnest. His words have no artificiality about them. He has not to "get up " any fervor, or to strive to become impassioned: for it is the very volcanic energy of his conviction and emotion that makes him speak at all, and so he forgets himself in the object which he has in view. That which bears a man irresistibly along with it will generally, when it forces itself into expression, sweep others with him.

He is seen and known to be "emptied and lost and swallowed up" in his purpose; and so there is as much difference between his words and those of the mere rhetorician as there is between the mimic thunder of the theatre, and the roll of the cloud artillery, as it is redoubled and reverberated by the Alpine echoes. Nor is this quality in the speech of such a man recognized only by those who hear his voice. It is characteristic also of his words when reported and printed. We feel as we read the discourses of Peter on Pentecost and other days that he spoke just as he felt, and that awakens in us kindred emotions even at this distance of time. Earnestness was not in them any more than it can be in us a thing got up for the occasion, to be manifested by rant and roaring; but it was the irrepressible in them making for itself an outlet, — the irresistible overflow of the heart into the speech; and that, whenever or in whomsoever it is observed, is real eloquence.

But again this quality of irrepressibility in the convictions and emotions of the Apostles explains very largely their courage. No doubt they had strong faith in the presence and grace of their unseen Lord. Like Moses, "they endured, as seeing him who is invisible," and no explanation of their boldness of speech will be satisfactory which leaves that out of the account. Continually it was with them as with Elisha. Their inner sight perceived that which was unseen by others. They knew, they saw, that "the angel of the Lord encampeth round about them that fear him and delivereth them;" and so no matter how numerous their foes might be they could say, "They that be with us are more than they that be with them." Whensoever, therefore, they were tempted to quail before their adversaries, they were upheld by that. But my point here is that while yielding to this irresistible impulse in them, they had for the time being lost all consciousness of self. They had not even any such sense of themselves as to be afraid for themselves. All they cared for was that what in them was forcing its way out should get out in appropriate expression. It made no matter, therefore, where they were, whether before councils or kings, whether in the presence of men who, like Cornelius and his company, were sincere inquirers after truth, or in the face of those who were bitterly opposed to Jesus and his Gospel, they were equally lifted above all trouble for themselves by the fact that the testimony that was in them compelled itself to be spoken by them. The little child that is full of some new thing which he has just experienced, loses consciousness of all externals in his eagerness to tell it out; so that in spite of the restraints of etiquette, or the frowns of parents, or the "hush" of elder people, out it comes, often to the confusion and perhaps oftener still to the amusement of all around him. The irrepressible within him has made him unconscious of all else, and sweeps away all barriers. Now similarly it was with the Apostles and the great all-important testimony which they had to give to their Lord. They felt for themselves what their Master said on a memorable occasion about the children in the Temple, that if they should hold their peace, "the stones would immediately cry out," and so they —

> "Heeded not reviling tones,
> Nor sold their hearts to idle moans;"

but whether men would hear or whether they would forbear, whether they themselves were persecuted or whether they were treated with kindness, they "spoke the things which they had seen and heard."

Still again this quality goes far to explain their persistence. You cannot easily stop a bird in the middle of his song. He pipes to give his gladness vent. It is in him, and it will whistle itself to its final note. So these Apostles held on in their testimony to the very last. That which they had to do they did, because their hearts, their consciences, their perception of the needs of their fellow-men, and the promptings of the Holy Spirit, would not suffer them to give up.

So once more it explains their naturalness. You are struck as you read their utterances with the total absence of the artificial. They were so truly and perfectly themselves that you never think of *them*, but only of their words, while you are reading their sayings. They did not by any device thrust themselves upon their hearers; but because in their eagerness to say that which they could not keep back, they lost all consciousness of self, their hearers also forgot their manner in their matter. Now when we put all these qualities together, their earnestness, courage, persistence, naturalness, and remember that the Holy Ghost was on them and in them and with them, we are at no loss to account for their success. Nay more, if we are ever to get back Apostolic scenes, in the proclamation of the Gospel message, it can only be when, as ministers, as missionaries, as teachers, as Christians, we get back to this "cannot but" of my text, and seek in connection therewith that we may all be endued with "power from on high."

It becomes then a most important question for us all, and especially for those among us who are in any way engaged in the propagation of the Gospel, for those who are in the ministry or who are looking forward to it, and for those who are teachers in our Sunday-schools or elsewhere, how we are to get to this most desirable state of heart and mind, how we are to attain to such a disposition concerning the Gospel that we shall feel that "we cannot but" speak it in some way or other to our fellow-men. In the search for an answer to that question I will spend the remaining time at my disposal in this discourse.

And first, as an indispensable factor to the production of this irrepressibility of which I have been speaking, I name positive convictions as to the truth itself. Uncertainty of belief from the very nature of the case produces hesitancy of speech. He who has not made up his own mind upon a subject cannot speak to any purpose upon that subject. If, therefore, one has no positive convictions on any matter, he had better keep silence on it until he gets them, and when he gets them they will make for themselves a manly and earnest utterance. Remember Paul's words, "We having the same spirit of faith, according as it is written, I believed and therefore have I spoken, we also believe and therefore speak." Mark that "therefore." It is the hinge on which all true efficiency of utterance must turn. Without personal convictions a man's words will be little better than drowsy tinklings: with them they will be like his of whom the poet writes, —

> "His words did gather thunder as they ran,
> And as the lightning to the thunder
> Which follows it, riving the spirit of man,
> Making earth wonder,
> So was their meaning to his words."

I may be quite wrong, but in my view it is just here that many preachers fail. They go into the pulpit with things about which they are uncertain. They give utterance to speculations concerning things in regard to which no certitude is possible, or they produce their doubts or their disbeliefs; and so they are neither in earnest themselves, nor the means of producing earnestness in others. As Dr. Johnson said of Priestley, "They unsettle everything, and settle nothing." But what is needed to-day is the positiveness that springs from personal conviction. Nothing can be so effective as that, for conviction is infectious, and the very perception of it in a man who is known for moral integrity and intellectual vigor will often of itself produce the result that is desired. But doubt leads to dumbness. When the conviction drops out of the heart, it is as if the "but" fell out of the text, and there remain only the words "we cannot speak."

But in the second place I name as another factor in the production of this irrepressibility a vivid realization of the fact that without the Gospel our fellow-men are perishing. The danger of her child makes a mother forget everything else, in the eagerness of her effort for its deliverance; and when we attain to such a perception of the danger of sinners as that, and have withal such love for them as Christ inspires, we shall not be able to keep from telling them the good news of salvation. Look at the difference between Paul's letter to the Galatians and his other epistles. Mark its passionate energy, its scathing invective, its rapid movement, its parental tenderness in some of its appeals, and its condensed power throughout. How do we account for all this? I do not say that the great Apostle was not in earnest in all his letters; but 1 do say that he was particularly so in that one, and you will find the explanation in the circumstances of those to whom he wrote it. He saw that the fundamental principle of the Gospel was endangered, and that those beloved ones, over whose conversion he had rejoiced, were imperilled by the influences at work among them; and so he was in haste to rescue both. Then that eager, impassioned spirit pushed itself irrepressibly into his words, and so "the arrows of his thoughts were headed and winged with fire." Now it is the same still. The well-known story of the dumb boy who gained the power of speech in a moment because of his overmastering impulse to warn his parent of a tremendous danger that was threatening him, may not be true. But even if it be a myth its lesson, as such, is an enforcement of that on which I am now insisting, for the perception of the fact that without the Gospel men are under condemnation and in danger of being eternally lost, will cast the dumb spirit out of the lethargic Christian, and make him "instant in season and out of season" in his efforts to secure their salvation. There is no mistaking the earnestness of him who rushes from the burning dwelling to cry, "Fire! fire!" He sees the evil. He knows that if means be not promptly taken to extinguish the flames the house will be destroyed; and so he does not take it leisurely, but he rushes with all his might to open the nearest alarm-box he can find. And when the salvation of souls shall be felt by us to be a matter of as urgent and imperative importance, we shall get to the "cannot but" of the Apostles in my text.

But finally, here an equally important factor in the production of the irrepressibility is a sense of personal responsibility. We find Paul's whole Apostolic and

18

missionary life explained in these words of his to the Romans, "I am debtor both to the Greeks and to the barbarians, both to the wise and to the unwise." God had given him the Gospel in trust for his fellow-men, and he was determined not to be a defaulter where such interests were at stake. Therefore he was always on the outlook for opportunities of paying this debt. He was not afraid to speak to men in high position, like Sergius Paulus or Festus or Agrippa, and yet he was not above seeking the salvation of a runaway slave like Onesimus. He was equally earnest in the little prayer-meeting of women at Philippi where Lydia was converted, and on the summit of Mars' hill, where he was surrounded by the proud philosophers of Athens. He could not rest under this great responsibility, but went in obedience to its demands from city to city both in Asia and Europe until he reached Rome itself; and even there, when he was an ambassador in bonds, he found a congregation large enough for his ambition in the soldier who was chained to his right arm. He never saw a man without remembering that he had this debt to pay to him, and therefore not more for the benefit of the stranger than for the relief of his own soul he sought his highest welfare. But the same responsibility rests upon us. The same Gospel has been given to us by God in the same trust, to be kept in its purity, and to be proclaimed in its fulness to the uttermost parts of the world; and if in conjunction with our firm conviction of its truth, and our clear perception of men's need of it, we had also the sense of responsibility which made Paul declare himself a debtor to all men, we, too, would not be able to keep still, but would meet every attempt to silence us with the declaration that we cannot but speak that with which God has intrusted us for the salvation of mankind.

It may seem to you, however, that in all this I am dealing with what concerns the pulpit more than the pews; but while I cheerfully acknowledge its direct bearing on me, I would not have you miss its indirect reference to you. For in the long run the pulpit is influenced by the pew as really as the pew is by the pulpit, and there are more ways of publishing the Gospel than by the living voice. Suppose I were to read my text, "we cannot but" give for the propagation of the Gospel to our fellow-men at home and abroad, would it not be just as true of Peter and John as when they said, "we cannot but speak"? And if it be that it is the irrepressible in a man that makes him earnest in speech, is it not just as true that it is the irrepressible in a man that makes him liberal as a giver? Ah! when we shall see that form of it prevalent among Christians, then the treasuries of our missionary societies will overflow, and the conversion of the world will be close at hand.

Then again the same principles will be found to underlie earnestness in the Christian life. When we have clear convictions as to our duty and our obligations to Christ, we shall not be able to do otherwise than just as he requires. Vacillation in conduct, pliancy before temptation, general inconsistency with our Christian confession, would be impossible if we felt that we could not but follow where Jesus leads. That, indeed, was just what Paul meant when he said "the love of Christ constraineth us that we should henceforth live not unto ourselves, but unto him which died for us and rose again." The head and the heart and the life would unite in the service of the Saviour if we but thoroughly believed his words and heartily loved himself. Decision of character is the eloquence of life, and that is only thorough in the Christian when, like Peter's testimony, it is spontaneous and irrepressible. That which we have to *labor* after is not yet fully possessed by us; and fully to possess this decision in all cases where principle is involved, we need first of all to have Christian principle, and such love to Christ as shall impel us to keep it. So that which is first an Apostolic example to the preacher becomes in its ampler application a noble incentive to the Christian. And may God help us all, each in his own department of Christian life, to work toward this high attainment when the Christianity within us shall be irrepressible, and it shall be true of the Christ in our hearts as it was of him long ago in the Sidonian village that "he could not be hid." Secure that, and then your daily life will be a more eloquent presentation of his truth to the men around you than was ever made by the grandest pulpit orator.

XXII.

CHARACTERISTICS AND TRIALS OF REVIVAL.

When the Lord turned again the captivity of Zion we were like them that dreamed. — PSALMS cxxvi. 1-6.

THE date and primary reference of this beautiful Psalm are easily discernible in its contents. It belongs very clearly to the era of the Jewish Restoration under Ezra, Nehemiah, and their compatriots, and was designed to encourage the hearts and give direction to the prayers of the returned captives in their efforts for the reorganization of their national worship. The standpoint of the singer is indicated by the petition in the fourth verse, " Turn again our captivity, O Lord, as the streams in the South." Looking around him at the still desolate city of Jerusalem; contemplating the despondency of those who had been at first so enthusiastic in their labors for the rebuilding of the Temple and the metropolis; above all, having regard to the vindictive and persistent efforts of their enemies to prevent them from accomplishing their purpose, — the Psalmist cries, " Turn again our captivity, O Lord, as the streams in the South." As if he had said, " Everything with us at present seems to languish and droop. We are like the Negeb, or South country, in the summer, when all its brooks are dry and everything is withered; but let thy Spirit descend upon us, and thy favor be enjoyed by us, and then all will be revived, just as the land is freshened and its vegetation quickened by the rains that fill the channels of the streams." This prayer may be called the centre of the Psalm. All that goes before is designed to strengthen the faith of the people, so that they should be impelled to offer it; and all that comes after is intended to sustain them in the experiences through which they might still have to pass before the full answer to their supplication came. To impel them to offer the prayer, the Psalmist goes back to the issuing of the decree of Cyrus for the return of the exiles from Babylon to Jerusalem. That had so taken them by surprise that they could scarcely believe that it was real. Just as when Peter was led forth out of prison by the angel, " he wist not that it was true which was done by the angel, but thought he saw a vision," so these captives could not at first realize all that Cyrus had done for them; they were like men in a dream. But when they did take it fully in, they saw that their God had neither forgotten nor forsaken them, and their joy was so exuberant that even the heathen, who had aforetime taunted them with the powerlessness of their Jehovah to help them, were now constrained to say, " Jehovah hath done great things for them." But that only moved them to respond with deeper fervor, " Yea, the Lord *hath* done great things for us, whereof we are glad." When, therefore, they thought of all that God had done for them at that time, they might well be encouraged to cry in their new need, " Turn again our captivity, O Lord, as the streams in the South country."

But though an answer of blessing would surely come to such a petition, it might be for a time delayed. For a season yet they might be compelled to contend with Samaritan antagonists. Sanballats and Tobiahs and

Gashmus might continue to trouble them; and many a time they might be saddened, even to tears, as they saw "the walls of their city broken down, and the gates thereof burned with fire." But the work must not stand still for these things. "Weeping must not hinder sowing;" and they must labor on, taking this for their support, "They that sow in tears shall reap in joy. He that goeth forth and weepeth, bearing precious seed, shall doubtless come again with rejoicing, bringing his sheaves with him."

Such, as it appears to me, is the scope of this psalm in its primary application. But to-day I mean to take it as suggestive, first, of the characteristics of a revived church; second, of the trials which a revived church must expect to bear; and, third, of the comforts by which it is sustained under these trials.

Let us look, then, first, at the characteristics of a revived church as they are here suggested; and among these I name, first, its clear and distinct recognition of the fact that its revival has been the work of God himself. The restoration of the Jews to their own land had been brought about through the instrumentality of Cyrus, but in all the hymns of praise to which it gave birth nothing is said of the Persian monarch. That was not because the people were not fully sensible of his kindness, but because they looked above the earthly agent to their covenant God, in whose hand is the king's heart. Now, in the same way, wherever under the Gospel dispensation a revival is genuine, those who have been blessed by it give all the praise to God, and affirm that he hath turned back their captivity, and done great things for them. The preacher who has been the instrument in the revival is esteemed very highly in love for his work's sake, but the whole praise is given to God. The revived ones do not regard themselves as the converts of any man, however great may be his gifts, but as the converts of the Holy Spirit; and whenever that disposition disappears, and they begin to give pre-eminence to men, — some saying, "We are of Paul," others, "We are of Apollos," and others, "We are of Cephas," — the blessing has largely died out, and bitterness and contention are beginning to take its place.

Now, all this is fraught with richest instruction to us, for it bids us when we seek revival to look away from instrumentalities to Him who alone can make any instrumentality efficacious. It bids us trust not in the coming of any man among us, but rather in the manifestation of God's power in the midst of us, in any manner and in connection with any agency which he may be pleased to employ. We are in no right spirit for the reception of revival if we connect our request for it with the condition that it is to come through the labors of a certain man, or in any other specified way; and if after a season of what seems to have been revival we give the honor to any earthly agent, we just so far discredit the work, and bring in envy and alienation where love and brotherhood should reign. Let the Lord make bare his arm as he pleaseth; and no matter though the blessing come through a Cyrus, or a Darius, or an Artaxerxes, let us give God the praise. If it be a true work of grace it will lead us to ascribe it all to him; but if the name of any man be uppermost in it, then let us take care lest, after all, it be only a man's work, and lest the frailty of its origin should be revealed in the brevity of its results.

But a second characteristic of a revived church, as here suggested, is joy. "Then," says this Psalmist, "was our mouth filled with laughter, and our tongue with singing;" and again, "The Lord hath done great things for us, *whereof we are glad.*" Indeed, so great was the joy of the returned captives that it attracted the attention of the heathen. Now, in the same way, when a soul is revived, or when a community is spiritually blessed, there is the utmost gladness. You remember that after Philip had baptized the Ethiopian, the new convert "went on his way rejoicing;" and after the same Evangelist had preached in Samaria, and had led multitudes to the Lord, we are told that "there was great joy in that city." So when God visits a church with a fresh baptism of the Holy Spirit we have always a new illustration of the truth that "the fruit of the Spirit is joy." We cannot receive favor from God's hand without being gladdened by the gift. New converts have the joy of pardon, reconciliation, and regeneration; and older Christians are delighted with the fresh experience of those who have recently been led to Christ. All this leads to a general consecration of the members to the Redeemer, and that elevates the platform of character among them to such a degree that men outside begin to take knowledge of them "that they have been with Jesus." Their very joy, from its peculiarity and its exuberance, attracts the attention of the worldling.

Now, this is a matter which, I think, is too seldom thought of by modern believers. We have not been so careful as we ought to have been to maintain a gladsome piety, and so we have given some little occasion for the calumny that the Gospel tends to moroseness and despondency. But if we have failed in this respect, may it not have been because of the low state of real piety in our own hearts? When the Church has little joy, when its gladsomeness ceases to be observed by those outside, are not these symptoms that it needs revival? "Then were the disciples glad when they saw the Lord." So writes the fourth Evangelist of the meeting between Jesus and his followers on the evening of the Resurrection Day. But always when the Lord visits a church in the power of his resurrection, to quicken and revive its members, the same thing may be said. If, therefore, we are lacking in joy; if our praises falter; if, as the hymn has it, "hosannas languish on our tongues and our devotion dies;" if there be among us little of that spirit of glad enthusiasm which is quick to accept responsibilities, and eager to carry on new enterprises for the Lord, — then we need revival. Nothing but that will give us gladness. We may get up any number of entertainments; we may have all manner of social gatherings; we may have festivals of this sort and of that; but all these shall be only so many signals of distress, betokening the absence of that of which they would fain be taken for the expression. All these will be powerless in themselves to remove the evil. All these will but mock the malady which they are used to cure. The true and only specific for the removal of sadness is the presence of the Lord among us. Let us be but thoroughly revived by his Spirit, and we shall have joy enough in ourselves to lift us above the temptation to turn the church into a place of amusement, and to make us independent of the pleasures of the world.

But we have brought before us in this psalm, also, some of the trials which a revived church must expect. After the Jews returned into their own land, and began the work of rebuilding their metropolis, they were assailed by many adversaries; to such an extent, indeed, were they hindered by their enemies, that many years elapsed before their work was accomplished. One wonders if, sometimes, they were not tempted to say, " Did God indeed intend that we should come back? If he did why does he permit us to be thus opposed?" But whether they were thus tempted or not, we know that their experience is not at all singular. You remember how the disciples sent off by their Master to cross the Lake of Galilee were immediately required to contend with the waves raised by a storm of contrary wind. You cannot have forgotten either, how after Paul had gone to Macedonia, in response to the vision of the man who cried, "Come over into Macedonia and help us," he encountered antagonism wherever he went,— was shamefully entreated at Philippi, was hunted out of Thessalonica, was smuggled by night out of Berea, was laughed to scorn at Athens, and was dragged before the judgment-seat of Gallio at Corinth. That seemed a strange welcome for Greece to give to the Apostle; that looked almost as if the vision which he had seen at Troas had been a delusion. But in reality, the whole experience was only an illustration of the common law that *revived effort in the cause of God quickens the opposition of his enemies*, and it was permitted to come upon Paul just to harden him for new suffering in his Master's service. Now it was not different with the returned captives to whom we have so often referred. If they had been content to let Jerusalem lie waste, the surrounding tribes would have let them alone. But because they set themselves earnestly to reorganize the worship of Jehovah there, and to refortify the city itself, they were hindered and attacked. And in like manner, when a revived church puts forth its new strength in testifying to Christ; when it is fearless alike in its advocacy of truth and in its assaults on error; when it lifts up its voice like a trumpet to show the men of the world their iniquity; when it pushes on its missionary activity into the streets and lanes of the city so effectively as to dry up the gains of those who live on the vices of the people, and to awaken the enmity of Demetrius and the craftsmen,— then it will be assailed. Efforts will be made on every side to hinder its usefulness. Slanderous stories, for which no better authority can be given than this, " It is reported among the heathen, and Gashmu saith it," will be circulated to the defamation of its members, and possibly a new enthusiasm for some one of the world's Dianas may be made the excuse for a crusade upon them.

But all this when it comes is only the world's way of bearing its testimony to the genuineness of the church's life. If that was a make-believe, the world would let the church alone; but because it is real, the world is bitter. In the wake of every genuine revival, therefore, you may look for some kind of assault from the enemies of the Cross; and if that do not come, you may conclude that the revival has not gone so very deep after all. Indeed, it may be accepted as a general principle that the church which stands well with the world has no great spirituality in it. You remember the words of the Lord Jesus, how he said, " Woe unto you when all men speak well of you," and you cannot have forgotten the unqualified assertion of his Apostle, " The friendship of the world is enmity with God." Now it is in perfect keeping with these utterances to affirm, that when the ungodly see in the church the spirit of compromise, they will speak well of it; but when they are confronted with its emphatic and unqualified testimony against respectable wickedness, then they will begin to condemn it, and will oppose its efforts by every means on which they can lay their hands. When a church is afraid of its reputation with the outside world, its aggressive force has gone. It is then in captivity as really as were the Jews in Babylon. But when its members become unbending in their loyalty to Christ and unwearied in their efforts for the conversion of their fellow-men, then they will not care for what men say concerning them, or they will prefer the frown of the world to its favor, for they see in that the seal of the divine approval. How is it, my brethren, in this respect with us? Is not the present tendency among us in the direction of the cultivation of the good opinion of the world? Are we not too often tempted to meet it a good deal more than half-way? Do we not weaken the emphasis of our protest against its wickedness and lessen the weight of our condemnation of its iniquities, because we fear its opposition? How few among us would care, for example, to be put in the pillory of an unscrupulous press for our adherence to that which we believe to be right, and how weak one's condemnation of prevailing evils becomes when one of the evil-doers has it in his power seriously to injure our business interests! Ah! are not all these signs that we need revival, genuine heaven-born revival, to break up our friendship with the world and give us the blessing of its antagonism? At all events, this is true, — that if we were thoroughly revived by the Spirit of God we would be more clearly seen to belong to the Lord Jesus, and would know something more by experience about the opposition of the world.

But now, in the third place, let us look at the supports of the revived church under these trials, as these are suggested in this psalm. The first of these is prayer; for, as we see, the inspired singer cries aloud, " Turn again our captivity, O Lord, as the streams in the South country," and the reader of the history of the period knows full well how much the spirits of both Ezra and Nehemiah were upheld by their communion with their God. They believed that He who had opened their way back to Jerusalem and had moved them to go thither, had a work for them to do there, and would sustain them until it was accomplished. They were confident that He who had broken the power of Babylon and turned the heart of Cyrus, was able also to preserve them from the enmity of the Samaritans and the plots of Sanballat, and so they called on Him in prayer.

And in the same way, the mightiest means of defence which the church can employ is prayer. It lies back behind all other efforts which the people of God should make against their adversaries. It will keep their assaults from doing harm; for just as a wet hand can with impunity lay hold of a bar of iron that is heated to the white, so no evil can injure the church that is bedewed with the spirit of prayer. But besides all that, it will guide to the use of those means which shall most surely checkmate and defeat the plottings of her enemies. Who can read the life of Nehemiah without being convinced of that? And in the record of the labors of such a man as Felix Neff, the pastor of the Ban de la Roche, one can see how his courage and his inventiveness, his wisdom and his readiness in resource, were all stimulated and directed by his constant waiting upon God in prayer. So amid all the attacks of infidelity, and all the slanders of calumny, and all the sneers of ridicule, the church's first and strongest defence is prayer. In *that* all true revival begins, to *that* all true revival tends; and the church is safe in the proportion in which constant and confidential fellowship with God is maintained by its members.

But the other support of the church under the assaults of its enemies is in the assurance that no work for God is ever without fruit. This is the meaning of the beautiful figure with which the psalm concludes. That figure is so simple as to need little or no explanation, but it may thus be interpreted. "The Hebrew church is compared to a farmer with a basket of seed in spring; the soil is hard and firm, and most unsuitable for the reception of the seed, for no rains have descended to furnish a moist bed. He sows with tears, with grief and anxiety, for so dreary is the prospect of harvest that sowing seems a waste of labor, a kind of tempting of Providence. Would it not be wiser not to sow at all? But he remembers the promise given to Noah, that the earth's harvest would never fail, and the seed is cast forth from his hand. Afterward the clouds pour out their treasures, and soften the soil; the sun sends down his genial influences; and the seed sown with so much misery and almost with despair springs up. The fields wave with yellow corn; the harvest is abundant, and the reapers bring in the sheaves with gladness." [1] So it was indeed with the returned exiles. Through many troubles they wrought their way to success; the city was built, the Temple was restored, their worship was re-established. But it was in " troublous times." They had many difficulties to encounter, they had long delays to endure. But they conquered in the end, and the gladness of their hearts at the Dedication added another to the number of the great feasts of their ecclesiastical year.

Let us not forget that work for God is never lost.

[1] The Pilgrim Psalms, by N. McMichael, D.D., p. 145.

Sometimes the harvest may fail in the husbandry of earth, but it never fails in spiritual fields. There are no exceptions to this rule; we may work amid many discouragements. Often the seed we sow, may be moistened with our tears, and occasionally too, there may be long delay between the sowing and the reaping; but in due season the harvest shall be gathered in. The sower perhaps may not always be himself the reaper; but always there will be a crop, and always the feast of harvest-home will be full of gladness. Therefore, whatever may betide, see that you labor on at the work which God has given you to do. Never mind though everything may seem to be against you; God is with you, and that is enough. As Miss Hopkins has said, " If you are sure that it is God's will that you should do it, then ' I can't ' must be a lie in the lips that repeat, ' I believe in the Holy Ghost.' "

So let each of us in his own sphere take the comfort of this thought to himself. Parent! though your children may be wayward, and may seem to be rebellious, *sow on* in prayer and patience and holy example and loving expostulation, for you shall see at length the reward of your labors in such a form as shall fill your hearts with gladness. Teacher! though your scholars may seem careless and indifferent; though they may laugh at your tenderest admonitions, and treat your solemnest words with ridicule, *sow on* in love and perseverance, in long-suffering and meekness; for the day is at hand when you shall " come with rejoicing, bringing your sheaves with you." Pastor! though you may see little present fruit of your labor, and may often go to your closet or to your couch with the prophet's words coming broken from your lips, " Who hath believed our report? and to whom hath the arm of the Lord been revealed? "

sow on, sow on, for you shall not be forgotten in the day of final ingathering; and among the surprises of that glorious time none will be to you more gladsome than the sight of the blessed fruit that has sprung from seed which you thought had been utterly unproductive. Here is a song which has often sustained me; let me pass it on to be a comfort to you.

>   Went ye not forth with prayer?
>   Then ye went not forth in vain;
>   "The Sower, the Son of Man," was there,
>   And his was that precious grain.
>
>   Ye may not see the bud,
>   The first sweet signs of Spring,
>   The first slow drops of the quickening shower
>   On the dry hard ground that ring.
>
>   But the harvest-home ye 'll keep,
>   The summer of life ye 'll share;
>   When they that sow and they that reap
>   Rejoice together *there*.

XXIII.

THE PLAGUE OF THE HEART.

Which shall know every man the plague of his own heart. — 1 KINGS viii. 38.

THE prayer from which these words are taken was offered by Solomon at the dedication of the Temple. It is remarkable for many things, but for none more than for its wonderful combination of brevity and comprehensiveness, with specific adaptation to many varieties of experience. Ordinary men are apt to become tedious just in the proportion in which they endeavor to include different forms of individual necessity in the petitions which they offer as the leaders of public prayer in the great congregation. If they try to be specific, they become diffuse; while, on the other hand, if they wish to cultivate brevity, they become general, and offer supplications which, like ready-made clothes, are so constructed as to suit everybody in a loose way, but fit nobody exactly. Any man can be brief and comprehensive if he is sufficiently general; but to have such individuality of detail as shall meet the personal case of each suppliant, while there is no lack of comprehensiveness and no infringement of brevity, — that is one of the rarest and at the same time one of the most desirable qualifications for the conduct of public prayer.

Now, that qualification Solomon seems to have preëminently possessed; for here, on the greatest occasion of his life, he does not suffer himself to be led away from the matter in hand by any temptation to the display of himself, but within the short compass of a few minutes he goes round the entire circumference of national necessity, whether present or prospective, while by his minute and suggestive phrases he touches the keys of individual hearts and makes each one vibrate with the tone of a personal petition.

It would be an interesting and profitable thing, especially for those among us who are called to lead the devotions of the sanctuary, to study this prayer, with the view of finding out if possible how this result was reached. But I do not enter upon that now. I only take time to remark that in the clause which I have selected as my text we have an illustration of one of the means by which it was attained. For such a phrase would startle every one in the vast assemblage; it would send each one in upon himself to search for the hidden plague, and bring him out again to join with deeper and devouter earnestness in the prayer with which it was associated. Yet, you observe, it does not name any detail. It is specific not because it is enumerative of particulars, but because it suggests to each person what the precise detail in his own case is, and sends him to join in the general prayer with that distinctly in his view. It was thus not so much an intercession for the people as an incitement to them to unite in the prayer which he was offering with them; and in that respect it is worthy of imitation by all who are called to lead others in general supplication.

But though I could not permit myself to overlook this remarkable quality in the prayer of Solomon as a whole,

I do not mean to dwell longer on it now. My business at this time is with the meaning of this particular clause, if haply I may be able to bring something out of it that may be profitable to our own souls. I have heard of men as having been converted through the instrumentality of an expression in a minister's public prayer; would that a similar effect might follow the setting out into distinctness here to-day of this deeply suggestive utterance in that of Solomon at the dedication of the Temple!

Let us notice, then, in the first place, that each man's heart has its own plague. Now here the question at once emerges, what we are to understand by that "plague" in this particular connection. Plainly, it cannot be meant for a designation of what has been called the *original depravity* of the soul, for that is generically the same in every man, while this, as the language of the text clearly implies, is specifically different in each. *That* is a nature; *this* is the particular outcome of the nature in different instances. *That* is a soil; *this* is the form in which the quality of the soil reveals itself in each of the different sorts of plants which are growing out of the soil; or to illustrate from a precisely analogous case, that is general debility, this is a disease. Depravity is in the soul, just as mortality is in the body, from the beginning. All men are depraved, just as all men are mortal. But precisely as the mortality of the body works its way out into some organic disease which takes its form and character from the constitution and habits of the man, so the depravity of the heart concentrates itself in and works its mischief through some particular "plague," the form of which is determined by something in the individuality of the man himself. Nay, more, just as, despite his belief in the mortality of the race, a man comes first and most distinctly to the realization of his own mortality by the knowledge that he is suffering from a dangerous disease, so in the same way a man comes most vividly to a sense of his depravity by the perception of the particular plague of his own heart.

What that plague is may be dependent on many things in himself. Thus, his constitutional temperament may have much to do with it. I do not enter now into the consideration of the mysterious action and reaction of soul and body on each other in our complex humanity. I simply note the fact that what we call temperament is a real thing. It is true that the spiritual part of our nature acts in a powerful way on the physical; but it is equally true that the physical reacts mightily on the spiritual. I believe that there are individualities of soul as well as of body, and that when a spirit with its peculiar characteristics is united to a body it assimilates its habitation to its own requirements; while, on the other hand, the body acts through its organs and appetites upon its great inhabitant. Even if man never had fallen there would still have been what we call constitutional differences between individuals, though in that case they would have been manifested in different aspects of holiness, whereas now they have developed themselves into different forms of sin. Take, for example, the man who is ardent and impulsive, and in him you find a tendency to explosiveness of temper, rashness of conduct, or hastiness of speech. Over against him you may place the melancholy individual whose inclination is to look on the dark side of things, and who as one result of that is apt to yield to fretfulness and discontent. Then, again, there is the sanguine person who is always so sure of success that he is prone to begin to build without counting the cost, and so is rarely able to finish. Perfectly distinct from all these is the lymphatic man, who loves his ease so well that he counts it a trouble to say "no," and so from mere indolence is inclined to "drift" with the current. While as another variety you have the stubborn, contradictious man, whose disposition is to be opposite to other people, and who is so constantly on the *de*fensive that he is apt to become peculiarly *of*fensive. Now, these illustrations may serve to show how much temperament has to do with the determination of that which comes to be pre-eminently the plague of the heart. Just as in certain people there are predispositions to some forms of physical disease, so there are in some men tendencies — hereditary, constitutional, or temperamental — to some particular sins.

Then, again, this plague of the heart may be partially accounted for in many men by the circumstances in which their lives are spent, or what certain modern philosophers would call their "environment." Just as some diseases are traceable to climate, some to locality, some to exposure, to infection, and so forth, so the particular heart plague of some men may be determined very largely by the surroundings in which we find them. The poor have their peculiar dangers, and the rich have theirs. What these are on both sides has been admirably set forth by Agur in his beautiful prayer, "Give me neither poverty nor riches; feed me with food convenient for me;" not riches, "lest I be full and deny thee;" not poverty, "lest I be poor and steal, and take the name of my God in vain." The man whose sphere of labor is on shore has one class of evils to contend with, while the sailor has quite another. The lawyer, who sees so much of the worst side of human nature, is prone to become universally suspicious. The medical man, who is working so constantly on the body, is apt to degenerate into materialism. And the minister of the Gospel, whose daily occupation requires him to deal with spiritual things, and to be much in devotion with others, needs to be particularly on his guard lest he lose all sense of their importance and become an empty formalist.

So, again, as tending to give specialty to this plague, there are influences which are connected with the time of life at which we have arrived and the spirit of the age in which we live. The youth at the birth-time of the appetites and passions, with his vehement self-assertion, his constant reading of the declaration of independence, and his utter contempt for advice, is apt to have this plague in one form; the old man is just as liable to have it in another; while the man of middle age may have it in one that is different from either. Moreover, the particular dangers of all are aggravated by the influence of the age. Its popular ambitions, its prevalent idolatries, its fashionable unbeliefs, its pestilential customs, — all combine to give intensity as well as form to the plague in each man's heart. Just as there are times when certain dangerous diseases are terribly prevalent, so there are seasons of spiritual epidemic, when special forms of sin seem to pass with some sort of contagion through a community and sweep off their victims in unusual numbers. But I need not dwell further upon this point, for it must be patent to all that, however we may account for the diversity between different individuals in the matter, each man has his own plague of heart.

I advance a step farther, therefore, and go on to remark in the second place, that it is a great thing when one knows the plague of his own heart. Every man has not this knowledge. Disease of the heart, physically speaking, is proverbially insidious. Many a one has it, and knows nothing about it until it carries him off; and in the spiritual department it is often similar. Sin is deceitful. Habit blunts consciousness. We are blind to that which we do not want to see. We are ignorant of the strength of that which we have no wish to resist. And the longer we indulge in any evil the heart becomes the more hardened to the sense of the evil. Thus one may have a very serious plague in his own heart without the consciousness of any particular attachment to any form of sin. But God has many ways of revealing a man to himself. Sometimes, even before he has become an overt sinner, God permits him to be subjected to the strongest temptations of avarice or of appetite. He lets him be led up almost to the very point of yielding, and then at the critical and decisive moment he opens his eyes to that which he was about to do; shows him its enormity, its ingratitude, and its results, and all with such tremendous power that he starts back aghast at the mystery of iniquity which he has discovered within himself. It is as if he had been walking in the darkness over a rugged mountain pass, and a flash of lightning had revealed to him that he was just about to step over a fearful precipice into a horrible abyss, and he flings himself back with the exclamation, "The heart is deceitful above all things, and desperately wicked. Who can know it? Lord, what is man? and what am I?"

Sometimes, again, after a man has been for a while indulging in sin, God opens his eyes to the plague of his heart, through his own efforts at reform. We never know the strength of a habit until we try to break it off. You do not feel bonds while you are asleep; but so soon as you awake, and endeavor to move, they force themselves upon your consciousness. Many a poor drunkard has thought that his "plague" was only a slight ailment, until he sought to rid himself of it, and then, for the first time, its seriousness has revealed itself to him. And the same is true of other evil habits. While we indulge them we think that they are but threads; but when we seek to break them, and the agony of the effort reveals to us the severity of the plague, we find that they are cables.

Occasionally again we may be brought to the knowledge of our heart plague by the prevalence of adversity or affliction throughout the community. That, indeed, is the particular case described by Solomon in my text. He supposes that there has come over the land a time of " pestilence, blasting, mildew, locust, caterpillar;" or that an enemy has invaded the country, and besieged its cities ; and that the people, led thereby to self-examination, had come every man to the knowledge of the plague of his own heart, and had spread forth their hands to God in prayer for deliverance. Nor is this by any means an unusual case. Individual affliction has often issued in individual conversion ; and national calamity has frequently led to national revival. It is not good for a community any more than for an individual to enjoy uninterrupted prosperity. When men have "no changes," then they "fear not God;" and oftentimes even the sore calamity of war has been the means of leading a nation to the discovery and acknowledgment of its sin, and to its hearty and entire repentance thereof. Darkness is often necessary to the success of a chemical experiment; and in like manner, when God would show us the enormity of our heart plague, he puts us into affliction that we may see it the more clearly. What Manasseh could not see in the light of the Jewish palace he soon discovered in the darkness of the Babylonian prison. What the prodigal could not perceive in the brightness of his father's house he was at no loss to descry amid the privation of a swineherd's life. Few things open the eyes more thoroughly than adversity. It is often a terrible ordeal, but it is usually effectual.

Then to mention only one other way in which God reveals a man's heart plague to him, he may bring him into direct and immediate contact with his own truth. "The entrance of God's word giveth light," — and the first thing *that* light does is to show the man to himself. A single passage of Scripture flashed in upon the soul by the power of the Holy Spirit has been enough to send a sinner away in the agonies of an awakened conscience, crying, " What must I do to be saved?" When the woman was brought face to face with Christ she said, " He shewed me all things that ever I did;" and when, whether by the incidental quotation of a part of it, or by the faithful proclamation of some truth taken from it, a man is brought face to face with the word of God in such " a narrow place" that he cannot evade the issue, he discovers forthwith the plague of his own heart. It is in this way not unfrequently that God answers the prayer, " Search me, O God, and know my heart; try me and know my thoughts; and see if there be any wicked way in me, and lead me in the way everlasting."

But now in the third place, supposing that a man knows the plague of his own heart, what is he to do about it? The one great indispensable thing to be done is to bring it to God in prayer. The man cannot cure it himself. He must apply to God in Christ for that; and there are many promises given for his encouragement. Thus the prophet Ezekiel has said in Jehovah's name,

" A new heart also will I give you, and a new spirit will I put within you ;" and Jeremiah has said in similar phrase, " I will give them one heart and one way, that they may fear me for ever;" and again, "I will put my fear in their hearts, that they shall not depart from me;" while the Evangelist John has declared concerning Christ, that " to as many as received him, to them gave he power to become the sons of God, even to them that believe on his name ; which were born not of blood, nor of the will of the flesh, nor of the will of man, but of God." To get rid of the plague of the heart, therefore, we " must be born again," and to be born again we must believe in him who has been lifted up, " that whosoever believeth in him should not perish, but have everlasting life." This faith unites the man to Christ so that he is " in " him; and " if any man be in Christ, he is a new creature ; old things are passed away, and all things are become new." Thus the discovery of the plague of our own hearts to be of lasting benefit to us must be combined with that of " the kindness and love of God our Saviour," who has shown us that " not by works of righteousness which we have done, but according to his mercy he saves us, by the washing of regeneration and the renewing of the Holy Ghost." The knowledge of the existence of the plague within us would only sink us into despair, unless it were also associated with the perception by us of the love of our Great Physician, who alone can deliver us from its danger, and work a cure in us by his renewing grace. Beautifully has one said: " He who prays, Shew me *myself*, Lord! should take good care to add, lest self-knowledge should plunge him into despair, Show me also thyself. The knowledge of the plague in our own hearts will lead us to the conclusion that the heart which showed so fair without is a whited sepulchre, — an Augean stable which it requires a moral Hercules to cleanse; but blessed be God, the love of Christ, and the blood of Christ, and the grace of Christ are stronger than ten thousand corruptions, though fastened down to the soul by the chain of evil habit. And when God exhibits to the soul his love as mirrored in those bleeding wounds, and the omnipotence of his free grace, the energy which is felt there is great enough to crush any and every foe. The gentlest touch of God's finger upon the soul is like the touch of the dawn upon the dark horizon. Birds waken and trill their notes, and leaves flutter in the fresh breeze; and there is an electric thrill of joy and hope through the whole domain of nature. My hearer, thy whole soul shall leap up at that touch; holy affections shall lift up their hymn of praise within thee, thy heart shall flutter with mingled awe and joy, and thou shall know that thou hast found thy Lord."[1] Let no one therefore despair. The plague need not be mortal. There is "balm in Gilead;" there is a Physician there. That remedy is potent for every form of the malady; and there are no hopeless cases in that Physician's practice. The only incurables are those who persistently refuse to make application unto him. When he was upon the earth he healed all that had diseases and came to him; and these miracles of his were signs or acted parables to teach us that he can cure every form of plague which the human heart can know. Go to him, then, and he will be to you "Jehovah Rophekah, the Lord that healeth thee."

As I dwell on this thought there rises up before me the vision of that scene which I have always re-

[1] Thoughts on Personal Religion, by Dean E. M. Goulburn, pp. 209, 210.

garded as one of the most beautiful in the Gospel narratives: "Now when the sun was setting, all they that had any sick with divers diseases brought them unto him ; and he laid his hands on every one of them and healed them." Was there ever anything more delightful? The westering sun, just disappearing behind the mountain, was reddening with its softest radiance the surface of the Galilean lake, and the sick ones of Capernaum were carried to his feet, while their bearers united with themselves in pleading for his help, and — no niggard he in the dispensation of his blessings — "he laid his hands on every one of them and healed them." But as I gaze on, the vision widens from Capernaum to the world, and still I see the blessed Redeemer exercising his divine and chosen vocation as the Healer of Humanity. From "every clime and coast" the sin-sick sons of Adam, "every man that knoweth the plague of his own heart," come to him, — the guilty, the backsliding, the burdened, the forlorn, the tempted, the victims of evil habits, and the worn-out votaries of pleasure; and "he lays his hand on every one of them and heals them." My hearers, why should you not join the throng? With some of you the sun may be setting; in some of you the malady may be of the most virulent sort; but none of you yet are beyond his aid. Take that heart plague, then, to him, and "he will lay his hands upon you and heal you."

THE END.

www.ingramcontent.com/pod-product-compliance
Lightning Source LLC
Chambersburg PA
CBHW022105230426
43672CB00008B/1284